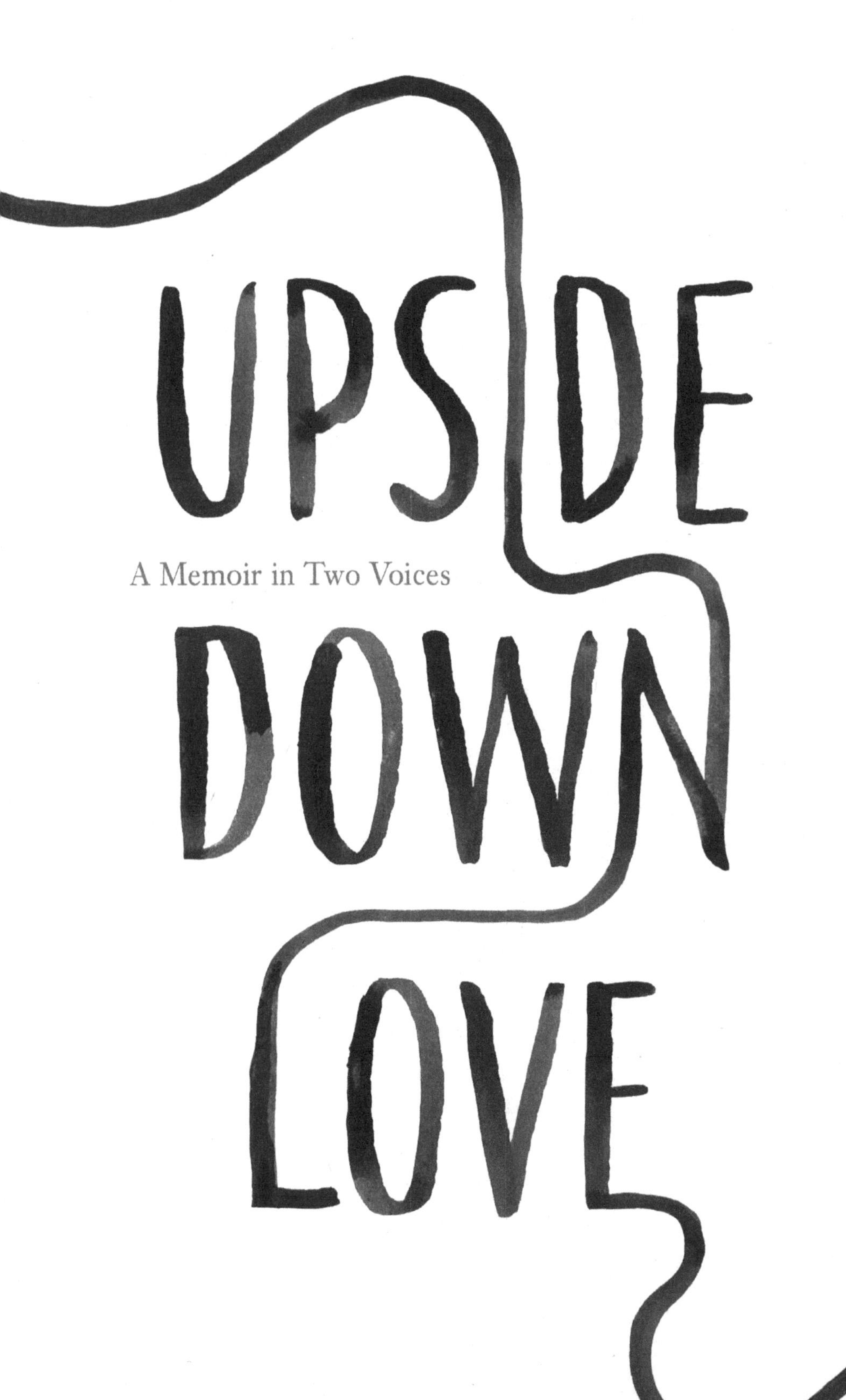
UPSIDE
A Memoir in Two Voices
DOWN
LOVE

Sari Bashi

UPSIDE-DOWN LOVE

A Memoir in Two Voices

BLACK STONE
PUBLISHING

Published in 2026 by Blackstone Publishing
Cover and book design by Alenka Linaschke

Some names and identifying details have been changed to
protect the privacy of individuals.

Printed in the United States of America

First edition: 2026
ISBN 979-8-228-59005-2
Biography & Autobiography / Cultural, Ethnic & Regional / Arab & Middle Eastern

Version 1

Blackstone Publishing
31 Mistletoe Rd.
Ashland, OR 97520

www.BlackstonePublishing.com

To Dr. Tally Kritzman-Amir ("Yael") of blessed memory—
I feel your presence in the light and song you have brought into the world.
And to the beloved people of Gaza, with hope and apology.

Contents

Introduction to the English Edition

In 2006 I was a thirty-year-old Israeli-American lawyer. I had recently founded Gisha, a human rights group, based in the Israeli city of Tel Aviv, that provided legal assistance to Palestinians in the Gaza Strip who needed permits from the Israeli military in order to travel into and out of Gaza. I fell in love with one of my clients. This book, originally published in Hebrew in 2021 (Asia Publishing House, masterfully edited by Rivka Yogev and Avri Herling), chronicles that love story, told in two voices—the voice of my partner and my own. For this English translation, I have added short explanations and context within the narrative to help orient readers. And I'll begin with the following radically simplified summary of the political and historical context in which the book takes place, from my subjective point of view.

In 1948, as the British withdrew from historical Palestine, or the biblical Land of Israel, the Zionist movement declared the establishment of the State of Israel. At the time, approximately 1.3 million Palestinians and 630,000 Jews inhabited the land. In the ensuing war, about

700,000 Palestinians fled or were forced out of their homes as part of a policy by nascent Israeli authorities to ensure a large Jewish majority in the areas under their control. The newly founded Israeli government did not allow them to return home at the end of the fighting. Some of them settled in refugee camps such as the Jabalia refugee camp in the Gaza Strip, part of historic Palestine but outside the internationally recognized borders of the State of Israel. In the wake of that war, the Egyptian military occupied Gaza, while Jordanian authorities ruled the West Bank. In 1967 the Israeli military captured and occupied Gaza and the West Bank, including East Jerusalem. The Israeli government instituted military rule over the Palestinians living in those regions and began establishing civilian Israeli settlements there, in violation of international law, which prohibits an occupying power from settling the occupied territory with its own civilians.

Over the years, Israeli authorities increasingly restricted movement into and out of Gaza and the West Bank. In 1994, as part of peace accords negotiated in Oslo, Norway, the Palestine Liberation Organization and the Israeli government established the Palestinian Authority, a local government designed to run daily affairs within Gaza and the West Bank for a five-year transitional period, under the overall control of the Israeli military. The transition period concluded in 2000 without Israeli military rule over Palestinians ending, but the Palestinian Authority continued its operations. In 2005 the Israeli military ended its permanent ground-troop presence in Gaza and dismantled all Israeli civilian settlements there, withdrawing to the perimeter to continue to control the movement of people and goods, the population registry, and the tax system. In 2007 factional fighting led to a split in the Palestinian Authority, with the Hamas movement controlling local government functions, including security, inside Gaza, and the Fatah movement controlling local government functions inside the West Bank. As the years passed, the Israeli government intensified its restrictions on Palestinian travel within and between those areas. To this day, the Israeli government prohibits Palestinians from traveling between Gaza and the

West Bank, or from entering Israel but for exceptional circumstances, and it does not allow Palestinians in Gaza or the West Bank to operate an airport or seaport for travel abroad. Israeli forces operate permanent and temporary checkpoints and physical barriers inside the West Bank to prevent Palestinians from entering areas that the authorities designate as Israeli-only.

The Israeli government and the Palestine Liberation Organization designated three regimes of control within the West Bank. Area A consists of primarily Palestinian cities, in which the Palestinian Authority controls local policing as well as civilian governmental services. Israeli citizens, Israeli residents, and foreigners granted visas to enter Israel are forbidden from entering Area A without a permit. In Area B, the Israeli army exercises full security control, but the Palestinian Authority is responsible for local matters, such as school systems, zoning and construction, sanitation, and infrastructure. Area C, comprising 60 percent of the West Bank, is under full Israeli security and civilian control and includes most of the Israeli Jewish settlements. Since 1967, Israeli authorities have taken over large swaths of land to create civilian settlements inside the West Bank, off-limits to Palestinians, where about seven hundred thousand Israelis now live. Israelis living inside the West Bank are subject to Israeli law, while Palestinians living in the West Bank, except for East Jerusalem, are subject to the much more restrictive Israeli military law.

For the most part, Israeli law does not permit Israelis to enter Palestinian cities, and it doesn't permit Palestinians to enter Israel. A 65-kilometer (40-mile) barrier, part fence and part concrete wall, encloses the Gaza Strip, and a mostly completed 700-kilometer (450-mile) barrier, made up of fencing and concrete walls, runs through the West Bank, encircling large parts of the region and cutting towns and cities off from each other and from adjacent agricultural land. Israeli authorities control all travel into and out of the West Bank and most travel into and out of Gaza. Permits are required for Palestinians seeking passage.

These were the circumstances that brought Osama and me together.

PART ONE

It's Upside Down

Sari

No Movement

I met Osama because he was trapped in the West Bank city of Ramallah. Ramallah was his home and also his prison.

Osama was born in the Gaza Strip two months after the Israeli occupation began. That explains his name. His father fled to Egypt during the fighting, and so, in August 1967, when his mother gave birth, it was up to his uncle to name this baby whose father was missing because of the military occupation. His uncle chose a strong name: *Osama* means "lion," the animal that no other creature on the savanna can defeat.

Because Osama was born in the Gaza Strip, in the Jabalia refugee camp, that is the address listed on his Israeli-approved identification card, even though he moved to Ramallah back in 1985 to study at university and has lived in that West Bank city continuously for more than two decades. The State of Israel does not allow Palestinians to change their addresses from Gaza to the West Bank.

My area of legal practice is freedom of movement. In 2005 I co-founded an Israeli human rights organization, Gisha, that provides legal representation to people like Osama—Palestinians, mostly from Gaza, who need permits from the Israeli military to be reunited with family members, reach their jobs or universities, access medical care, or receive professional training. Coincidentally, or not coincidentally, my recreational passion is long-distance running. I'm a prominent female runner in Israel's modest and amateur ultramarathon community. In the early mornings and on weekends, I run for hours through cities, fields, parks, villages, and forests, and I feel a boundless sense of freedom, constrained only by the limits of my body's endurance. During the week, I lead a team of lawyers and advocates who help people like Osama overcome restrictions on their freedom to move and travel. When I met Osama in 2006, he had put off his studies for years. He wanted to advance his career, but his world had shrunk to the streets of Ramallah, surrounded by soldiers.

The army's laws didn't permit Osama to stay in Ramallah, and he feared getting stopped at a checkpoint if he were to try to leave. Arrest would mean removal to Gaza with no way back. He sought my help in obtaining permits from the military that would let him leave Ramallah to attend a doctoral study program in London and return to the city on breaks. I submitted a petition to the High Court of Justice and reached an agreement with the state, via a friendly lawyer in a hostile system, to allow Osama to study in London, visit his home during the course of his studies, and return to Ramallah at the completion of his degree program. At that point, he was to resume being trapped.

We were lawyer and client. He was different from any man, Israeli or Palestinian, whom I had ever met. He was quiet, gentle, smart, sensuous. He had strong arms that could hold me. Black eyes that looked at the world with curiosity. Delicate facial features and a trim goatee, the open, innocent smile of a boy. We knew what we longed for was forbidden—that it could never happen. The more we tried to separate, the more ways we found to stay close.

Osama

Turning the Pot Upside Down

My theory about Palestinian society—and I think it's true of Israeli society, but in a different way—is that life there is upside down. Maqluba is a Palestinian-Arab dish that has almost everything: generous layers of spiced chicken or beef, vegetables, rice, and potatoes, stacked on top of each other. There are many ways to prepare maqluba. That's a good thing, but it confuses people like me, who don't really know how to cook. When it's ready, you serve it upside down, meaning you turn the pot over onto a large serving platter. That's why it's called *maqluba*, the word for "upside down" in Arabic.

It was my first trip abroad—to a place that felt right side up—that made me start to realize how upside down things are here. In July 1998, I got a rare permit from the Israeli military to travel to the United States for a two-week tour organized by a US educational institute. I was thirty-one, and I went to an airport for the first time in my life, the Ben Gurion Airport in Lydda. I left behind my wife, Nisreen, and our baby son, Firas. At least they were spared the awful security check I underwent. At first I was pleasantly surprised—an Israeli security officer called me "Mr. Fahed" and pulled me out of the line at the airport. I had never been called "Mister" by someone in uniform and had never heard respectful words from Israeli men bearing guns. But then he took me behind a partition and made me strip to my underwear in front of two other men. They searched everything in my suitcase and left its carefully packed contents strewn across a table.

It was my first time on an airplane—my first trip to a new country. At the airport in the United States, I had a strange feeling of comfort, devoid of fear. I am far from the Israelis . . . wow. No need to carry an ID card! Despite my poor English, I began to walk around the airport as if I were one of the people for whom it was built. I heard my name over the loudspeaker, inviting me to come to the information counter. I felt a tap on my shoulder and turned around to see a woman in uniform addressing me as "Mr. Fahed." Wow.

How far I had come from my family's house in Gaza! I'm the fourth of five siblings, the son of a single mother, a refugee. For as long as I can remember, I knew we had a father who had left us to live in Egypt, but I don't remember my mother telling me that. My uncle would sign our school report cards, except for my fourth-grade card, or maybe it was third grade, when my father came for a visit. I remember he was tall, and my mother seemed quiet. He was interested in my eldest sister, Hayat, who had been eight years old when he left us. He stayed for a few weeks and then returned to Egypt.

I learned about Egyptian life and culture from watching Egyptian movies on Fridays in the home of a wealthy neighbor who had a television. All the people in those movies not only had electricity in their homes but also televisions. Relatives who visited my father in Egypt told us he had two televisions in his house. I grew up with a strong sense of injustice and insecurity and a desire to protect my mother and to help her in my childish way. When I was twelve, I started to work as a helper in a workshop so she could be less dependent on her brothers for financial support. As a teenager, I was able to earn more money working on construction sites in Israel, and I gave her all my wages. It was only after I left the refugee camp that I realized we lived in economic hardship, because all our neighbors lived the same way.

When I was seventeen, I wrote to my father to ask for his help in submitting an application to study at the American University in Cairo. I had only met my father twice, but I sent him a letter through a relative traveling to Egypt. He wrote back to say that he had tried but couldn't help, that I shouldn't come to Egypt. By that time, it was the summer after my high school graduation. Seeing my disappointment at this response, my mother suggested, "Why don't you apply to study in the West Bank, like your brother Omar?"

There were no universities in Gaza at the time. I didn't really want to study in the West Bank—it felt unfamiliar enough to provoke anxiety but not foreign enough to be interesting. But by the time Omar left home at the end of the summer, I gave him my application to submit. I was accepted to the university, but not to engineering, even though my grades were very high. Someone told me the university didn't like to accept students from Gaza to prestigious programs like engineering. I don't know if that's true. My mother seemed anxious when I left. I spent the next eight years going back and forth between my mother's home and the university. My studies coincided with the First Intifada, or uprising, against Israeli military rule, characterized by massive street demonstrations—public strikes and boycotts—and I would return to Gaza during the frequent periods when the Israeli military closed my university or banned travel from the Gaza Strip. In my first year, I completed just one semester. For three years, I couldn't make it back to the West Bank at all. When I finally graduated, I was offered a teaching job in a secondary school in Gaza, but I found work in Ramallah instead. And I have been in Ramallah ever since, until that first trip abroad.

When I reached the United States, I visited a museum for the first time, the California Museum of Science. Everything was so orderly and thoughtfully curated, inviting visitors on a journey of discovery. I fell in love with museums. I wandered around Beverly Hills, rode amusement park rides, and ate in an Iranian restaurant and a vegetarian Vietnamese restaurant. I experienced so many firsts on that trip. I saw that life could be different. There was so much open space, huge roads stretching long distances. I felt as if anything were possible. I wandered around without fear. Everything seemed easy, even though I didn't know the place. Maybe it only looks easy when you're a visitor. I also discovered that almost every person in the United States has at least two televisions in their home.

Two weeks later, I returned to wait in a special line marked for "Arabs" at the Israeli airport in Lydda. Everything went back to the way it had been, but I was different. I saw that there were places in the world that weren't ruled by soldiers. There were people who were safe enough and rich enough to create beautiful things and to treat me with courtesy. My world had expanded, and I couldn't shrink it back to what it had been.

Years passed, and one day the Roberts Foundation in London called to tell me that I'd won a scholarship for a PhD program. My son, Firas, then eight years old, was next to me. I hung up the phone and looked at him, shocked. We jumped, celebrated, screamed. Firas called his mother, Nisreen, who was still my wife then, at her work in Jerusalem to tell her.

But that joy was confusing. A three-year program in London was much longer than a two-week visit to the United States. I was worried about traveling so far away and taking Nisreen and Firas with me. I had also been accepted to a PhD program "inside," as we call the part of Palestine that is within the Green Line, the internationally recognized borders of Israel. That program was just sixty kilometers away and wouldn't have required me to uproot my family. But the Israeli authorities refused to give me a permit to reach the campus at Tel Aviv University. I met a young lawyer named Sari Bashi, and she petitioned the Israeli Supreme Court on my behalf, but we lost. The court accepted claims—based on evidence that neither Sari nor I were allowed to see—that I was involved in unspecified "terrorist" activity.

"There's nothing we can do," Sari told me on the phone, on her way back from the court hearing. "If the Shin Bet insists, the court will do nothing. But we can still try to get you to London." Her voice was emphatic, even harsh, and her tone surprised me. After I got to know her better, I realized she must have been upset.

Weeks later, Sari told me that the Israeli authorities had agreed to let me travel to London and come back, but they still wouldn't recognize my residence in the West Bank. I hesitated. I was afraid that if I traveled, they wouldn't actually let me back. Even if they did, I was also afraid to be free for so long and then to resume being trapped in Ramallah. But our South African friend Ann Marie, who had lived in Palestine for years, persuaded me to accept the offer to study in London.

"You have the right to study in Tel Aviv, Osama. That is the right of return, but if they won't let you do that, then travel outside Palestine, to the UK," she said.

Ann Marie and my wife, Nisreen, organized a farewell party. Firas remained glued to me. We hugged and kissed each other a lot, because we knew we would not see each other for weeks, until after his school year ended, when he and Nisreen would join me.

The day after the party, I left the West Bank for the Queen Alia Airport in Jordan—a bypass route around the Israeli Ben Gurion Airport, which, beginning in 2000, was closed to Palestinians.

At the border crossing with Jordan, an Israeli army officer rattled my nerves by telling me I was banned from traveling. I waited for more than two hours at window number ten. I texted Sari repeatedly, and she told me to keep waiting. *Maybe it would be easier if they didn't let me travel, if I just went home*, I thought. The travelers around me raised eyebrows. Window number ten is for intelligence interrogations and Gazans, so they told me. *Wait. We are checking. Wait.*

I waited. And then they let me cross.

At the age of thirty-eight, I found myself, for the first time, in an Arab country, on my way to a European country. I was thrilled but also terrified. How would this trip change me, and who would I be when I returned?

Sari

The Sea

TEL AVIV

You could say that I founded the human rights organization Gisha, which means "access" in Hebrew, because of the sea. I was twenty-eight years old, finishing up a clerkship at the Israeli Supreme Court, and I had an offer to continue working there as a legal advisor. The idea of accepting the offer depressed me. I did not want to draft court judgments that approved and legitimized the actions of Israel's security forces. Nor did I want to continue living in Jerusalem, which felt heavier than when I first moved there as a twenty-one-year-old in 1997. In the seven years that had elapsed since then, Jerusalem had become more religious, more tense, and more violent, and I was still recovering from a breakup with an Israeli man I had loved very much, who had been my anchor in the city.

Together with a more senior colleague, David Fried, I began dreaming up a project to provide legal assistance for people subject to travel restrictions in the occupied Palestinian territory. We didn't know how we would pay for it or what we could offer. David seemed to trust me, but I worried that I actually didn't know what I was doing. I considered taking the job at the court. I considered moving to New York and trying to work for a big human rights organization that would provide me with a desk, a job description, and a supervisor. One day, in conversation with a friend, I described the vaguely defined project David and I had started to develop. I told her that all my life I had wanted to live by the sea. At the very least, if I were to spend a year working on the project, I could live in Tel Aviv, where David's office was located, and rent an apartment within walking distance of the Mediterranean Sea. And that's what happened.

The sea is my savior: I begin my day with a morning run along the beach, at the end of which I bathe in the sea, letting the water wash away the sweat and stress. I turn my back on the noise and dirt of central Tel Aviv, stare at the endless horizon of sea and sky, and muster up the optimism I will need to get through another day of dealing with the military authorities. I drink in the sense of expanse and possibility that helps me reconnect to the purpose of the work that I do. The freedom that the sea represents is the flip side of the restrictions that I spend my days trying to overcome.

Osama's refugee mother was expelled from the sea of Ashkelon, from the village of al-Majdal, as it was called before Israeli forces captured it in 1948, to the sea of Gaza, to the Jabalia refugee camp. Together with the rest of the village's nearly twelve thousand residents, she fled the small stone houses and citrus groves, close to the sea, that had been her home. Her new home was a tent in the crowded Jabalia refugee camp. Her parents received sacks of flour, rice, and sugar and bottles of oil from the United Nations, which eventually built small tin shacks to replace the tents. When she became a teenage wife and mother, she supplemented those rations with vegetables she bought from the camp's crowded, lively market to cook for Osama and his siblings.

Osama's status as both a refugee and an exile pushed him away from the sea—to the mountains and clear, dry air of Ramallah. When we first met, in January 2006, I quickly discovered that he shares my love of water, even though he hasn't been allowed to reach Gaza's sea for more than a decade.

"The sea was stormy this morning," I wrote to him in our first conversations that weren't about court petitions and military orders. My email was supposed to be about a request I was filing on his behalf to the Israeli military.

"I thought it might be," he had replied. "I felt the wind this morning on my way to the university."

In my heart, I measure a person's refugee status according to the distance it creates from the body of water where they grew up. The upheaval in the wake of the 1948 war uprooted my father from his childhood on the Tigris River in Baghdad—from walks with his babysitter along its banks and shabout fish that fishermen caught and roasted along the river, wrapped in paper and eaten at home with salad and pickled mango. At nine years old, as the Iraqi authorities cracked down on Jewish Iraqis, he fled with his parents to the sea of Tel Aviv. My father's migration to the United States fourteen years later, after he fought as an Israeli soldier in the 1967 war, took him far from the sea of Tel Aviv. He crossed the Atlantic Ocean and settled in a house in New Jersey, an hour's drive from a beach we could access only after paying an entrance fee. My childhood was one of highways and shopping malls, and the beach was a rare summer treat.

Then, at the age of twenty-nine, I migrated to the seashore of my father's youth. I rented an apartment not far from the small, dark Tel Aviv apartment that my father's aging immigrant parents had bought with the money they managed to smuggle out of Iraq, close to the broad expanse of sea and sky that shaped his sense of horizon and possibility.

The city of Tel Aviv, and the sea that borders it to the west, help me avoid collapsing under the weight of the empathy I feel for the people we are trying to help, an all-encompassing empathy that sometimes borders on a dangerous overidentification. Since Osama entered my life, it feels like that confusing boundary is getting closer.

Defending clients against Israeli military authorities scares me, maybe because of that dangerous empathy. In the first few months after David and I founded Gisha, I received a response from the Israeli government to the first series of petitions I'd submitted to the Israeli Supreme Court on behalf of students from the Gaza Strip who wanted to reach their occupational therapy studies at Bethlehem University in the West Bank. The military refused to let them travel, not because of an individualized security allegation but rather as part of a comprehensive ban on students from Gaza studying in the West Bank.

It was a Thursday afternoon in 2006. Winter. David was abroad, and I hadn't yet hired any other employees to help me. The fax machine spit out twenty-three pages dense with orders, case law, and military procedures describing absolute control over the West Bank and over the question of where Palestinians could live: "The petitioners have no vested right to travel from the Gaza Strip to the area of Judea and Samaria."

I was supposed to persuade three Supreme Court justices to allow ten young people from Gaza to reach their studies in Bethlehem, over the objection of senior military officials.

A light panic swept over me. I left the office and walked to a nearby playground, sat on a bench, and watched a mother lead her two-year-old son by the hand through the green paths.

"This is a dog," she told him. "This is a tree. That's a cat."

Together with the child, I repeated her words silently. I brought myself back to the ordinary life that I lived but that my clients under military rule did not: to a dog and a tree and a cat and parents who explain the world to their children.

Four years later, as Osama was becoming more than a client to me, I felt that boundary between empathy and identification blur again, despite my being more practiced in the legal profession. The Israeli military issued an order in 2010 authorizing soldiers to arrest people like Osama, whose addresses are listed in Gaza but who live in the West Bank, and to remove them to Gaza or put them on trial for the crime of "infiltration," punishable by up to seven years imprisonment. The Israeli authorities wanted not just to prevent travel from Gaza but also to punish those who had already managed to make it to the West Bank, like Osama. I felt an irrational, uncontrollable instinct to protect Osama with my body, to insert myself between him and any soldier or police officer or judge who would try to hurt him. I was scared of the army and scared of my feelings for Osama.

Trying to detach from the pressure of fighting the military authorities and the emotional burden of managing the distress of people who are trapped, I look toward the horizon of the sea of my father's childhood, the sea that Osama yearns for and the sea that he's banned from reaching.

Our shared love for the sea brings Osama and me closer but also separates us. In our phone conversations, I was always ambivalent—should I tell him that I swam this morning? Should I describe the clouds, the waves, and the morning sun spilling out over the beach? Will he be able to feel, through my words, the initial shock of rushing into the cold waves and then the salt water washing over his skin, its scent filling his nostrils?

My name is Sari Bashi, and together with Osama Fahed, I am writing this book, *Upside-Down Love* (*Maqluba*). We want to document things that have happened and are still happening around us, to orient ourselves in a volatile and upside-down world. We begin writing in the winter of 2010.

Osama

LONDON

2006

Talya waited for me at the arrivals terminal at Heathrow Airport. I recognized her from the photo that Ann Marie had given me—a forty-something women with shoulder-length, salt-and-pepper curly hair and a warm smile. Ann Marie had arranged for me to rent a room in her flat. On that first day in London, she took me to her friends' housewarming party. There, for the first time, I saw a gay couple, two men, kissing with great intimacy . . . welcome to London.

"What was it like for you, the first time you met openly gay people?" Sari asked me years later.

"I liked it," I said, and my smile was probably shy. "I like that they resist the established order."

I would have loved to see the faces of the Israeli and British intelligence officers as they read Osama Fahed's permit and visa applications, a Palestinian refugee from Gaza listing his address in London at the home of Eli Levy and Talya Cohen.

At one of my first dinners with Talya and Eli, Eyal, their middle son, saw me drinking wine and whispered, "Isn't he Muslim?"

Talya told him: "Osama is Muslim like we are Jewish."

I wrote in my journal: *People in London forget that they live in London . . . A boy comes out of the corner store, a newspaper tucked under his armpit. Maybe his father sent him to buy it. He doesn't seem to notice his surroundings or display any sign of wonder or amazement about the fact that he's in London!*

My thoughts wandered to the Jabalia refugee camp, to a different boy whose mother sent him to the corner store. Did this British boy feel as ordinary in London as I felt in Jabalia, buying kerosene for the lamps we used at night to do our homework?

How can a person describe the feeling of freedom without comparing it to the lack of freedom with which they live?

Women in London bring their children to day care in the morning, go to work on the tube, and come home laden with grocery bags . . . Soho. I'm walking on Wardour Street. A man in his eighties, wearing a suit and hat, apologizes to a flustered woman for the minor car accident he caused: "I'm sorry. I'm a new driver."

At the orientation for foreign students at the King's College history department, the English-language professor began by asking what London meant to each of us.

"Freedom," I told him.

"Where are you from?" he asked.

"Palestine."

My commute to the university took forty-five minutes by bus or tube, and on the way, I had time to observe people from different countries and cultures. There are so many languages in the world and so many different kinds of people. It made me think more about Palestine and what it means to be a refugee. I met other refugees—from India, Afghanistan, and Pakistan—and they were also searching for something in London. I saw that other people suffer, not just Palestinians.

Months later, I met Ann Marie in Paris and strolled with her along the banks of the Seine. We passed towering Gothic buildings, swank cafés, and a brightly lit boulangerie. In her familiar, graceful accent, she said, "Can you believe that you're here, Osama, you Gazan, you refugee?"

Sari

Conversations with My Father

TEL AVIV
2010

My father visits Israel every two years. Before each trip, I compose and store a collection of conversational subjects in my head that I can raise each time we descend into silence. My father and I are good at being silent together. We have been practicing for thirty-five years.

While I sometimes wish my father and I had more to say to each other, when it comes to my work with Gisha, promoting the right to freedom of movement in the occupied Palestinian territory, I welcome my father's silence. Years ago, before he fell silent on this topic, my father used to scream at me about my work. How could I betray my own people. How could I help the enemy. Later, when he realized that screaming at me made him too angry, he began screaming at my brother, Samuel, on my behalf. I was OK with that development, but I'm even more OK with the silence that, in recent years, has replaced my father's screaming about our different worldviews.

Since I was a child, my father and I have peppered our silence with loud arguments when we stumble into subjects of disagreement. One such subject is my father's story about participating in the capture of the Old City of Jerusalem in June 1967, two months before he left Israel for good and immigrated to the United States. My father was a reservist in the Israeli paratroopers. He was called up to fight in the war just weeks before he was set to graduate from the Technion Institute in Haifa. At the last minute, his commanders sent him and the other members of his unit to Jerusalem—a change from the original plan to send them to the Sinai desert—and he fought the Jordanian legionnaires in a bloody battle to capture Ammunition Hill in East Jerusalem, which at the time was controlled by Jordan. My father survived. His unit received orders to continue to the Old City of Jerusalem, where they were supposed to "secure" Damascus Gate, a key entry point to the holy sites of Jerusalem, which were at that time still in Jordanian hands. The word "secure" is how my father put it; I would say that he and his fellow soldiers were sent to capture the area, as part of the Israeli conquest of East Jerusalem and the rest of the West Bank. They had some kind of map, but because they weren't supposed to have been sent to Jerusalem in the first place, they didn't know where the gate was. A Palestinian resident of the neighborhood appeared and offered to show them the way. My father objected, telling his commander that it was bound to be an ambush. The commander ignored his warning and followed the man. My father froze in place as a sniper shot the commander, killing him and another soldier.

My father would tell me this story, one of the few details he related about the war, and at the end he would share what he felt was the obvious conclusion: "You see? You can never trust Arabs."

Even as a child, I would suggest—meaning I would scream—another, more universal interpretation: "That's racist. Maybe your commander shouldn't have trusted the friendly advice of someone whose city you were in the midst of conquering and occupying!"

"I know Arabs. I grew up with them. Don't you tell me about them!"

Usually, our conclusions and interpretations were drowned out by screaming—the screams of an adolescent girl and her out-of-control father. We have both matured since then. I'm no longer an adolescent, and my father is a retiree. We don't lose control anymore.

When we used to scream, we screamed in English, my father's fourth language. He spoke Arabic and French as mother tongues and Hebrew as a language of study and then immigration. But now my father passes as an American, and the only thing that could give him away is the absence of a regional dialect of American English. My father seems to pass everywhere. It's part of his survival instinct, the same instinct that kept him alive in June 1967. He doesn't have an accent in Hebrew either. He understood the need to assimilate when he arrived in Tel Aviv with his older, Arabic-speaking parents in 1953. Maybe my father forgot French and Arabic in order to make room for Hebrew, which he needed for his new life, in the reality created after 1948, the Palestinian *Naqba* ("catastrophe") and the subsequent impossibility of most Arab Jews remaining in their homes.

My father and I once visited the mother of a Druze friend of mine, who doesn't speak Hebrew. I struggled to communicate with the elderly lady using the three hundred words in Arabic that I knew at the time. My father sat beside me, without contributing a word, even when I clearly struggled. I believe that he genuinely can no longer speak Arabic. But as I conjugated sentences in broken Arabic, he corrected my accent mercilessly.

Osama and my father share an affinity for unforgiving criticism of my accent in Arabic. They have never met, and I'm not rushing to make introductions. The meeting I'd be really interested in witnessing would be between my father and Osama's father, even though that's impossible. Osama's father passed away in 2004 without Osama ever getting to know him, except during three short visits from Egypt to Gaza, including the one in which Osama's younger and very charming brother, Mohammed, was conceived.

"What was your father like?" I asked Osama once.

"I don't know," he said.

I wonder if my father would have understood Osama's father's Arabic. I need to ask Osama if his father had adopted an Egyptian accent in the years in which he lived with the new family he started in Cairo, after he fled Gaza in 1967.

Would our fathers have talked with each other about the 1967 war, in whose wake they both left their homes for good? After they both left their homes in the wake of the 1948 war? In 1967, as young men, they each left their homes for such different reasons, but for Osama and me—equally unexplained.

It was 2008. My father was visiting, and we didn't know what to do together. We found ourselves in East Jerusalem on a Saturday, on the plaza of the Western Wall in the Old City. We stood outside the Jewish prayer area in the sun for two hours, while my father told me his 1967 war story, but this time in detail. It was the most my father had told me about his experience of the war. He said that he and the other students were watching the news and waiting for orders. He said he was hastily called up from the Technion Institute and told to report to a location in Tel Aviv with the rest of his reserve unit, with whom he fought until he was suddenly, confusedly, released to his mother's small apartment in Tel Aviv. He remembered being afraid to die, watching as his friends were shot to death and Jordanian soldiers lay dying. He repeated the story of the suspiciously friendly bit of directional advice and the ambush on the way to Damascus Gate. He repeated his conclusion about Arabs, and I repeated my accusation that he was racist. The adolescent girl and her out-of-control father made a brief reappearance. Our conversation ended with my father shouting, "Would you have preferred if I had been killed?"

We continued to Ammunition Hill. We found the site closed for the Sabbath, but to my surprise, my father agreed to climb the fence and sneak inside with me. We walked along the wall that protruded above the Jordanian legionnaires' trenches and bunkers. My father described how the Israelis had charged the legionnaires in a tough battle in which, he said, both sides fought valiantly. The Israelis fired in the direction of the small, fortified, square positions inside the trenches, which he called "pillboxes," and they continued to shoot until the firing from inside ceased. My father told me that he never let down his guard and would continue to look behind him, even while charging forward, in order to keep an eye on the pillboxes that had supposedly been neutralized—and from which the shooting would sometimes resume.

"I've always been very cautious," my father told me. "And I think that's why I'm alive today."

That was the first time, since I was ten years old, that I saw tears in my father's eyes.

"I want you to understand who I am, the experiences that shaped me," he said.

After that, I preferred to believe that the value of caution was his real conclusion, the lesson indelibly impressed on him, not just from the battle on Ammunition Hill but also from his survival of the fatal ambush near Damascus Gate. I think my father and I are trying to love each other, while hating so much of what the other believes.

When my father came for another visit, in October 2010, I tried to decide which was more stressful: the silence between us or the possibility that we would speak to each other. Osama and I were no longer lawyer and client, but it wasn't clear what we were to each other or what we might be. My father knew nothing about that, of course, but I particularly didn't want to hear him make racist comments about Arabs.

I was invited to Northern Israel, to the wedding of a work colleague that I felt obliged to attend. It was scheduled for Friday of the weekend I was supposed to travel with my father. I suggested we incorporate the wedding into a trip to the North, to Galilee, and my father agreed.

We got lost and arrived late to the wedding. We almost missed the Palestinian town of Rama, marked on the map as a small village, while in reality it was the biggest town in the area. As we approached the bright lights and wide roads, my father, who was holding the map, told me that it couldn't be the right place, that it must be another city, and that we were very lost. I explained that the Israeli mapping authorities tend to mark Jewish towns prominently, even if they are small and insignificant, while large Palestinian towns barely show up on the maps at all. He started to respond, but he fell silent as we pulled into the huge wedding hall at the entrance to Rama.

I worried about my father meeting my colleagues at the wedding, Palestinian and Jewish citizens of Israel, but in the Christian village of Rama, where the bride and groom were from, his skill at fitting in was on full display. The Gisha staff guests sat at one large table, and my father chatted with them, asked friendly questions, and even danced. The people at our table were the only ones dancing, while the guests from the village remained seated. I joked about it with my father. "Isn't it funny that at this wedding, only the Jews and Muslims are dancing, while the Christians sit politely?"

"Muslims?" my father asked, and his body went rigid in his chair. "Who here is Muslim?"

In a gesture that I hoped was discrete, I pointed to Layla and Diana, two members of Gisha's staff who sat opposite my father and had chatted him up all evening about our trip, life in the United States, and also about what I was like as a child. Like most of the female guests, they wore party dresses with lots of sequins, bright lipstick, and high-heeled shoes.

"Layla and Diana, for example, are Muslim," I told him.

"That can't be," he said. "They speak Hebrew like native Israelis."

"Yes. They were born here. Layla's from a village in the North, and Diana's from Lod."

Layla noticed us talking about her, smiled at my father, and asked if we wanted to dance some more.

On Saturday night, which was also the end of the last of the Jewish high holidays, Simhath Torah, we began the 150-kilometer (100-mile) drive back to Tel Aviv. The dimly lit roads wound around hills and mountains, with signs marking turnoffs for nearby towns. As we descended from the heights of Galilee, the breeze turned warmer, typical balmy weather in October. I warned my father that the holiday traffic would be heavy, with Sunday marking an end to the long holiday period. We somehow got to talking about the dangerous subject of Israeli politics, but there was no explosion. I tried to describe the Israeli political spectrum from a neutral, informational perspective. My father asked about the orientations of various parties in the Knesset, or parliament, and I told him that there are nationalistic parties—most of the parties are Zionist Jewish, and there are a handful of Palestinian nationalist parliamentarians—but that some political parties believe in equal citizenship, without privileging one group over another.

"There's no contradiction between a Jewish state and having equality and democracy," my father said.

I tried to be careful. "Some people argue that there can never be true equality if the state is defined as Jewish, and that it will inherently discriminate against non-Jewish citizens, Palestinians in particular," I said.

"That's ridiculous. Maybe there are a few problems here and there, and they should be addressed, but Israel should remain a Zionist, Jewish, and democratic state," my father proclaimed.

It was hot in the car. My father tried to turn up the air-conditioning of our budget car rental, but it barely blew cool air, because we were sitting in a traffic jam. "Is the traffic going to be this bad all the way to Tel Aviv?"

"It should clear up in a few kilometers. This road is dotted with entrances to the Arab towns around Umm al-Fahm. When we pass them, the traffic should start to flow."

"Which towns?" my father asked, looking at the map. "I don't see anything here."

"There are dozens of Arab towns here. But in your Jewish and democratic state, in which all citizens are equal, the mapping authorities don't mark those towns on the map."

My father didn't argue or yell at me. He laughed.

Osama

In the winter of 2009, my scholarship was about to end. I had lived in London for three years, but I couldn't disconnect from Palestine. I watched the war in Gaza on television and looked at the headlines of the newspapers in the tube station kiosks. I was hysterical with worry for my family. "Thank God, we are fine," my mother said over the phone, but I could hear the sound of explosions in the background. It was the widest scale Israeli attack on Gaza in my lifetime, with hundreds killed, including families in their homes as they slept. Other homes in the Jabalia refugee camp were hit by missiles. Some of my friends moved their families to relatives' homes because they lived close to a government building that they feared would be attacked; because they lived close to the beach, within range of the Israeli warships; or because they wanted to minimize the risk of the whole family being wiped out in a missile attack—by dividing family members among different locations. The distance between them and me—my reality and theirs—felt wider than ever.

"We're still alive," my younger brother, Mohammed, said, and I heard his triplet babies screaming in the background. I had never met them, nor met his wife.

Some of my non-British colleagues from the doctoral program began looking for positions in the UK and applying to research groups, requesting grants—anything that would let them stay in London. My advisor offered to cosponsor a research grant application with me.

"I'd like to keep working with you, Osama," she said. Other mentors sent me links to teaching positions in Europe.

"They're looking for someone with your qualifications," Richard told me.

Terrified, helpless, I watched the destruction wrought on the Gaza Strip. My relationship with Nisreen was also ending, and Nisreen had taken Firas back to Ramallah. I missed him desperately. I understood that if I returned to Palestine, I might never be able to leave again. I wrote to Sari, asking her to help me go home immediately—but not to Gaza. Sari was just my lawyer then, and I trusted her, but I knew she couldn't get me into and out of Gaza. She had promised that the Israeli military would let me return to the West Bank. She replied to my email but transferred my case to another lawyer in Gisha—she apologized, said she was busy because of the war. I asked him to help me get a permit from the Israeli military to return to Ramallah, an hour-and-a-half-long drive from my mother's house, a distance that I would never be able to travel.

It took several weeks to get an answer from the military. Sari wrote to me and told me not to worry, that her colleague was taking care of it. The war ended, and my family survived. I got an email from Gisha confirming the date the Israeli military would let me cross into the West Bank from Jordan. I packed up my life in London to return home, to resume my previous life.

Sari

Is-Said ("Mister")

Sari Bashi

"That guy needs to change his name," said Jacob, my beloved American younger brother, when he saw Osama's photo in the Rite Aid envelope and asked about him. I was visiting my mother and brother in New York, where they had moved from the home where I'd grown up in New Jersey years earlier. My brother was now a young professional in a law firm, and my mother had become a proud Manhattanite.

It was the summer of 2010. I had printed a digital photo of Osama with the cake I'd baked to celebrate his submitting his PhD dissertation. It was the first photo I had printed of him. Jacob's reaction reminded me of my own associations the first time I encountered the name *Osama*, in a petition assigned to the judge for whom I clerked at the Israeli Supreme Court in 2003. I had imagined a bearded petitioner, religious, dressed in white and having no sense of humor. Pretty much the opposite of Osama, who did indeed become a petitioner in the petition I filed at the Supreme Court.

I first met Osama, in his living room in Ramallah, at a meeting of

Gazans in the West Bank, as we called them at Gisha, on a sunny January day in 2006, a few months after I had cofounded Gisha. He had smiled and graciously welcomed David and me, his Israeli visitors. His goatee was trim, his eyes warm. He was dressed in a blue button-down shirt and jeans. He introduced us to people who, like him, hadn't left Ramallah in years and wanted us to help them reach their studies, travel abroad to get married, visit a sick father in the Gaza Strip, or take a job in a nearby West Bank city without fear of being removed to Gaza during their commute. I thought I saw compassion on Osama's face for me, oddly enough, running between the petitioners sitting on the couch, in armchairs, and around the kitchen table; writing down names and recording details; doing an improvised triage according to the severity of the situation and the dates people needed to travel. His son, Firas, then age eight, hid behind Osama's legs, and his wife, Nisreen, who was born in Umm al-Fahm, a Palestinian city in Northern Israel, served everyone coffee and spoke to me in charming Hebrew.

I didn't say any of this to my brother, Jacob, who long ago stopped being Jacob. Just before beginning law school, he became Samuel, and that's how he is still known outside our family. The circumstances of his name change are typical of my brother, whatever you call him. At the time, my brother was unemployed and supporting himself through clinical trials. One evening, he was talking to a friend, Cedric Windsor, with whom he was participating in a clinical trial for a huge pharmaceutical company. Cedric told Jacob that he wanted to change his last name, which was his stepfather's name, so that people would stop assuming his stepfather was his biological father. But he didn't want his biological father's name either, because Cedric had never met him. My brother suggested that Cedric take our last name, Bashi.

"I only have sisters, and I don't plan to have children, so our last name will die out, and that's a shame. Take it."

"I can't take your last name," Cedric objected. "That's too weird."

"It is weird," my brother agreed. "But Cedric Bashi has a nice ring to it. You know what? As an act of solidarity, I'll change my first name."

"You would do that for me?" Cedric asked.

It's possible they had both started to feel the effects of the experimental drug.

"It's too complicated to change it on official documents, but I'll use my middle name, Samuel. I'll become J. Samuel Bashi—basically, Samuel."

And that's what happened. His friend became Cedric Bashi, and Jacob became Samuel.

It was a strange outcome for my brother, because there was little meaning in the choice of Samuel as his middle name. In 1978, as my parents expected their third child, they chose the name Jacob because they liked how it sounded. They selected his middle name for my paternal grandfather, who had died when my father was eighteen. My grandfather's name was *Salah*, which means "goodness" in Arabic, but after he died, his legacy was Hebraized: My cousin was named Sa'ar, and Jacob was supposed to get the middle name Shmuel, from the Bible. But my parents must have felt that Shmuel was too Hebrew for the reality of New Jersey in 1978, so they Americanized it to Samuel.

I didn't even know that my grandfather's name was Salah until my first visit to the Israeli Ministry of Interior, when they figured out that my father was an Israeli citizen and issued me an Israeli passport. "Was your grandfather's name Salah?" the clerk asked, and I stuttered a hesitant affirmation, because suddenly it made sense.

Names are easy to change, and my brother was apparently continuing a family tradition. My eldest uncle, Shafiq, chose the Hebrew name Aryeh as far back as his days in the pre-Israeli state Zionist underground in Baghdad. Twenty years later, when he was about to travel to Europe with his wife to work for the Israeli Defense Ministry there, Aryeh became his official name, to which he was supposed to add a Hebrew family name to print on his passport, as per a policy requiring government employees working abroad to adopt "Israeli" names. Within twenty-four hours, following a quick search in the telephone book, Shafiq and Aziza Bashi became Aryeh and Ilana Tal, which is how they are still known today. I once asked my Aunt Aziza which name she prefers. She said that when someone calls her Ilana, she feels like a teenager, because in the 1960s, Ilana was a popular name for pretty young women, and that's why she chose it.

My parents chose an ambiguous name for me, a name that can invite others to decide who they want me to be. In 1998, while working as a journalist in the Jerusalem bureau of a news agency, I developed a professional friendship with Nadim, the correspondent in Beirut. We covered the occupation of Southern Lebanon together, until the Israeli forces withdrew in May 2000. Two or three times a week, we worked together to write a news report on the fighting there. We composed the story together, using his Lebanese sources and my Israeli sources, but we weren't allowed to speak by telephone, because getting a phone call from Israel could get him into trouble with the Lebanese authorities. We communicated by email, and if we needed to get in touch quickly, we would call the AP bureau in Cairo and ask one of the reporters there to pass along a telephone message. So for years we chatted, groused, consulted with each other, and exchanged jokes over email, but we never heard each other's voices.

One day, I got a message from Nadim: "Forgive the question, but are you a man or a woman? I was talking to the Cairo bureau, and they referred to you as a 'she.' I told them that couldn't be, but which is it?"

I wrote back: "Sari is a somewhat unusual name for a Palestinian man or a Jewish woman." Then I added: "You guessed wrong."

Osama

Sunlight

I awoke to street sounds I had almost forgotten. The sound of drilling and snatches of conversations in Arabic among construction workers renovating the building next door, the shouts and laughter of children as they walked to school. Within just two days, London had become far away. I opened the shutters, and the light in Ramallah—even on this winter day—flooded the room and blinded me.

Groggy, I made coffee. London was many things to me—a place of stupendous personal and professional growth, meeting people from all over the world and seeing the world through their eyes. When I was trapped in Ramallah, it was a wish, the subject of my dreams, some of which I even fulfilled, but most of the time it didn't feel like home.

On my last night in London, friends organized a farewell gathering in a crowded flat full of books, rugs, and wooden furniture. I felt sad to leave, full of longing, and worried about the future. I left the party and headed for the tube, accompanied by my good friend Madeline. We walked together for about fifteen minutes in that generous and fascinating city. It didn't rain, but the cold was piercing. We talked about the possibility of her visiting Palestine and wondered if we would ever meet again. I didn't know if I would see any of my friends again. I descended into the tube feeling like I was giving up my sense of belonging to London's streets.

I was home, but I felt out of place. Nisreen and Firas had left London six months before I did and had returned to the apartment we bought together. We hadn't yet officially divorced, but I returned to Ramallah separated from her. I missed the sense of stability that my marriage had provided. I worried about how I would maintain my relationship with Firas if I couldn't make him breakfast in the morning and nudge him to get dressed for school. I was a PhD student with all but my dissertation completed, looking for a rented apartment, trying to make my way alone for the first time in ten years.

Sari

First Date

In early February 2010, Osama asked if I would come to Ramallah for a rare in-person meeting to talk about next steps in his legal case. I made the appointment for Friday, the beginning of the weekend in Ramallah and Tel Aviv, so that we would have time to talk without me having to rush to another meeting. I'd started speed training two months earlier and was discovering that I was capable of a lot more than I'd thought.

Osama asked me to meet him as his lawyer but also as his friend. In his email, after he wrote "friend," he added a caveat in his charming English: "If you allow me to say so."

In a phone conversation to finalize the details of our meeting, I asked how Nisreen was doing. I had always liked her and would have liked to get to know her better. Osama replied that she was fine but would not join us, that they had separated. I felt compassion for him.

The driving rain slowed my trip, and I arrived late. He was sitting at a table at the Ziryab restaurant near Manara Square, his delicate face absorbed in reading an English-language article. When he saw me, he immediately rose, kissed me on both cheeks, and ordered me a coffee.

We talked about his case. I tried to deliberate with him, not just as a lawyer but as a friend offering advice about completing his dissertation, applying for a postdoc, considering how to time his requests to the military to maximize the chance of them letting him travel. It felt new to think of myself as his friend, but I liked it. When he asked me about myself, I spoke about running, a subject I often chose to avoid answering personal questions. He listened and asked questions. I found myself sharing with him my feelings from that morning's training session. I told him about the sixty-kilometer training run that I was planning the next day, my last long run before a one-hundred-kilometer race that I hoped to run the following month, a distance that instilled in me a sense of fear and awe. Still practicing being his friend, I allowed myself to bring up his wife, their divorce. I allowed myself to quote Jorge Luis Borges, the Argentinian writer who, after he went blind, began to learn ancient languages through cassette tapes and with the help of students reading aloud to him. Had he not lost his sight, Borges wrote, he never would have discovered that rich world of ancient literature.

"When something ends," Borges wrote, "we should think: Something is beginning. It's good advice, but difficult to implement, because we know what we are losing but not what we can gain. We have such a precise, sometimes even heartbreaking picture of what we have lost, but we have no idea what will come or happen in its place."

Later, a group of colleagues whom we both knew from Ramallah's nonprofit community entered the restaurant. Osama and I split up in order to join their large table, but our eyes met as we searched for each other from time to time, in between conversations with others. Toward the end of the evening, I came to sit next to him, as if we were a couple reuniting.

The rain had begun falling again, and the wind blew cold. A winter night in Ramallah. Osama walked me to the taxi that would take me to Jerusalem, a way station in the impossible transition between Ramallah and Tel Aviv. As the taxi drove into the fog, I watched him through the rearview mirror, watching it leave.

On the outskirts of Ramallah, on the way to the checkpoint, I got a text message thanking me for the visit and the advice. I thought about the meeting as I watched the hills surrounding Ramallah and Jerusalem, covered in fog and rain clouds.

The next day, I went on an eight-hour muddy run in the forest, after which I would begin the "taper," the rest period before the 100K race. When I returned home, tired and proud, an email from Osama was waiting for me. I answered it, and another one arrived. We started to write to each other, about his case, but also about poetry, running, the sea. I found myself waiting for his emails. I delighted in them. I was terrified by my attraction to him. This was impossible. He was my client. Palestinian. Living in Ramallah. I couldn't deny my yearning for contact with him.

After four years of knowing him, I fell in love with him instantly. I realized I would do anything to be close to him, regardless of the consequences.

Osama

Opposite Spaces

Beyond right and wrong, there is a field.
I'll meet you there.

—Jalāl ad-Dīn ar-Rūmī,
1207–1273

Sari has the striking ability to see things from multiple angles. Upside down. As someone who grew up in the United States and came to live in Israeli society, and as a human rights activist, she found herself in an upside-down reality with me, someone who was born into it and has lived it ever since. I'm drawn to the nimbleness of her thinking and her movements. When I talk to her, I travel through different worlds.

We live in opposite spaces. She can come to me. She can see the sea whenever she wants. Her mother lives in New York, and she can visit whenever she wants. I last saw my mother ten years ago. I haven't seen the sea of Gaza in fifteen years.

I'm not sure I'll manage to describe the upside-down reality in which I live right now, but I'm sure that it's not the reality I would choose. Maybe by writing, I can turn it right side up.

I knew that Sari could be everything—and that it's impossible for her to be anything to me. And still I wanted to keep a part of her for myself, if only my description of her on the page. I will try to write. That's something we can do together.

Yes, I will try to write.

Sari

Crossings

When I return to Tel Aviv after visiting Osama, I have to cross the Qalandia checkpoint, which separates Jerusalem from Ramallah, a city forbidden to Israeli citizens by a "temporary" military order issued in 2000 and still in force.

I take a taxi to Manara Square in downtown Ramallah, or sometimes Osama gives me a ride. From there, I board a public taxi, a minivan that ferries ten passengers to and from Ramallah's city center, crowded with shops, restaurants, and an outdoor produce market. In telling the driver where to let me off, I replace the Arabic *ha*, which I can't pronounce correctly, with the American "h," rather than the Israeli *khet* that would give me away. People hear my cautious accent and assume that I'm foreign, perhaps a well-meaning peace activist, brimming with goodwill and seeking an exotic volunteer experience.

The checkpoint is a gap in the concrete wall that separates East Jerusalem, which is off-limits to Palestinians, from the rest of the West Bank. There are vehicular lanes where cars undergo inspection by teenage soldiers and then drive through the opening in the wall, and a building, sandwiched into the wall, where soldiers check documents to determine whether to allow pedestrians to cross. I enter the pedestrian checkpoint, crowded with male laborers trying to get to work on time. Everyone pushes in order to enter the narrow lanes, surrounded on all sides by iron bars that direct traffic into long columns leading into the security inspection area. Sometimes a passenger with the wrong ID card or without a permit is turned back, and if he is too big to squeeze past us in the opposite direction, we all file out of the long metal cage to make room for him to go back to Ramallah. Those who pass inspection arrive at their destinations in Jerusalem: work on a construction site, an appointment at the hospital, attendance at a university lecture hall.

One morning, when the public taxi arrived at the checkpoint, a young woman gets off with me and asks a question in rapid Arabic. I don't understand. I answer her in English, and she smiles broadly, surprised.

"Where are you from?" she asks in charming English.

"I live in Tel Aviv."

"Welcome."

"Thank you," I say.

"Are you American?"

"Also."

"Welcome to Palestine," she says.

Later, inside the checkpoint, she approaches me and offers detailed instructions on how to prepare my US passport for security inspection. I thank her and walk to a faraway inspection lane so she won't see me take out my blue Israeli identity card.

I didn't mean to lie to her. I didn't lie to her. What was I supposed to say?

Then I am in the narrow lane, surrounded by soldiers with guns, waiting in the long line enclosed by bars that, I am told, protect my security. The soldier pacing slowly up and down, resting a hand on his gun and scrutinizing us—I know him. He's the nephew of the office manager at work; he stands in front of me in line at the supermarket in Jerusalem, takes out a fifty-shekel bill, and pays for a pack of Noblesse cigarettes and a chocolate bar; he and his friend sit on a bench on Allenby Street in Tel Aviv, catcalling, "Come here, sweetheart," as I pass them on my way home; he'll finish his army service and serve tapas in the restaurant where I'll celebrate a good friend's thirty-fifth birthday.

The soldier's gun is enormous, slung across his shoulder. He shouts. He's afraid of the crowds in the checkpoint. He opens the "humanitarian lane," an additional lane that is supposed to expedite passage for people with special needs. He inspects documents and allows women, elderly men, and schoolchildren to continue on to the security inspection area. The women and elderly men push each other in order to reach the soldier, but after a few minutes, he closes the gate and returns to the booth on the other side of the bars. We, the people with special needs, continue to wait. More people arrive; the line gets longer and bifurcates; and elderly women, dressed in headscarves, push aside the few mostly elderly men, their broad bodies staking out positions in anticipation of the soldier returning to open the gate.

Usually, I avoid the humanitarian lane and stand in the regular line, between the iron bars, together with the male workers. The lone woman there, I choose the longer line to avoid contact with the soldiers. I'm afraid of the humanitarian lane, where the soldiers talk to people, where they might notice that the birth date on my ID card is listed according to the Hebrew calendar, one of the many indications that I'm a Jewish, not Palestinian, citizen of Israel. They might ask me where I'm coming from. I can't say, "Ramallah."

Shoving. Pressure. The line breaks up; people are shouting. I'm pushed in different directions. The man standing next to me extends his hand to protect me and another woman who joined us by cutting in front of the others who had been waiting.

"*Niswan*," he says to the men pushing us. "Women."

When do I resume being Israeli? When I take out the blue ID card and press it against the bulletproof window of the security cubicle to show the soldiers inside? After I emerge from the last revolving gate to the waiting area for Israeli cars? On the bus to East Jerusalem when, for the first time, I dare answer a telephone call in Hebrew? When I cross the invisible Green Line, the international border that divides Israel from the West Bank, into the western part of Jerusalem? At the Zion Square station for taxis to Tel Aviv? The taxi drivers ask Arab passengers to show identification to make sure they have a permit that allows them to go farther.

Until the taxi pulls out of the station, on its way to Tel Aviv, I do everything I can to let those around me decide who they want me to be. I avoid exposing myself with an error in word choice or accent that would arouse curiosity or suspicion. I have come to learn that if people like you, they associate you as belonging to their own group, making assumptions about your character and identity. They don't like to be proven wrong.

Osama

Names

I have always been curious about Jews from Arab countries, like Sari's father, who, in order to adjust to their new lives in Israel, had to give up their names and their language.

My first encounter with Iraq was through an Iraqi woman I met in the Israeli city of Holon—or Bat Yam; I get confused between them—while I was working in construction. As I mixed cement, she called out to me from her open second-floor window in an Arabic that was so strange and unfamiliar I couldn't understand a word. I asked her to speak to me in Hebrew instead.

Later, Sari told me about her uncle and his wife, Shafiq and Aziza, who reminded me of characters in a novel by the Iraqi writer Khalid Kishtainy, *By the Rivers of Babylon*. The main character in Kishtainy's book is Abdel-Salam, a loving and devoted Jewish doctor, and his story of exile, together with his wife, Tufaha. Abdel-Salam has a close Christian friend, George. The Iraq in Kishtainy's novel was able to contain them and their friendship, until 1948, when Abdel-Salam and Tufaha fled or were expelled from their homeland and culture, together with most of the Iraqi Jews.

I saw, in the novel, the story of Sari's family too. I could visualize Sari's Uncle Shafiq in the description of Abdel-Salam embracing his friend George for the last time as he prepared to board a boat that would smuggle him out of Iraq and into Iran at night. I could imagine Sari's Aunt Aziza in the scene in which Tufaha took Abdel-Salam's arm to help him into the boat, and he turned around to take one last look at his Iraq. I could imagine the anger that Shafiq must have felt when they made him change his name to Aryeh, while he wanted to protect what remained of his identity and selfhood.

Except that Sari told me that Shafiq said he was glad to become Aryeh, and that her father, if asked, will say that he was born in Israel.

I heard a story of another Iraqi Jewish immigrant, a man named Latif, who apparently willingly gave up his language and culture for a new life in Israel. At the end of his life, as he lay in his hospital bed, he returned to his native language, to the alarm of his loving wife, Aliza. "But Moshe," she said, using the only name she knew for him. "You know I don't understand Arabic!"

Sari's father also insisted on a new name and new citizenship, twice, leaving behind not just one but two languages. And I guess there's no way back.

I wonder if Gershon remembers his real name, from the time when he was still Tunisian.

What name would I choose?

Maybe I'll look in the telephone book!

Sari
The Wadi

Osama is not able to travel to the sea, because he can't leave the West Bank for fear that he won't be allowed to return. Until we petitioned the Israeli Supreme Court and got the army's temporary permission for him to stay in the West Bank, Osama couldn't even leave the Ramallah metropolitan area for fear of being arrested and removed to the Gaza Strip. Gaza has a sea, but it doesn't have his son, his apartment, or his position at the university. Ramallah has all those things, but no sea.

A few weeks after I started coming to Ramallah to see Osama, not as his lawyer, I promised him a visit with me to a freshwater sea, in the southern West Bank—to Wadi Qelt, a river that flows between Jericho and Jerusalem, through a number of Israeli settlements. This was the only place I could imagine where we could swim. If soldiers were to stop us there or on the way, Osama had a temporary permit—a "staying permit" that I got him, which would provide temporary permission to live in his house. They wouldn't remove him to Gaza.

On a Saturday morning, I informed him that we were going to hike with a positive attitude. We were going to have a good time. I promised that on the Jewish Sabbath there would be fewer settlers in the wadi, and even if we encountered armed Israelis, we would not let them interfere with our fun trip. The occupation, I told him and myself, was not invited to our outing. Osama would taste the water, feel it on his skin, I instructed him. We would linger in that no-space space where we could swim together.

I hadn't been to Wadi Qelt in ten years, since the outbreak of the Second Intifada in 2000. Before that, when I still lived in Jerusalem, I hiked there in the hope that the occupation was just about to end. I rehearsed my trips there as a guest, as a tourist in the State of Palestine. I remembered the peppermint fields, the deep cold pools, and the stunning view of the desert. I remembered that the nicest pools ran near the settlements, but before the separation wall was built, they were accessible to all. Israelis and Palestinians both hiked in the area, as if with every step, each side tipped a scale that had yet to reach its final equilibrium.

I packed food and drinks into a bag and tried to persuade a nervous Osama to leave the house. I showed him the map I had bought from the Israeli Society for the Preservation of Nature, with details of the area's topography, attempting to assuage his fears of the unknown the way you show a child exactly how the nurse is going to stick in the needle to draw a blood sample. He found reasons to delay. We left late.

We boarded a public taxi to Jericho and asked the driver to let us off near the Israeli settlement of Vered Yeriho, where there was a path leading down to the wadi. Osama laughed when he noticed me trying to cover the map with my hands so that the other passengers wouldn't see it was written in Hebrew. He doesn't understand why I am careful in Ramallah, why I try to hide signs that would identify me as Israeli, like Hebrew writing on my bag or shirt, the screen of my telephone, or a water bottle on which the Hebrew word *Neviot* is printed. Osama would understand very well the confusion, fear, or hostility that seeing an Israeli could inspire in Palestinian passersby. But only that day did I realize that Osama had resisted identifying me as Israeli. Until that day, he didn't see me as being, among other identities, also Israeli.

We arrived at the entrance to the path, near the main road, overlooking a vast expanse of rugged mountain and below, in the wadi, a trail of green tracing the path of the life-giving water. We began the descent. A Bedouin hawker left a group of English-speaking tourists to offer us "authentic" souvenirs. He addressed me in Hebrew and seemed confused when Osama asked him, in Arabic, if this was the right path to the spring. Then he smiled a tolerant, pluralistic smile and pointed the way. As we progressed along the deserted path, I paused at a switchback, took off my jeans, and put on a pair of shorts for the hike, all of which greatly alarmed Osama. "But you're in the middle of the street!" he said, as if it were a crowded urban thoroughfare.

Blue skies, mountains, the winding wadi, a sense of space. Osama couldn't believe that it was so beautiful here, so nearby. He began to take photographs of the rocks, the cliffs, insects, the bend of the riverbed. He photographed a rock on which thousands of years of dripping water had created ridges shaped like DNA spirals and proclaimed it "the biology rock."

We walked a path that traversed the riverbed from above and met a young Israeli man and woman eating breakfast near a tent they had erected on the bank. They invited us to join them, and I politely declined. Osama was startled to see them on the path but also charmed by the idea that they had spent the night there. "They're just hiking," he agreed. We kept on walking toward flowing water—visible for the first time in the stone aqueduct built a century ago by Jerusalem's well-established Husseini family. We walked alongside it, passing the stone house where a Bedouin family still lives deep in the valley, in an oasis of water amid the desert mountains.

When we reached the first pool—small, shallow, but bursting with cold water from a waterfall—Osama jumped in and knelt, splashing water everywhere, laughing like a child and shouting in celebration.

Graceful lizards darted among the rocks, their tan color partially camouflaging them. My heart filled with joy, as if our simple and common love for water were stripping away the layers of difference between us and cutting through our halting attempts to understand each other's social and cultural norms. I wanted to make Osama happy, and I wanted to get closer to him, to create a shared happy memory.

We continued walking toward Ein Fuar, a spring relatively close to the road and therefore popular with casual hikers. The hikers we passed greeted us, offered water, and asked about landmarks, all in Hebrew, and I engaged with them easily and naturally, as I had on dozens if not hundreds of hikes in Israel. Osama became increasingly quiet. Five young men—teenagers, really—approached and asked us in Hebrew, heavily accented with Arabic, how far to the monastery. I showed them on the map, and then Osama joined the conversation in Arabic. They stared at us, stunned. One of them started speaking rapid Arabic to Osama, which I couldn't understand, and I offered his friend a bottle of water. He took the bottle, and they continued on their way. Osama said one of them asked if I was "Jewish or foreign," and he didn't respond. We kept walking.

A fortysomething man and two younger men passed us, one of them carrying a baby in a carrier on his shoulders. They responded to my hello hesitantly, sizing us up, and then disappeared around a bend. A few minutes later, we encountered them at the first deep pool of the trip, fed by a surging waterfall. Without hesitation, I stripped down to my bathing suit and jumped into the cold water. I stood under the waterfall and laughed out loud at the water's force. Osama photographed me but stayed on the edge of the pool. I swam to him.

"Why don't you jump in?" I asked. "The water is wonderful!"

"Let's go," he said. His face was closed. I climbed out of the water and dressed. As I sat down to lace my shoes, I found myself eye level with the pistol strapped to the waist of the older man who stood next to the pool. Osama had already rejoined the path, and I raced after him.

"I'm sorry," I said to Osama. "I didn't see it."

We repacked the backpack and continued walking, now in water that reached our knees. We didn't see any more Palestinian hikers. I counted two more armed Israeli men, bearing huge guns that you couldn't miss resting on their shoulders and strapped to their chests.

I tried to talk to Osama about anything. I mentioned how refreshing the water was, that the sky was blue, and the stones white and smooth. The silence between us deepened.

When the path widened, we again encountered the group of young Palestinian men who had been on their way to the monastery. They heard me speaking to Osama in English, our habitual language of communication. Again they tried to figure us out.

"Are you her translator?" one of them asked Osama, and again he didn't respond. We bypassed the crowded area of the pools and put distance between ourselves and Ein Fuar. Another passing hiker promised a beautiful, isolated pool a kilometer and a half away. I persuaded Osama to continue on the path rather than return to the main road at Ein Fuar. I wanted to re-create the childlike joy he had showed jumping into the first pool, before we had to justify ourselves to Israeli and Palestinian hikers trying to categorize us as with them or against them.

For the first time since the morning, the path became quiet. Serene. We climbed up and down a narrow trail along the cliffside. The exertion masked our silence. We reached the pool and found two groups of young Israelis sunbathing and laughing. We stepped into the cool water, and I watched Osama smile as the water touched his skin, hot from the sun. But after a few minutes, he got out and asked that we go home.

We walked back to Ein Fuar, where six kilometers still separated us from the main road. I suggested we try to find a ride—I often hitchhiked out of hiking areas to get to public transportation on main roads—and we searched for a car that had Palestinian license plates, white or green. We didn't find any. I heard the rattle of an engine behind us, and I moved toward the street, intending to ask for a ride, but Osama took my hand and said, “Not that car.” His smile was genuine, amused. It was a Border Police jeep.

We ended up hitching a ride with a young Israeli woman and two young Israeli men returning from a short walk in the wadi. They were happy and lighthearted. I offered them some of the wild mint I had picked, and we each described the route we had taken. They asked where we were from.

“The Jerusalem area,” I said.

“Where?” the young woman asked.

“Each of us from a different place,” I said. I didn’t know what would have happened if I had said, “Ramallah.”

Osama thanked them in Hebrew when we got out of the car.

“*Shalom*,” he said.

We found a public taxi to his apartment. He said he had to get to bed early in anticipation of a busy week.

“How are you?” I asked.

“Fine,” he said.

“I’m sorry about today. I didn’t realize it would be like that.”

“It’s fine,” he said.

“Can we talk about it?”

“There’s nothing to talk about.”

I tried some more and managed to extract this:

“It was strange for me to see that you feel more comfortable with Israelis than with Palestinians,” Osama said to me.

It was true. I had a common language, even with the Israelis who went for a hike armed with guns. I knew how to talk to them. With despair, with helplessness, I realized what I imagined Osama had already realized—that if we were to encounter danger, I would be the one to protect us. I would be the one to save us, with the language and identity I shared with the people who terrified Osama.

I left for work the next day and didn’t return to see Osama until the following weekend. I didn’t suggest we go out again. While Osama was at work, I found in his apartment a book by Raja Shehadeh called

Palestinian Walks. It had a chapter on Wadi Qelt, describing the author's trip to green space that had been occupied. Territory occupied belligerently. Territory occupied with love. Territory occupied with violence.

There was no space for us to walk in Wadi Qelt together. I felt stupid, naive, as if I had forgotten it was occupied and had forgotten who I am and who Osama is.

Osama

A List of Things to Be Angry About

Sari, I'm sorry.

I'm angry. Very angry.

I believe that those who hate hurt themselves. Still, I hate Israel.

I don't hate Israelis. I am angry at them and sad for us and for them.

I hate Israel as an occupying power. I hate Israel because I miss my mother and my brothers and sisters, and my friends, my childhood, Gaza.

I don't want to be a tourist in my own land. I want to get to know every part of it, to feel it and to sow love and hope within it, to go with my son anywhere I want in my country, to swim with him in the sea whenever I want, to drive my car anywhere or nowhere without someone detaining and humiliating me.

I love people and don't want to be afraid of them. I want to say my name anywhere and anytime, to walk in Wadi Qelt whenever I want, to swim in its waters, without the threat of a gun.

I don't want to miss Gaza over the phone, as I have been doing for seventeen years. I want to miss its messiness, the smiles of its residents, their jokes—the way a person misses his people or city after being away from them for a week or a month.

I want to visit Faya, Wendy, and Garo, my friends from the English-language course for foreign students, who live in China and Taiwan and Korea, and even Silvie in Argentina. The world is full of countries and cities that I will never have the freedom to visit and people I will never be able to see again.

I want to plan a men's trip to Aqaba, without the word "Israel" coming up. We'll talk about women. Or be together and say nothing.

I don't want to be reminded, while sitting in my office, of the interrogations and torture that I underwent in Israeli detention, to be terrified when a door slams from the pleasant breeze of a summer day.

I don't want to jump in fear when I hear fireworks.

I want to swear at my workplace as I drive there in the morning, without scanning the sides of the road, afraid of seeing blue and white and khaki.

I don't know the dimensions of the space in which I live my life. I have no idea how far Ramallah is from the villages that surround it.

I want to know the path Sari will run in her ultramarathon—160 kilometers in Southern Israel, not far from Gaza, a distance I can't even see in my imagination.

I want my geography and my history. I want my own dreams. I don't want to dream about soldiers. I don't want to take revenge on Jews or wish for them to be persecuted again. Not them and not us.

I want the freedom to want.

I'm sorry, Sari. I don't know how we can make this work.

Sari

JUNE 2010

Recipe for *Fatat Dajaj Ghazawieh* (Gazan chicken on a bed of bread and rice)

Ingredients: Kosher and halal chicken parts, preferably frozen so they don't spoil during the bus and public taxi ride from Tel Aviv to Ramallah. Gazan pita, thin and fresh; fresh garlic; hot peppers; lemon; salt and black pepper (white pepper also works); rice; olive oil.

First, persuade Osama to eat the kosher chicken, despite his denial of the existence of God and his opposition to organized religion. Then clean the chicken and marinate it in lemon. Boil the chicken in a pot. Add salt and pepper. Crush the garlic and hot peppers and place in a small bowl. Add lemon juice and set aside.

Osama asks, untrustingly, how I'm managing.

Osama

God Is Kosher

When I was in fourth grade, in the UNRWA (United Nations Refugee Works Association) school, my teacher brought his adult son in at the end of the year and asked him to calculate our class rank. I think he was training his son to teach in the school. According to the son's calculation, I had earned the highest grade, but the teacher manipulated the numbers so that another boy, who was not a refugee, would rank first. His son pointed out the discrepancy, and they discussed it in front of us. The teacher prevailed with an intentional miscalculation, and they ranked the other boy first. We were children, but we knew something was wrong. This was the religious studies teacher who taught us how to do wudu—the ritual ablutions of hands, face, and feet—to purify ourselves for prayer.

A few years later, when I was twelve years old, I worked for a rich family in Gaza, assembling silk flower bouquets in their workshop. It was Ramadan, I was fasting, and I was shocked to see the family members eating. There I was, a child, fasting every day while working, and

I was still a refugee and still poor. And the head of the household, who had lots of money, was eating. All my life, adults taught me that God blesses those who obey his commandments. But if that guy was not fasting, how could God bless him with so much money?

There must be something wrong with that God, I thought.

Sari

Precious Chickens

Remove the chicken from the pot and grill it at a very high temperature on both sides, until it browns. You can do that in a small, portable metal oven that you plug into a household electrical socket—it mimics the flames that Osama's mother used to light to cook food in the courtyard of their house in the Jabalia refugee camp.

Toast the pita in the oven until crisp.

Fry a little of the rice in olive oil on a high flame until it browns. Add water, salt, and the rest of the rice, and cook on a low flame.

That's it. When everything is ready to be assembled, break the crispy pita into pieces and scatter them in a baking tray. Add the rice in a layer. Place the chicken on top of the rice. Pour part of the soup from the chicken over the tray and add some more to the small bowl with the lemon, hot peppers, and garlic. Adjust seasonings and serve the bowl as a sauce for guests to add as they wish.

Eat the *Fatat Jaj Ghazawieh* with Gazan tomatoes, prepared as follows: Sauté hot peppers. Add garlic and tomatoes, cut into quarters or sixths, until the spiciness of the peppers is absorbed into the tomatoes, and the peppers take on the acidic neutrality of the tomatoes. See how easy it is for something to become something else?

Persuade Osama that Gazan tomatoes are indeed part of the chicken recipe, despite his protest that they require a separate recipe and therefore a separate chapter. He should write his own chapters and let me write mine.

Here's a suggested topic of conversation during the meal: Ask Osama to tell the story of the hunger strike he began one Friday, the day that families in the Jabalia refugee camp made chicken for lunch, in protest of his mother's refusal to let him play football. To the best of my recollection, the strike succeeded in the sense that his mother released him from the meal to play football, but by the time he arrived, the game had already ended. And when he got home, he discovered that lunch had ended too—the chicken was all gone.

Osama

She

Easy to describe, hard to understand.

Kind, shy, patient, supportive, deliberative, stubborn. Persistent. I kept a copy of her training program for the 216-kilometer marathon she planned in the North, near the Lebanese border. She made a list of all the details, down to the minute, every point where she expected to refill water or change socks or meet a friend who drove food supplies to her.

She is also impulsive and doesn't wait. She pushes me to places I'm not ready to go.

She loves people—their different ways of life and how they express themselves. If I mention a friend or family member, she insists on knowing their names and seeing their photographs. She likes when they identify with each other, and with her. She likes stories. Likes exploring. She doesn't argue with me but challenges me with affection.

She needs me without saying so, needs me in her way. I saw that in her face, when I asked her not to come to Ramallah next week. She didn't ask me why, and she didn't come.

Try to get close to her without forgetting all of what she is.

Gentle. Compassionate. Tough. Friendly. Cold. Distant. Close. Loves to eat. Loves chocolate. Loves to run. Delights in those she loves.

Sari

Proofreading

AUGUST 2010

Five months after Osama and I began our halting, start-stop attempts at an impossible love relationship. It's thirty-one degrees Celsius and humid. I made myself a pot of herbal tea with a lot of sugar and sat in front of the computer at the kitchen table of my apartment in Tel Aviv. I drank hot tea, sweated, and proofread Osama's doctoral dissertation.

To me, it's beautiful research that demonstrates curiosity, listening, and genuine interest in students and the way they understand and learn about the world of science. How students' and scholars' approach and access to language influence their abilities to engage in scholarly discussion and the way their work is received by others. I imagined the committee members at King's College reading the text and being moved by the sensitive and brilliant researcher, who adopts a lighthearted tone and peppers his words with exclamation points and enthusiasm for the journey into the world of ideas. Israel has to allow him to remain in Palestine. Palestine has to allow him to challenge its educational system—to inject new ideas into it and to insist on high standards.

I worked on the dissertation in sessions of several hours each time. I forced myself to concentrate and didn't tire. I dove into the words to connect to Osama's world, making his English-language sentences more precise and encouraging him to explain himself fully.

Every few days I sent him the computer files, and we discussed them, working through my comments. He complimented me on my "charming criticism." I didn't visit him in Ramallah, hadn't seen him in many weeks, but rather restricted myself to Skype calls, with Osama's electronically reconstituted face on one screen and his dissertation on the other, switching back and forth between the person and his words: "Who Joins the Club? Language of Publication and Ownership of Scientific Research."

When I reached the fifth chapter, I realized I was proofreading his dissertation because I was in love with him.

Osama

Open-Book Exam

The astonishment was apparent on their faces.

One of them asked, “You mean we’re allowed to cheat?”

“If your definition of ‘cheating’ is opening the book and reading it during the exam, then yes, you are allowed to cheat,” I said.

Another student asked, “Can we bring our outlines?”

“And also half the books in the library, if you want,” I responded.

The discussion continued in that vein for a few minutes, until a student asked, “OK, if all the material is on our desks, what are we supposed to do, Professor?”

“Could there be something important to recognize about this whole process of teaching and learning?” I asked. “What about trying to see yourselves as important here—as the most important part of this. Your opinions, your ideas and way of thinking, are what’s important on this exam.”

“What do you mean, Professor?” a student asked.

“What we’re asking, Professor, is what should we do?” another student added.

I felt a pang of guilt that we, the lecturers in the universities and the teachers in the high schools, and the Palestinian educational system in general, are failing our students. We're rewarding them for memorizing the words of others and failing to encourage them to challenge and engage with what they read and hear.

The first student who asked me about the exam brought the textbook with her, as I'd told her to do, but she left it in her bag as she wrote the exam. She had already memorized its contents and reproduced them in answer to the exam questions.

Sari
In Re:

I wrote the letter and got David to sign it, because I don't put my signature on Osama's letters anymore. I stopped being his lawyer, but I'm not sure what I am to him instead.

Date: August 17, 2010

To: First Lieutenant Nathan Liver, Officer Advisor—
Legal Advisor, the West Bank

Dear Colleague,

Re: HCJ 23503/07 *Osama Mustafa Fahed v. Defense Minister*—
Coordinating the petitioner's travel via the Allenby
Bridge.

I write to request that you coordinate the exit of my client, whose details are above, via the Allenby Bridge, to allow him to defend his doctoral dissertation in the United Kingdom, and also coordinate his return to the West Bank upon conclusion of his doctoral studies.

You will recall that, in the context of the agreement reached in the above-referenced petition, the state committed to allowing my client to be present in the West Bank for visits during his doctoral studies, and that "after he completes his studies, the petitioner will reenter the area of Judea and Samaria as a visitor." My client is currently about to complete his doctoral studies. He must participate in an oral defense of his dissertation before a committee of the Faculty of Education at King's College, which will convene on November 23, 2010.

In order to facilitate his participation, my client was issued a visa to the UK.

The defense of his dissertation (the "viva") is the last stage of my client's doctoral studies. Afterward, he requests to return to the West Bank, and from there to ask the Israeli authorities to recognize his residence there, pursuant to the arrangements reached by the parties in HCJ 23503/07.

Kindly confirm that my client's exit and entrance via the Allenby Bridge will be coordinated for the requested dates.

Respectfully and with thanks in advance,
Attorney David Fried

Osama

What If . . .

NOVEMBER 2010

How do you know if you're in love? When can you let yourself love again, after your heart has been broken?

I met her in midlife, a divorced father. I felt many things for her: desire, joy, laughter, curiosity. Also fear. I felt that my habits and customs limited me. Did the smell of my cooking fish bother her? What did she expect of me? She's foreign, Jewish, Israeli. I didn't know what she knew about me and my society, and it was hard for me to reconcile what I knew about hers with my feelings for her. Maybe we both were flooded with stereotypes.

She said that, after a number of failed attempts, she was ready for a relationship. I wasn't sure about that.

After the bitter experience of my separation and divorce from Nisreen, I felt as if the ground were not stable beneath my feet. I lost trust. I'm afraid of people. Afraid of love. I try to create a safe distance between myself and others, but I fail at that miserably and find myself dangerously close to others. I'm afraid of being vulnerable to new pain.

And then she showed up.

I wanted to see her all the time—and that terrified me. I was fascinated by the way she thinks, the way she gets to know new places by running through them.

"There's a stone castle on the other side of the mountain," she told me, returning to my apartment from a morning run. And: "I found a bakery in the Old City that has real whole wheat pita, no white flour."

I prefer to take my time. It can take me hours to decide whether to buy something in this store or that store—and she's in a rush, and that's her right. "We're going to Wadi Qelt tomorrow," she said. And: "I'll come to Ramallah on Friday."

I told her frankly: "I can't be in a relationship with you when I'm prevented from traveling, and you are not."

If we can't travel together, and if I can't come early in the morning and wake her up, or visit her in the middle of the night to go for a swim, or just drop by to eat hummus and falafel in the middle of the day, I don't see how we can be in a relationship. My not being able to travel put a strain on my relationship with Nisreen, even before we went to London. For seven years, she traveled to the North, to the sea, to Jerusalem, with and without Firas, and I didn't leave Ramallah. It ate away at me. I did things that I'm not proud of, and I don't want to repeat them.

These doubts are killing me.

What if she leaves me? What if she cheats on me? What if she cuts me down? What if I cheat on her? What if they send me to Gaza? What if I feel, after some time, that I'm not ready for love? What if . . .

I think I'll never embark on another adventure, that I'm no longer capable of taking any risks. As if I'm more than a hundred years old.

I like my space. I like my isolation and privacy.

I don't dare to talk about my sexual practices and my views on sex. It's a very private space. Will I dare share that with her?

I'm the son of a refugee camp. The children of refugee camps have a special scent, enticing and complex. We love people—that's the first thing that comes to mind. We're used to being crowded together, never alone. We love loud voices and raunchy jokes. We live in such close proximity that we know what's happening in each other's lives without needing to be told. The walls between homes are so thin we hear the farts of our neighbors in the bathroom and laugh. We protect the camp and our neighbors. We prefer death over humiliation, or at least that's how we used to be in the First Intifada, when my friends and I held our ground in the alley, even as the soldiers advanced. I fall apart if someone disrespects me, even inadvertently. I like to help and accept help from others—but only when I request it.

It's been two months since Sari last came to Ramallah. I miss her. Is that longing the first sign of liberation from an old pain, or perhaps the beginning of a new pain?

Sari

Note in the Mailbox

Osama motivated me to learn Arabic. The things that I asked about his past, about his feelings for me, the things he refused to tell me—he wrote. In Arabic. Not even the spoken Arabic that I'm haltingly learning, but formal, literary Arabic. I'll kill him. He wrote down his thoughts about "What if" we were to try to be in a love relationship, uploaded them to the *Maqluba* book's Dropbox, and then flew to London to defend his dissertation.

It's strange that he is the one traveling for work and I'm staying put. I've only ever seen him in Ramallah and Wadi Qelt. I wish I could see him at the airport in Amman. Suitcase in hand. Presenting his passport at the check-in counter. Reaching the gate and handing over his boarding pass. "Mr. Fahed," the flight attendant would address him, and she would smile a British smile. I'd like to see him wearing a winter coat. Opening an umbrella. Walking the streets of London.

Even before he traveled, I hadn't seen Osama for two months, because he erected an obstacle that I couldn't overcome—his unwillingness to love me.

"I can't do this," he told me early that Sunday morning as he dropped me off at the taxi station for the long journey to my office in Tel Aviv. We'd stayed up late the night before talking, or trying to, because Osama would start sentences but not know how to finish them, and my questions left us both frustrated and exhausted. "I'm sorry."

If Osama would give me permission to love him, I would fight. With the same patience and stubbornness with which I ran my last ultramarathon. But Osama needs to understand—Osama needs to agree—that in a 160-kilometer race, you can't avoid pain.

I want Osama to be happy. Maybe there, in London, he would be happy.

I don't want to leave this land.

I didn't write this earlier, but on the evening we returned to his apartment from our trip to Wadi Qelt, Osama made up a separate bed for me.

He wrote of loving me as he flew to London. Will he still love me when he returns to our maqluba world?

Osama

Gloves

Again I'm at a border crossing. I know that some people arrive at an airport and rush to the duty-free shops, sip a cappuccino, and buy souvenirs for their children. In movies, traveling to another country represents freedom. But the stench of garbage at the border crossing between the West Bank and Jordan reminded me of the stench at the home-based factory that belonged to that rich family in Gaza, where I worked assembling silk flowers when I was twelve. One day, the owner's sister-in-law asked me to take out their garbage, which was not part of the job description I had agreed to. The garbage bag was smelly, it leaked, and I was angry. I left their house, threw the garbage into the dumpster, and continued walking all the way home. The owner came to my house to find out what had happened, and my mother spoke to him. "That boy is stubborn," she told him. He promised they would never again ask me to take out the garbage.

I very much wanted to get to know Jordan, but the authorities are incredibly creative in putting up obstacles and making people angry, making them hate. At least, that's what they do when they see the word "Gaza" in your passport. *Go into that room. Sit. Where are you going? Where do you live? Do you intend to stay in Jordan? When is your flight? Why are you flying?* I took a taxi from the West Bank border straight to the airport. By the time I left Jordan, I hoped never to come back. I felt the same way at the Israeli airport in Lydda in 1998, where they separated Palestinians from Israeli Jews and subjected us to humiliating bodily searches, and I hoped that I would never have to return to Palestine.

The universe was too narrow to contain me. I flew and flew, and I arrived at Heathrow.

I was glad that this time, the city was no longer strange to me. I remembered how it had looked just a few years ago. The style of houses reminded me of the houses we drew as children, made of brick and wood, with sloped roofs and a chimney sticking out. The red double-decker buses intimidated me. I didn't know where to get off and when to ring the bell to request a stop, and I didn't want to make a mistake. It took me a month to dare ride the bus.

Then, as now, taking the tube was easy. No need to make decisions. Euston is Euston. Marx is buried outside the Highgate stop. East Finchley, West Finchley, and then my flat was a three-minute walk from Woodside Park. I remembered how much I loved watching the other riders listening to iPods, wearing suits, reading books. Except in the mornings, when they were so pressed against me in the crowd they were just bodies. I wondered what languages they spoke and what the inside of their homes looked like.

London reminds me that Palestine is a human problem like any other. Our oppression is specific but not unique. People are suffering in India; people are suffering in Thailand; people are suffering in Ethiopia, in Bosnia, in Pakistan; and people are suffering even in Europe and the United States.

I ask myself, *How can we identify with others?* Identification is first and foremost recognition and familiarity. But Gazans don't even know West Bankers; West Bankers don't know Gazans; West Bankers don't know Palestinians inside Israel; Palestinians inside Israel don't know what is outside Israel. Palestinians don't know Palestinians. I saw "Free Palestine" graffiti on the wall of a tube station and wished I could meet whoever had written it to learn more.

The two weeks in London flew by. I passed my dissertation defense with a request for revisions. I did a little shopping, had some last meetings, and rushed to board the train to Heathrow Airport. A text message from Sari arrived: "Waiting for you." Her name on my phone screen flooded me with excitement but also self-doubt. Will she like the gloves I bought her? Will I have the courage to invite her to Ramallah to receive them?

Sari

Ultramarathon

Osama returned to Ramallah, but we haven't seen each other. I offered to pick him up from Jericho, to come to his university in the middle of the week, to visit him for a quiet and intimate Friday.

"I need my time," he said.

The text messages he had sent me from London were full of joy. Also longing, but not for Ramallah. He wrote that he slept soundly there, didn't wake up in the middle of the night. He walked the streets like the rest of the anonymous people, presented his work at the university, and rubbed elbows with colleagues who encouraged him, who saw him as a brilliant scholar with some technical problems traveling—they didn't really understand the details.

Maybe the return home shook him. I felt him slipping away from me.

After he sent me that letter daring to love me, just before he left for London, I felt a change. I had a "Congratulations!" balloon sent to him on the day he defended his dissertation. He told me that he told his London friends about me, and I got a friend request on Facebook from one of them. Osama and I spoke on Skype every day, also about the future. We had turned our nonrelationship into a relationship. We gave up the protection that denying our relationship had given it, to blossom, unfettered, in a twilight zone where no one could harm it, because it didn't really exist, and Osama and I couldn't break up, because we weren't together. We decided to have a relationship inside our there's-no-space space, the only place where it could exist.

I raced forward, but maybe it was too fast for Osama. Our relationship, I'm realizing, is not just a relationship but also an ultramarathon. And Osama and I are running at different paces and with different strategies for reaching the finish line.

After founding Gisha, I started to run very long distances. Ultramarathons of 100, 160, and even 200 kilometers. These runs take hours, even more than a day, and to complete them, I have to be slow, patient, and calculated, but also unrestrained. To succeed, I need to stay hyperaware of my weaknesses while simultaneously believing that I can do the impossible.

When my nonrelationship with Osama became a relationship, I searched for the route. I discovered not only that it was much longer than any race I had run but also that my running partner and I had no shared understanding of the terrain.

"I told Firas about you, in an indirect way," he told me while he was in London. "And Nisreen as well, although I didn't give many details." I had told my closest friends months ago, but no one else. It seemed too fragile, until London, until our relationship started to seem real.

But when Osama withdrew, I started to believe that our relationship was over or, more precisely, that it had never existed.

It's hard for me to believe in the existence of things I create. Five years ago, during the early phases of founding Gisha, when I was working day and night to breathe life into the organization, a friend invited me to watch a movie with her. I declined, as I almost always did during that period, explaining that I had to work. She said, "Sari, the organization will still exist tomorrow, even if you leave the office before ten p.m."

With time, the realness of the organization helped convince me of its existence—people's lives had been changed after we helped them travel, including Osama's. Just this week, at the end of a long day, as I locked the dark office, I looked at the desks and chairs and computers and realized they belonged to staff members of an organization that I created, that exists.

I didn't believe I could run 160 kilometers, but I did. I didn't believe I could create an organization with a professional staff and mission that would help hundreds of people, but I did. I wanted to believe I could build a love relationship with Osama, but I think I was wrong.

Osama

Sixty Kilometers

It's early evening, and the restaurants in Ramallah are preparing for New Year's parties. People are getting out of their cars dressed in their finest, the men in button-down shirts and the women in sequined dresses. And I haven't even showered yet today.

The distance between us is sixty kilometers, and an entire world separates us.

I wanted you to come to me, for us to celebrate the new year together. I didn't want you to come to me, because I can't come to you. I was afraid of how much I wanted you.

The running gloves that I bought for you—with the special pocket to hold your house key—are still wrapped in the Harrods box. I was overcome with an impossible desire: to come to you now, in my car, ten o'clock at night, to Tel Aviv. I think my car can manage the trip.

Yeah, I know that . . .

And anyway, could an impossible act like that alone save this relationship?

Sari

Love Experiments

"The Israeli military is arresting people from their homes and removing them to Gaza by force," I said to Orit, the director of Gisha's public outreach department, working through my talking points for lectures and meetings for a planned work trip to the United States.

"Can you soften your tone a bit? You sound angry," she said. "Remember that many Americans have a positive view of the Israeli army. Especially when you go to Washington, DC. Can you use the passive voice? Say, 'People are being forced from their homes,' and let your audience feel sympathy for that before you reveal that it's Israeli soldiers taking them away."

She studied me from across my desk, checking to see if I took offense. She'd been with Gisha for two years and was skilled at getting our unpopular messages into Israeli TV, radio, and print media. Apparently, she understood US audiences as well.

"I'm lucky to have you," I told her, and typed away at my computer, making her revisions.

In breaks between preparations for my trip, I wrote to Israeli academics in the fields of science history and science, asking if they would write to the defense minister and urge him to permit Osama to continue to live in his home. Five months had passed since Osama's successful trip to London. The committee approved his dissertation, and the university issued his diploma, so he should now be referred to as Dr. Osama Fahed, and that's how I wrote his name in the letter to the defense minister. But with his graduation and new title, the military's commitment not to remove him from Ramallah expired. The agreement I had reached with the state attorney's office was valid for the duration of his doctoral studies only.

In other words, Osama was again trapped in Ramallah, as an illegal resident in his home.

"Sari, you're not displaying empathy for the security concerns that travel in and out of Gaza creates for many people," Orit said with a hint of frustration. This was a second practice round in advance of my trip to the United States, and she was still not satisfied. "We need to show that we see ourselves as part of the Israeli public, working out of love for the society in which we live, with all its flaws."

"I'm trying," I said, and went back to revising my talking points.

Her reproach reminded me of a conversation I had with a Saudi human rights activist named Abdulaziz, whom I met at a conference abroad. Abdulaziz had been tortured in a Saudi prison for his activities, among other things, working to protect LGBTQ people. In some Saudi families, the parents lock up their gay children and abuse them physically, using violence to try to root out the forbidden sexual orientation. Abdulaziz didn't even try to preach tolerance or to get the Saudi authorities to protect the threatened men and boys, but rather, he concentrated on trying to smuggle them out of the country to more tolerant countries or at least places where they are not known to be gay, in order to save their lives. I asked him how he deals with the huge gap between his values and the values of the society in which he lives, which he is trying to change.

"With a lot of love," he said. I felt a wave of admiration for him, together with a strong sense of inadequacy, that my ability to love was inferior to his.

I'm trying to love the mother of an acquaintance, a professor at Tel Aviv University, to whom I wrote on Osama's behalf. Osama had been accepted years ago to Tel Aviv University for doctoral studies but couldn't study there after the military authorities refused to allow him to reach the campus. Now I wrote to her and others at Tel Aviv University, asking them to petition the Israeli defense minister to allow Osama to remain in Ramallah and use his newly obtained doctorate to teach there.

I sat on my couch, an open but still empty suitcase on the floor next to me, and typed out my plea.

"Your daughter gave me your contact information and told me what a strong supporter you are of academic freedom," I wrote. "We're trying to show the defense minister that Israeli academics are in solidarity with him." I threw some sweaters into the suitcase and went back to approving expense payments for Gisha when I saw that she had written back to me, expressing support for Osama's right to remain in Ramallah, but with a caveat:

> A few months ago, I invited Professor Peters, a friend and colleague from London, to give the keynote speech at a celebratory conference at Tel Aviv University. Professor Peters agreed, but then three months before the conference, he canceled his participation, saying that he does not want to participate in a conference at a university sponsored by a state that discriminates against his Palestinian colleagues. He explained that he had heard that one of his doctoral students from London would be barred from attending the conference and hearing his lecture, because the student was Palestinian, and that was unacceptable to him. As far as I understand, that's the same person you want me to help. And a few years ago, to the best of my recollection, that same person was accepted to study at Tel Aviv University, and he got permission to reach the campus

> (I know that from an official source), but he refused to attend. So I'm aware of the difficult situation in the territories, and it pains me, but if, in both cases, it's the same person you want me to help, I want to clarify a number of things before I try to mobilize my colleagues on his behalf.

Israeli academics viewed boycotting Israeli academic conferences as an existential threat, and I considered giving up. But my friend had said her mother was open-minded, and she was also well respected and could bring others along. I made myself a cup of cinnamon tea, took three sips and a deep breath, and responded:

> I represented Dr. Fahed in his request to reach his studies at Tel Aviv University. He was accepted to the university in 2006, but the military refused to give him an entrance permit into Israel. I petitioned the Israeli High Court on his behalf, but the High Court refused to intervene, and so he transferred his studies and scholarship to the UK.

Then I added:

> I'm not familiar with the story of Professor Peters, but I also don't understand what it has to do with the appeal to the defense minister to allow Dr. Fahed to continue his academic work in the West Bank. I think the question of supporting Dr. Fahed's ability to work in the field of science history in the West Bank is a separate question—is he entitled to remain in the West Bank or not, and should Israeli scholars express their support for defending that right, in the hope that it will influence the Defense Ministry's decision?

I brushed my teeth and went to switch off my computer for the night, but I saw that the professor had already responded:

"In my opinion," she wrote, "he has a right, like all Palestinians, to travel freely . . . but before I mobilize support of other academics, I want to know what his role was in the boycott by the professors of Ramallah and the Palestinian academy against Israeli professors."

Here she raised another issue—beyond the boycott of Israeli academic institutions by foreign academics, Palestinian universities have a policy not to work with Israeli institutions, to avoid normalizing the occupation. I wrote back: "Is his opinion relevant for you in making your decision whether or not to sign the letter to the minister?"

She said it was. "I understand from my colleagues here that the professors of Ramallah really declared a boycott, and even when we got funding and wanted to work together with professors in the West Bank on education and advanced technologies, we faced boycott and calls not to cooperate. And also I want to understand—would he really want to work with us if he could?"

I had asked myself a similar question at the beginning of our relationship, when we grappled with the fact of our maqluba world that Osama couldn't come to see me at home. I showed him, through the Skype camera, my small but quaint apartment, the double window that looks out onto a tree that shades the outdoor market below, the compact kitchen with the slightly crooked ceiling, the single window that opens out to the roof of the building next door, the dimly lit bedroom with thick stone walls, and the refrigerator he saw behind my chair when we spoke, with magnets holding electricity bills that I haven't paid yet.

The Israeli military didn't take his wishes into consideration, and maybe, for that reason, it's hard to know what they are. Would he really want to visit me? Would he want to travel to Tel Aviv? It had been years since he'd entered Israel. Would he fear the Israelis he would see here, especially those carrying guns?

But this Israeli professor took a different view of who is boycotting whom.

"I'll ask him," I wrote. "If you are talking about the university, then yes, it's university policy not to work with Israeli institutions or to permit university cooperation with Israeli academics . . . I can ask him what he thinks about it. I'll also ask him if he was in touch with Professor Peters . . . It was very hard for him, when they refused to allow him to reach Tel Aviv. He had counted on it and also got a scholarship, so it's a bit like opening up old wounds."

She responded, "I want to know if he boycotts academics from Tel Aviv University in any way. If so—it would be difficult for me."

I tried to think how best to raise the subject with Osama so that he'd understand her question to him, but when I tried to explain it all on Skype, I found myself exploding into laughter—at her, at us, at the upside-down situation—such that Osama barely understood what I was trying to ask.

"I'm sorry," I said. "It's really not funny." But it was, and his expression on the Skype screen grew more confused as my eyes teared up and giggles splurted out.

"She supports your right to live in Ramallah but wants to know if you want to study in Tel Aviv," I said, still laughing.

"But they wouldn't let me study in Tel Aviv!" he said, still confused.

"Yes, but she wants to know, if they would allow you, would you want to?"

"I tried to study there. I applied, registered, and got a scholarship," Osama said, and his earnest face suggested that he really wanted to understand her and me. I tried to pull myself together.

"She wants to know what you think about academic boycotts in the UK and also about your university's anti-normalization policy before she agrees to help."

"I'm in love with an Israeli-American woman who wants to have children, and she wants to know what my position is on normalization?" My ears burned, and I struggled to focus on the conversation. Osama had finally invited me to visit him, several weeks after his return from London. He'd even introduced me as his "friend" to Firas, a sweet, shy boy who shook my hand politely and then left to go to the *balad*, the downtown, with his friends. Osama and I were trying again.

I brought myself back to the professor.

"She wants to know if you accept her," I improvised.

"But they didn't accept me."

In the end, he sent an email directly to the professor, which included an invitation for her to visit him in his unlawful home in Ramallah, but asked her not to send the letter on his behalf if her decision about doing so depended on his position regarding boycotts and normalization.

The professor went ahead and sent the letter to the minister of defense and even mobilized some of her colleagues to do so as well. My friend was right—her mother was open-minded and well respected. And Orit was right—my ridicule of her fears lacked empathy and almost cost us an opportunity to put pressure on the Israeli authorities for Osama's case.

Osama told his colleagues at the university about our appeal to Israeli academics, and they said, "Isn't that normalization?" Osama told them he didn't think it was. He showed them, and then me, the definition of "normalization" as described in the official policy of Palestinian civil society: it concerns joint projects in which Israelis and Palestinians are presented as if they were on equal footing, without reference to the occupation. He agrees that so long as the occupation continues, joint work between Israeli and Palestinian institutions should focus on resisting the occupation.

"Sometimes I want to tell my colleagues about Israelis—I learn so much from you, from Yehudit and Talya and Eli, and Rami and Itamar . . ."

And I thought about normalization, about how far our situation here—mine, Osama's, the professor's—is from being normal.

I finished packing my suitcase and waited until the last minute to tell Osama that I was also going to see my mother in New York.

"Regards to her," Osama told me. I didn't ask him about his mother.

Osama

“We Will Not Permit Normalization”

Yesterday they declared a general strike in Ramallah.

A friend called to tell me while I was already on my way to teach at the university. I decided to return home through the center city. The shop owners were lowering their shutters and locking their doors. I asked one of them for the reason behind the strike. She said that she didn’t know, but that she had heard a dance troupe in the city had agreed to accept Israeli dancers and choreographers.

Another shop owner heard our conversation and gave me a flyer he’d received, which announced the following:

Dear Citizens,

Residents of our Heroic City: It wasn’t enough for the so-called theater director to accept funds from world Zionist organizations. Now he is hosting a delegation that is pushing our honorable dancers into the darkness of normalization in the heart of our beloved city. These attempts at normalization will not succeed, and we will demand accountability from anyone who even thinks about normalizing our lives with the occupation!

This didn't really explain the situation, as it wasn't clear what the delegation wanted or who they were.

Another store owner said, "There's an activist here who knows the reason for the strike." He pointed to a young man who was talking to the owner of a hummus restaurant, trying to get him to close the place.

"Let the people finish eating," the restaurant owner said, even though his restaurant was empty. When I approached the young man, he said he wasn't sure, but he had heard that someone named so-and-so was supposed to direct a show about coexistence (or had submitted a proposal for it) with a Jewish choreographer whose name he didn't know. That was the best answer I had heard so far. I continued on foot to the dance theater, where a small group of artists were demonstrating outside.

First protestor: "We will not allow normalization."

Second protestor: "We are not talking about normalization that has already taken place, but rather about new attempts to normalize, and we are doing this out of fear and concern . . ."

Third protestor: "We will burn down the theater . . ."

The third protestor got applause from most of the onlookers, including from those with whom I had spoken.

On my way home, I saw a group of activists pressuring shop owners to close their gates. I stopped to talk to them and asked, "Do you know that there is more than one Jewish person who joined the PLO, and a few even held senior positions in it, and that there is a street in Ramallah named after such a person?"

"Don't be ridiculous, man," one of the activists said.

In the residential areas of Ramallah, far from the center of town, the shops were open. I stopped in the supermarket. The woman ahead of me in line began to unload the groceries from her cart. I watched her put onto the conveyer belt two cartons of Tnuva milk, Straus sweetened yogurt, and a big bag of Osem Bamba—all Israeli products for which there are local alternatives. I remembered the cooperatives we created during the First Intifada and the commercial boycotts we led, to wean ourselves off dependence on the products that the occupation industries flooded onto our tables.

We have more work to do in order to figure out what we mean when we talk about normalization.

Sari

Personal Narrative

I write letters to be signed by another lawyer, one who is not in love with Osama. Today's letter makes a big ask: for the Israeli military to recognize Osama's right to live in Ramallah permanently.

"I write to you with a request to recognize the permanent residence of my client, whose details are listed above, in the city of Ramallah, where he has lived for the past twenty-one years."

At Gisha, I remind our lawyers to make compelling factual presentations. To write personal narratives that encourage identification with our clients and attempt to persuade the authorities that granting the requested remedy doesn't require a ruling on overall policies in the occupied territory. We're just asking that X reach her work, remain in her home, reunite with her son, travel to her studies. Granting the request won't shake the pillars of the occupation.

Two years ago, during a conference in Istanbul where I spoke about my job as a lawyer in the Israeli legal system, I was accused of collaborating with the system of oppression. Why do I ask the occupier for favors it has no right to grant or refuse? Why do I impart legitimacy to a system that presents a facade of justice? Why do I file documents before courts that serve merely as public complaint boxes, in which judges select a petition, read it, and sometimes pressure military officers but don't make rulings? These judges don't issue orders that would enact significant change.

I liked the conference-goers' vision of ideological purity. It probably feels good to declaim enlightened sentences about human rights and to spin off a brilliant analysis of the responsibility of a military commander who holds a territory under belligerent occupation. What I do is small-scale and practical: I want to help students to study, workers to work, and families to reunite. No letter of mine is going to end the occupation or even shake it up. But a letter from me might allow one person to do something she dreams of doing. Or not.

If I wanted to feel I was in the right, I would have chosen another profession. My profession is dirty.

Four years ago, I would have justified my appeal to the army by saying that giving Osama a chance to reach his studies would not only help him but also Palestinian society, which would benefit from his contribution to the educational and higher educational system. Even if I didn't appeal to the military, and Osama remained trapped in his home, the occupation would continue unfettered. Today I would be willing to do anything to protect Osama from the danger of removal. To remove his fear that the ground beneath his feet is not stable, because at any moment he could be exiled from his home, separated from his son, fired from his job.

Yesterday I dreamed that I was a Palestinian resident from Gaza living in the West Bank. The military knew I was there. I ran, I evaded, but the soldiers closed in on me. There was nowhere to escape. I woke up in a panic at three in the morning, looked at the curtain blowing in the window above my head, and reassured myself: I'm in my bedroom, in the Kerem Hateimanim neighborhood of Tel Aviv. It was just a dream.

I sprinkled the letter to the military with details from Osama's résumé, trying to impress Katie, the nineteen-year-old soldier who will give the letter to Assaf, the twenty-one-year-old commander, who will pass it to Liron, the twenty-three-year-old officer who will decide Osama's fate.

A few months ago, during negotiations with the military over extending his staying permit, I met Liron in the hallway of the Supreme Court. I explained to her that as part of the 2006 court petition, the military had already agreed to allow Osama to stay in the West Bank as a visitor until the completion of his doctoral studies. At her request, I outlined Osama's course of study, his timeline, field research, and dissertation, which at that point was not finished. We agreed that I would write a follow-up letter. I tried to speak with her calmly and logically, to soften her opposition to allowing more Palestinians to remain in the West Bank.

I spoke in a pleasant tone of voice but wanted to scream: *Who do you think you are? What do you know about the semantic foundations of communication in the study of science, and why do I have to explain it to you in order to get you to allow a person to live in his house?*

Now I wrote, calmly and logically: "There is no allegation that my client's residence in Ramallah endangers state security."

Osama

Ramadan

I need a vacation from the vacation, I thought. Ramadan. Ramallah. June and July.

At eight in the morning, they started to bring the children to the summer camp held in the building in which I'm lucky enough to live. The parents were tired from a sleepless night and irritated from a morning without water, coffee, or a cigarette, in the heat of summer. The counselors were also irritated, and I heard their screams all day, together with the crying of the children. It got quiet in the late afternoon, when the last parents collected their kids, and it stayed quiet until the iftar meal breaking the daily fast. At dusk, I heard the clattering of dishes and the clinking of glasses. At that point, I was already exhausted and wanting to sleep, to prepare myself for the nightly round of chaos that continues until five in the morning. Fed, quenched, and having smoked a cigarette, the neighbors wanted to celebrate all night above my bedroom, and I had to leave at least a small window open to let in some air.

They were setting off fireworks to celebrate getting the results of the

Tawjihi, the high school matriculation exam, which happened to coincide with the Muslim holy month of Ramadan. The barking of dogs all night long, together with sorties of buzzing mosquitoes zooming in for attack, added to my frustration.

When did I become sensitive to noise? When did I start needing peace and quiet?

I grew up in a refugee camp in which loud background noises were a part of life. We were eight family members in a two-room house. I could hear the intimate details of my neighbors' lives on the other side of the thin asbestos walls.

In Jabalia, during Ramadan, I would sit outside during the preparation of the iftar meal, breathing in the smells of cooking and enjoying the quiet, as the men slept and the women cooked. After iftar, I would spend the night with my friends on the dirt paths, barefoot, walking on the sand, singing and playing.

"Where are you going?" my mother would ask me.

"Just to so-and-so's home," I would lie.

We prepared lanterns from empty tin boxes of ghee, punching holes to stick a candle inside. We imitated the musaharati, the men who took it upon themselves to wake people for the nightly breakfast before sunrise. Lanterns in hand, we roamed the dark streets, calling, "*Es-ha ya nayem! Wahed il Dayem! Ramadan Kareem!*"

"Wake up, sleepyheads! God is one! Happy Ramadan!"

In Ramallah, just before iftar, cars whizz through the streets to make it home in time to eat, and restaurant staff work furiously to prepare lavish buffets for Ramadan specials. Families arrive in private cars to the apartments of friends or relatives, laden with trays of food, boxes of sweets, and bottles of juice.

Even though I lay awake in my bed in Ramallah during the month of Ramadan, I didn't hear the musaharati at any hour. I don't know why.

Sari

Qalandia: The Last Crossing

The checkpoint system is getting more sophisticated, and I'm increasingly afraid of being arrested.

For the past few months, soldiers at Qalandia checkpoint have required travelers to electronically scan their identification cards, providing a computerized record of their crossings from Ramallah to Jerusalem. My crossings are recorded at six in the morning, together with permit-bearing laborers who, like me, are anxious to get to work on time. Otherwise, I try to hide my identity. If someone speaks to me, I smile or nod, but I don't let my accent give me away. People treat me with courtesy, a lone woman in a sea of men.

So long as the ID card is blue, Israeli, they don't examine it and don't scrutinize the date of birth, which, for Jewish Israelis, includes the Hebrew calendar date. I assume the soldiers believe I'm Palestinian, a resident of East Jerusalem, who also holds a blue ID card and therefore can enter Jerusalem. Sometimes, as we wait to enter the inspection area, soldiers patrol on the other side of the metal bars, examining us, examining me. I make eye contact with them, trying to learn something from the way they look at a Palestinian woman.

I got confirmation of a soldier's assumptions on one of the first days after they installed the electronic scanner. As I approached the inspection window, I didn't immediately notice the new machine and pressed my ID card to the window, as usual. The soldier ignored it. I waited silently in front of the window, and then he yelled at me in Arabic over the intercom, apparently annoyed that I was holding up the line. Even if I could decipher some words through the crackling speaker system, I wouldn't have understood his instructions in Arabic. A female soldier pushed him aside and yelled at me too, in Arabic, but she was kind enough to point to a small new machine installed next to the window that separated us, on my side. I recognized it as a scanner and put my ID card on it. The female soldier gave a victory smile to the male soldier. Before she turned off the intercom, I heard her say to him, in Hebrew, "You see? I told you I speak Arabic better than you do."

I continued crossing through Qalandia in the mornings, an imposter Palestinian, lousy at following directions, whose entrances from Ramallah to Jerusalem were meticulously recorded. If I wanted to know how often Osama and I saw each other, I could request a printout from the Israeli military.

One morning, in early spring, they changed the procedures. Even before I reached the concrete overhang that covers the entrance to the crossing, I saw the workers crowding and pushing. I thought they had closed the crossing, and that's why there was a jam. The crowd pushed toward the entrances to the cages (long, narrow aisles surrounded by metal bars) that funnel the traffic toward the manned inspection area. I stood on the side, wondering what to do. A handful of men, among the youngest and the oldest, also hung back from the throng swaying forward and backward as if it were a single creature, a creature that occasionally spit out a lucky person into one of the aisles. A mustached man pointed me in the direction of the "humanitarian lane," but the gate to the lane was closed. I wondered what would happen if I joined the throng of men. Would I be pushed? Crushed? Would they make an opening for me? Reproach me for undermining my feminine dignity? What about their dignity?

I waited by the humanitarian lane, and after a few minutes, I was joined by other women, older people, and a few young men. It got crowded there too. Every time a soldier came out of the booth and approached us from the other side of the bars, we surged forward toward the gate, anticipating its long-delayed opening. I found myself pushed up against the bars, crushed between them and the broad body of a very old and very strong woman who didn't take her eyes off the tall soldier surveying us from the booth. I think he was also startled by the crowd pushing up against the bars, everyone late, everyone pressured, everyone confused. Finally, a soldier began checking our eligibility, sent the young men away, opened the gate, and let us enter the inspection area, but it seemed as if there, too, the inspections was taking longer than usual. When my turn came, I placed my ID card on the scanner. A young soldier in a thickly padded winter coat looked at her computer screen and then looked at me. She picked up the telephone next to her. I didn't hear what she said, but as she spoke, another soldier sitting on the other side of the cubicle turned his head, looked at her, and then looked at me. Apparently, she received instructions over the phone to let me pass, and she pressed the button that opened the next set of revolving steel doors.

I didn't say anything to Osama.

Later that week, again returning from a visit to Osama, I arrived at the checkpoint earlier, but again throngs of people swarmed the gates. I realized they had changed some of the inspection procedures—made them more rigid or onerous. The lines moved slowly. Again I debated whether to push myself into the crowd of men—what was the difference between me and the smaller men, for example, who were also being pushed and crushed—but I imagined how a woman pushing and being pushed might look through the eyes of the men, and I didn't dare violate the social norm. In the humanitarian lane this time, a soldier took pity on us, or maybe he was startled by the crowds. He opened the gate immediately and motioned for us to enter quickly so that he could reclose the gate.

At the plexiglass window, I placed my ID card on the scanner. The soldier looked at his computer screen, looked at me, and turned on the intercom.

"Why are you crossing here?" he asked me in Hebrew.

Startled, I answered, "I'm a lawyer. I had a meeting in the parking lot." According to the maps of the Oslo Agreement, the parking lot of Qalandia is in Area B, Israeli security control, where Israelis are permitted to enter. He nodded, gave me a thumbs-up, and let me pass.

I waited until our evening Skype call to tell Osama what had happened this time and last time, that now they're scrutinizing ID cards. Someone once told me that it's harder to surveil Skype calls than phone calls.

"They know you are crossing into Ramallah," he agreed. "But no need to make it obvious."

I made inquiries about public taxis via the checkpoint next to Hizme village—the checkpoint used by settlers, far from Ramallah and open to anyone bearing a blue Israeli identity card. I knew that East Jerusalemites crossed there. From the Hizme checkpoint, you can't tell where people are coming from: from the settlements; the villages around Ramallah that, in theory, Israelis are allowed to enter; or from Ramallah itself, located in Area A, which, by military order, has been off-limits to Israeli citizens and residents since 2000.

A week later, I reached the crowded, chaotic parking lot of the Qalandia checkpoint and looked for the vans to Hizme that people had told me about.

"Yes, Hizme," the driver said. "Two for Jerusalem!" he shouted, until the van was full. He navigated his way onto the potholed streets leading around the concrete wall to another gate, the Hizme checkpoint, to which settlers and Palestinians holding Israeli ID cards were permitted access.

We in the minivans driving through Hizme belonged to a different population: richer, holding blue ID cards. Residents of East Jerusalem on their way to university classes, businesspeople, and older women traveling to visit their daughters. Sometimes a tourist would join us. The trip cost ten shekels instead of the five shekels and sixty pennies from Qalandia. We paid the premium for the privilege of a seat, protection from the wind and rain, and avoidance of the steel bars of Qalandia. Maybe we also paid extra for the beautiful view we got as the road wound up and down: clouds poking out over green mountains, little villages that dotted the Jerusalem hills.

A half hour later, we arrived at the Hizme checkpoint, the meeting point between the narrow access roads of the Palestinian villages and the broad, well-paved settlement access roads. Buses of settlers—organized transportation for students and employees of companies in Jerusalem—passed through the inspection lanes with a slight deceleration and a wave to the soldiers in the tollbooth-like structures. Even we—Palestinians in a white minibus—merely pulled over to the side so that a border guard could board and briefly make sure all the passengers had blue ID cards. We drove past the outer neighborhood of Pisgat Ze'ev, the traffic circles, the supermarket, and the parking lot of the community center—typical Israeli urban infrastructure. We continued to downtown Jerusalem, and from there I took a service taxi to my office in Tel Aviv.

After the next visit, just before dawn, as Osama and I left the house so he could take me to the public taxis, he urged, "Wear my hat. It's cold outside."

"No need," I said. "I've been upgraded."

Osama

The People Want to End the Division—Honey, Carob Juice, Honey

In March 2011, negotiations resumed between Fatah and Hamas to form a national unity government. A few hundred people gathered in Manara Square, chanting, "The people want to end the division," referring to the political split between the Hamas and Fatah factions, and, "The people want to end the occupation."

I almost cried when I saw the crowd, especially the teenage girls, dressed in their school uniforms of tan pants and white-striped shirts, who declared that they had decided to end the factional division: "We will succeed where our parents failed!" I felt gratified that things were passing from generation to generation—the younger generation still feels the occupation and wants to end it, but the factional division feels more acute to them right now.

"*Y'alla*, let's end the occupation!" I don't know why that call makes me angry. It makes me think of a very small and very privileged group of people vowing to stop eating chocolate for a half hour.

I was twenty years old when the First Intifada broke out. I was proud of the solidarity in the Jabalia refugee camp. We would run toward the occupation soldiers, as if they weren't carrying M16s, and as if the rock in my hand were a missile. In 1988 thousands of us ran into al-Mashru'a Street toward Beit Lahia to rescue a group that was under siege in the mosque. Most, if not all, of al-Mashru'a residents were from the Jabalia camp. No one was killed that day, but I will never forget the sight of the soldiers just a few meters from me, each of us holding back our weapons: their guns, our rocks.

At the age of twenty-one, I served a year in prison, mostly for distributing flyers with instructions to refugee camp residents about which products to boycott and when to strike, measures to demonstrate our cohesion and determination to control our neighborhood. Since then, our solidarity has disintegrated: Palestinians have become consumed by the internal factional split, and I have retreated from politics. I tell myself that my academic work is an act of resistance.

I liked seeing an elderly woman among the 2011 demonstrators. I liked hearing the carob juice peddler call out, "The people want to end the division," with the same rhythm of his usual call: "Honey, carob juice, honey."

Sari

The Culinary Version

I went to stay with Osama for the weeklong Passover vacation, slated to be the longest stretch of time we had spent together. I brought with me matzah, the unleavened bread traditional for the Passover holiday, when Jewish tradition forbids eating ordinary bread, and kosher chicken parts. I delicately informed Osama of my new dietary restriction. My identity must remind him of so many things he would prefer to forget.

The matzahs stayed on the kitchen counter—I don't find them tasty either—and we focused on the chicken. I told Osama we were going to prepare maqluba. We went out to buy cauliflower, eggplant, and potatoes for the vegetable layer. On the way home, we stopped at the rehabilitation hospital in Ramallah to make an appointment for Osama's sister, Hayat, who was trying to get a permit to come from Gaza to receive therapy here after suffering a stroke. Osama's mother, whom he hadn't seen in ten years, was supposed to accompany Hayat. We didn't talk about it much to avoid raising expectations that this would actually happen. Instead, I tried to get Osama to tell me about his mother, as if to make her presence real by describing her. I asked him if his mother was thin, and he said, "Yes," and then corrected himself. "She was thin. I don't know about now."

In the hospital courtyard, I consulted with a colleague by phone in Hebrew about applying for an entrance permit to Israel for Hayat. I didn't notice that a patient and his companion had come to sit next to me. When we left the hospital, Osama told me that the companion looked at me and then addressed his friend, saying, "It will rain today," only he injected the Hebrew word for rain into the sentence he spoke in Arabic.

"I want you to be careful," Osama said. "You're not in Tel Aviv."

We reached the car and discovered it wouldn't start. Osama's friend Hosni happened to pass by at that moment and offered to help. They worked on the car for an hour while I stood there silently. I know nothing about cars. When we were joined by the owner of a nearby shop and a passerby, who asked me where I was from, Osama answered, "From here." I guess he made a quick calculation that she would assume we were a married couple and chose the answer easiest to digest. For all of us.

What am I trying to say?

I was silent. I disappeared. I don't know who to be here, in Ramallah.

After they fixed the car, Hosni accepted Osama's invitation to join us for a meal of maqluba. At Osama's apartment, I stood next to the stove, absorbed in adding spices and frying. A breeze from the open window dispersed the tear-inducing vapors from the onions. My phone rang, and I answered it while cooking.

"Hello to you!" I said enthusiastically to a friend I hadn't spoken to in a long time. Osama motioned for me to lower my voice and closed the window.

"There are people right outside," he explained.

When Hosni arrived, he smiled at the packet of matzahs on the counter. "I remember those from prison," he said. "We used to eat them with chocolate spread."

I suppressed an impulse to apologize—for the matzahs, or the prison, or maybe for the entire Israeli occupation of Palestine.

I warned Osama and Hosni that the maqluba would take time to cook, but they refused my suggestion to start with a first course of soup and salad. "We want maqluba!" they insisted, like small boys. Hosni examined the pot and persuaded me to add water to the layers of chicken, vegetables, and rice. He said he had learned to cook from his mother and also from his stint in the Ketziot Prison, which held many of the Palestinian political prisoners arrested during the First Intifada. Hosni had been responsible for the prison kitchen.

"Soon my wife will take over the cooking," Hosni said, and told me that he was to marry a woman from a village on the outskirts of Qalqilya, whom he'd met after divorcing his first wife.

"I didn't know that!" Osama protested.

"Congratulations!" I said, smiling to myself at the silence of men. I had known Hosni for an hour, and Osama had known him for more than a decade.

"I saw her in a shop and asked about her," Hosni said. "People told me she was Issam's sister, and I know Issam well from prison." Hosni then blinked at me and seemed a bit bashful. "You know, it's not like the city, here in Ramallah. I had to check with Issam so he could agree for us to meet."

Yes, I thought. *It's not like here in Ramallah, where a Palestinian man and an Israeli woman—a Jewish, matzah-eating woman—who are not married can cook maqluba together.*

Finally, it was ready—the layers of chicken, rice, and fried vegetables, spiced with cinnamon, allspice, coriander, hot paprika, clove, and cardamom. We conducted a rescue operation with a coffee mug to extract the excess water. Hosni turned the pot over onto a huge platter, and not a single grain of rice spilled out onto the table. We ate the maqluba, drank wine, and laughed and chatted into the evening. I was impressed by Hosni, who treated me warmly and naturally, even if my presence did seem to remind him incessantly of an Israeli prison.

"You're a nice person," Osama said, after Hosni had gone home. "Hosni liked you."

Except for telephone conversations, Osama had never seen me interact with other people. Outside, in Ramallah, I am silent.

The next day, I rode in a public taxi, and when the driver heard my accent, he smiled widely and asked in English where I was from.

"America," was the answer that passed my lips.

"Welcome to Ramallah, Palestine," he said. "Palestine, not Israel."

"Thank you."

"How long are you here for? Have you visited Jerusalem and Bethlehem yet?"

"That's a good idea," I said.

"How do you find the people in Palestine?" he asked.

"Charming, warm, and nice."

In the center of town, crowded with pedestrians and taxis trying to inch forward along the narrow streets, I bought groceries for my Passover vacation and the slightly later Easter vacation that Osama's university and his son's school would have. In a dark, crowded shop that sold nuts and other dry provisions, I asked for dates, and when the seller repeated my question, I realized I'd pronounced the Arabic word for "dates" incorrectly, saying the word as it's pronounced in Hebrew. As I fumbled to correct myself, embarrassed, the Hebrew word for "where" came out.

I'm sure my face paled. I don't know if they noticed. OK, of course they noticed. I was so flustered that I couldn't find the dates on the shelf the seller pointed to, and he had to come out from behind the counter to bring me the box himself.

It's tricky for me to speak Arabic in public places because of its similarity to Hebrew. I'm always afraid of making a mistake—*tamar* (Hebrew for "date") instead of the Arabic *tamr*, *kol* ("all" in Hebrew) instead of the Arabic *kul*, *mayim* (Hebrew for "water") instead of the Arabic *maya*. I'm also afraid I might completely forget where I am and speak Hebrew, like the Hebrew "where" in the shop that came out of nowhere. Last month, while visiting Osama, I was absorbed in replying to a text message in Hebrew, and when Osama asked me a question,

I answered him in Hebrew. He and Firas started, alarmed, and then laughed. It was unexpected.

During this vacation, I had time to practice being in Ramallah, to try to discover who I was here. Who I wanted to be. Who I would be allowed to be.

Later, back at Osama's apartment, I told him that I was struggling with writing a *Maqluba* chapter about this current visit to Ramallah. In the kitchen, I sautéed garlic with the remainder of the cauliflower that hadn't fit into the maqluba pot. The phone rang, and I spoke with my Aunt Aziza, who invited me to a holiday meal for the last day of Passover. Osama had closed the window when I started talking and reopened it when I put the phone back down on the counter.

"The conversation got cut off; I'm going to call her back," I told him, pointing to the window.

He began closing it again and stopped himself. "Forget it. Let them wonder."

I told him that I was trying to write a chapter on language, on identity, on my attempt to find my place in Ramallah.

"I was worried about you today," he said. "I wanted to call you, but I stopped myself. It was strange. I usually don't worry about you."

"What were you worried about?"

"I don't know."

"Were you thinking about Juliano?"

"Yes, how did you know?"

Two weeks earlier, someone had murdered Juliano Mer-Khamis in Jenin, a northern West Bank city about ninety kilometers away. He was an actor and director who had moved to the Jenin refugee camp to live with the children to whom he taught theater. A gunman shot him outside the theater that his mother, Orna Mer, had founded. The identity of the killer and the motivation were still unknown. His mother had been Jewish, and his father was a Palestinian Christian citizen of Israel. Osama had seen Juliano perform in a play in Ramallah the night before the murder.

"I admired Juliano, but he was confused about his identity," Osama said.

"I didn't know him, but my impression is that he knew very well who he was," I said. "I think everyone else was confused."

I waited for Osama to say more about his worries, but he looked at me silently.

"Do you want me to tell you what I'm worried about?" I asked Osama. I was developing all kinds of techniques to deal with his silence. This time—the demonstration tactic. *I'll show you mine to get you to show me yours.*

"Three things," I said, because three is always a good number for lists. "I'm worried that someone crazy would try to hurt me. I'm worried someone would use our relationship to hurt Gisha. Already they call us traitors, antisemites, enemies of Israel. And the third thing I'm worried about is that I'll get arrested for entering the city of Ramallah. Because even if the Israeli authorities don't put me in jail, they can demand I sign a commitment not to reenter the city, as a condition of avoiding prison. And I can't sign a commitment like that."

That was the first time I had listed, even for myself, my fears about the things that Palestinians and Israelis could do to me.

Osama took my hand and stroked it, but my tactic had failed: Our conversation ended without Osama sharing his fears with me.

Osama

The Middleman

When I was twelve or thirteen years old, some friends from the camp and I waited in the Shuja'iya neighborhood, on the road where Palestinian middlemen selected day laborers to work jobs in Israel.

At four thirty in the morning, a middleman promised, "Five hundred liras for each of you," and we left in his van for an Israeli town on the outskirts of Gaza to work in the tomato fields.

By the end of the day, my hands were scratched and blistered, and my legs ached. The middleman brought us back to Gaza but subtracted fifty liras from each of our wages. We shouted at him in protest, but he said, "Either you take what I'm giving you, or you'll get nothing." We took what he gave us and came back the next day to work again.

Sari

Refusing to Keep Records

We left-wing Israelis prefer to have girl babies, not to resist patriarchy but to avoid the kind of military service that boy babies eventually do. The masculine overachievers will want combat duty: to patrol the occupied territory and checkpoints, to break into people's homes, shoot according to the army's rules of engagement. You can't stop these boy babies from turning into men. You can't explain to them that a few years after their military service—while staying at a guesthouse in India, touring the campus of a prospective university, mindlessly watching the Israeli political satire program *Eretz Nehederet* on the couch of their parents' home—they'll think about what they did. Digest it. Maybe regret it. Or not.

My colleague Yonah, also a human rights lawyer, told me his wife has already decided: If their toddler son turns fifteen without the occupation having ended, they will leave Israel. She won't risk him being drafted.

My beloved friend Josh, on the other hand, does reserve duty in the occupied territory: bears weapons at checkpoints, inspects documents, and prevents Palestinian residents from traveling inside the West Bank. He says that if he doesn't do it, someone else will take his place, and at least he treats people humanely. Josh is also an engineer with Palestinian colleagues. Once, a Palestinian researcher, an older man who'd worked with Josh on a desalination project, arrived with his family by car to a checkpoint that Josh was manning. "We shook hands, and it was really awkward," Josh told me. Josh is my closest girlfriend; I'm his best buddy. He is a good person, a better person than me. But he refuses to refuse to serve in the occupied territory.

Osama had spoken to Josh by phone without knowing all this, on the morning of the Tel Aviv Marathon, after I fainted at the finish line. Josh had arrived to meet me as I ran across the finish line, but instead he carried me in his arms to the paramedics' tent. He didn't say a word about my limp body being covered in sweat and even feces, because as I fainted, I lost control of my bowels. He followed the ambulance to the emergency room and waited as I received multiple infusions. He scolded me for pushing too hard, for endangering myself and making him worry. Osama, of course, was not allowed to come to the race, and Josh gave him telephone updates.

I told Osama about Josh in a conversation about dilemmas, trying to share what it's like to be Israeli. Osama felt betrayed, because he spoke to Josh without knowing all of that, because he trusted him.

"How could you hide that from me?" he asked, and the Skype camera transmitted his anger.

For God's sake. Hide? Osama didn't understand that if I had to tell him about all my intimate encounters with ugliness and oppression, we would talk about nothing else.

I could picture myself walking around with a notepad, keeping a precise record in order to report to Osama on all the things in my daily life that I repress in order to function, live, be happy, and also fight the occupation.

6:00 a.m.: I wake up and run speed intervals on the boardwalk, along a path that begins at the ruins of the Palestinian village of Manshieh and ends at the entrance to the Irgun (Zionist paramilitary organization active in the 1930s and 1940s) Museum, near the sign that describes thousands of years of Jewish settlement in Jaffa, deftly skipping over the hundreds of years during which Palestinians lived there.

7:30 a.m.: I return home and dress for work, while the radio interviewee explains that the Land of Israel belongs to the Jewish people, and that Palestinians are the invention of mendacious Arabs who want to massacre us.

8:50 a.m.: I cross the entrance to Nahalat Binyamin on my way to work, and when the security guard hears the accent in my "good morning," he lets me pass without checking my bag.

This is all before I start my workday, which is dedicated to requesting permits from the military authorities in order to temporarily allow Palestinians to travel within the Palestinian territory.

What else does Osama want me to reveal? Maybe I should stop "hiding" my little routine protest at the airport, where I try to avoid receiving preferential treatment based on my nationality. The security officers read the Arab last name in my passport and see that I was born in the United States. They have to determine, without asking me directly, if I'm Jewish. They need to make that determination in order to decide whether to give me sticker one—Jewish, no accompaniment or bag search—or sticker five—Arab citizen of Israel; search everything in her bag and accompany her from the check-in counter to the entrance to the gates. I deliberately make it hard for them because I don't want to cooperate with this system.

"How many years have you lived in Israel?" the security officer asks, smiling.

"Fourteen."

"Where did you learn Hebrew?"

"On Mount Scopus."

"And what kind of name is Bashi?"

"Iraqi."

"Did you belong to any community in the United States?"

"I don't understand the question."

"Never mind. Maybe . . . what holidays do you celebrate?"

"I'm not religious."

"Do you have relatives in Israel? What are their names?"

"Aziza Bashi, Shafiq Bashi, Naima Bashi," I answer, deliberately choosing the names before they were Hebraized. Once, at the Vienna airport, the young EL AL security officer, new to the job, seemed so distraught by my answers that I decided to ask her a question.

"Do you want to know if I'm Jewish?"

"Yes!" She smiled, and the relief was evident on her round, smooth face.

"Ask me," I said, knowing she wasn't allowed to.

"So, are you . . . ?" she asked in anticipation of my response.

"Ask me," I said again.

"So . . . yes?" She raised her hands in a gesture of filling in the blank, eyes wide, a tentative smile on her lips.

"Ask," I said.

Her face fell, and she went to consult with her supervisor.

Sometimes they decide I'm Jewish and send me to the check-in counter. Sometimes they decide I'm Arab and take apart everything in my suitcase. Sometimes they take so long to decide that by the time they begin the search intended for Arabs, I risk missing my flight.

Osama

Seam Line

I asked Sari to lower her voice when she spoke Hebrew. When she spoke with her aunt on the phone, I closed the window. I asked her not to speak Hebrew in the street. Not to dress in a certain way. Not to run in remote areas.

And then I hated myself, that I dared to ask her to change who she is.

How can I make her understand what she represents here?

When we're together, I'm on edge. Terrified.

I know she deserves an explanation, but I don't think she can fully understand what it means for me to be with her.

A friend said to me, "It's all in your head. You're not the first and certainly not the last to be with a Jewish woman."

I'm trying to see it that way, but I can't. My problem is not just fear of what others might think or do. As soon as I imagine Sari's life in Tel Aviv, her friends in Israel, the ease with which she moves from place to place, I'm forced to confront a discriminatory and painful reality. She gets into a taxi and crosses through gates in the walls and fences that surround the West Bank and keep me from my mother and the sea. I hear in her phone conversations the language of the prison guards. She walks through Ramallah fearlessly, as if she doesn't know what it means to spend your whole life feeling unsafe. My connection to a Jewish woman pulls me toward that seam line that divides our two worlds—and from there, I can see everything. From there, I have to acknowledge all the things that separate the occupier from the occupied, the master from the subject.

All because I love her.

Sari

The Honorable Retired Justice

I didn't want there to be secrets between us, but I can't disclose everything. Osama knows that. He's aware of the ugliness that surrounds me, and he also looks the other way; because otherwise, how could we touch each other? How could we drink our morning coffee together?

When I founded Gisha, I cut ties with an Israeli Supreme Court justice who had been a mentor during my legal studies and clerkship because I began submitting petitions to his court and wanted to avoid a conflict of interest. This justice eventually ruled on Osama's petition, and not in Osama's favor. Based on secret information submitted by the Shin Bet, the Israeli security service, he ruled that Osama's admittance to the Tel Aviv University campus would endanger state security because of Osama's activity in a terrorist organization. A few months later, in response to another court petition in which it was harder to allege dangerousness, the state admitted that its refusal to allow Palestinian students to study in Israel was not due to any individual security risk but simply applied to all Palestinians. But at the time of Osama's hearing, they preferred to argue that he was dangerous.

Last month, years after filing Osama's court petition and well into the justice's retirement, I invited him to lunch at my apartment together with a mutual friend visiting from abroad. I was nervous that my modest apartment in the Kerem Hateimanim neighborhood of Tel Aviv, tucked between hummus restaurants and spice stores and across from the open-air produce market, would not be respectable enough for esteemed guests. I scrubbed the surfaces and floors until three in the morning. I bought flowers and then returned to the market to buy a vase. I confessed to Osama over the phone that I didn't have a matching set of dishes. Osama, knowing very well who the judge was and what role he played in the court petition, reassured me over Skype. He praised the menu and reminded me of what I had told him: that the retired justice was an important person, but he was also warm and unpretentious, and he liked me and the other guests I had invited.

Indeed, the lunch was successful; the conversation was pleasant; and the guest of honor was the judge who had decided that Osama wouldn't be allowed to reach his doctoral studies, because he was a terrorist.

Osama knew. He chose not to discuss it.

I told him about the nationalistic, parochial ultra-Orthodox Jewish system in which my nephews were educated, and about what my oldest nephew, five-year-old Menachem, had asked me when I took them to the zoo. We passed an exhibit about tiger poaching, and I explained that there are people who try to kill tigers, but the zoo is protecting them.

"Who is trying to kill tigers?" Menachem asked, troubled.

"Bad people." I touched his head gently.

He screwed up his face in an attempt to understand. "Are they gentiles?"

I gave Osama the photograph I had taken of Menachem and his younger brother, Haim, holding a drawing of theirs on which I had written, in Arabic, "Hello, Uncle Osama!" I didn't tell Osama about another drawing on the wall near the entrance to their apartment—a printed picture of the Jewish holy site of Rachel's Tomb in the West Bank, which

Menachem had colored in kindergarten. The picture didn't show the Palestinian houses adjacent to the tomb; the Israeli military had built walls that surrounded the houses on three sides, closing their inhabitants off from the rest of the city to facilitate visits by Jewish worshippers to the tomb.

Was I hiding that from Osama the way I concealed Nir, my running partner, a charming and quiet guy who, during a run one morning in the Ben Shemen Forest just outside Tel Aviv, politely declined an offer to join me again the following Friday.

"I'm doing reserve duty next week, guarding near Ofra," he explained.

Osama's house wasn't far from the Israeli settlement of Ofra, in the West Bank, and during my long runs there, I'm careful to stay away from the settlement access roads. I avoid contact with the military jeeps that occasionally patrol the main roads and practice an American answer, in English professing ignorance, in case they stop and interrogate me.

"There are beautiful trail runs in that area," I had responded to Nir. "Especially now, in winter."

Does Osama really want a daily printout of confessions, a running disclosure of racism and oppression, including incidents involving people whom I love? He doesn't understand that acknowledging too much of that would make my life in our maqluba world impossible. It's not by chance that his friends in London—Rami and Itamar and Sammy—can allow themselves to feel clean. It's easier to feel clean in London.

Osama also wants to feel clean. He's looking for a job at a university in Europe, and I don't blame him. He says that he deserves a better life. He's right. But for now, my life is here, inside the ugliness. I look for the beauty within it, try to cultivate and celebrate it. I'm still trying to love Miriam, the professor from Tel Aviv University who ultimately did write to the minister of defense on Osama's behalf, recruited additional colleagues to join her, and sent me copies of each letter in her orderly way.

I love Menachem. I love my father. I love Josh. And I love you, Osama.

For God's sake, none of us is clean.

Osama

Confession

Even though, in many ways, our souls grew close, I was tough with Sari.

With myself, too, but mostly with her.

I couldn't say out loud: You should get out of here, before we become even more involved in each other's lives. Before we fall in love. Before the breakup—because there has to be a breakup—will be ever more painful.

I'm afraid of love. Before I got to know Sari, I failed in my marriage with a wonderful woman, whom I met at the right time and who came from the same society I did. I will never forget the pain I caused Nisreen and the feeling of failure that burned inside me. I didn't know how to make the relationship work. I remember how my hair turned white within a month or two. My choked voice. That metro station, where I felt for a few moments that I wanted to kill myself. I'd kissed Nisreen there for a long time, when we reunited in London after a long separation, and we kissed briefly there when we broke up, and she and Firas returned to Ramallah without me.

I loved Nisreen, but it was hard for me to show up for her consistently, when I felt the ground beneath my feet to be so unstable. When she could take Firas anywhere she wanted, and I was trapped. The knowledge that I couldn't protect them or myself consumed me, and only when we were on equal footing, in London, did I have the courage to separate from her.

I since did everything to avoid exposing myself to a new pain—and I mostly succeeded.

Then Sari showed up. And she wants children.

Sari

April 24, 2011

Letter of Complaint to the Israeli Postal Service
To: The Israeli Postal Service
Re: Serious and Strange Defects in Delivering Foreign Mail to My Home

Dear Sir or Madame,

I write to demand that you remedy serious defects in delivering mail from the United States to my home, Yehia Kapah 17/3, Tel Aviv 65600.

For the past many months, the delivery of mail from the United States to my home has been unacceptable, to say the least. Frequently, pieces of mail that have been sent to me disappear after I've been told that they have been sent. They don't arrive and are not returned to the senders. In other cases, items are returned to the sender, even though the address and postage are correct.

In addition, pieces of mail addressed to me at home—with my name and home address written in English on the envelope—are delivered to my work address, even though the name of my workplace and its address are not written on the envelope (because it's personal mail). I note that my workplace and my home are not served by the same postal branch office.

Attached is a photocopy of a letter that was delivered to my workplace, the Gisha organization, located at Harakevet 42, Tel Aviv 67770. Note that it is addressed to Sari Bashi at Yehia Kapah Street. The name of my workplace does not appear on the envelope.

Can you explain to me why a letter addressed to my home address, Yehia Kapah 17/3, was delivered to the Gisha organization at Harakevet 42? How does the postal service know that I work at Gisha? Why did the postal service decide to channel letters intended for my house to my place of work?

My request is simple. When an item of mail addressed to me at Yehia Kapah 17/3 arrives to the postal service, please deliver it to me at Yehia Kapah 17/3, consistently, without delay, and without sending it to other locations. If you are forwarding any of my letters to the Shin Bet (Israeli Security Agency responsible for counterterrorism), please ask them to send the letters back to me when they complete their work so that I, too, can read them.

Very truly yours,
Adv. Sari Bashi

Osama

I wrote to myself:

We parted a few minutes ago,
each one with their own tough feelings.

I expected the meeting to be difficult. I brought you the things you'd left in my apartment, aware that I was cutting my last ties to you.

I love you, Sari. That's what I felt and still feel.

You are different. A different kind of woman. A different kind of human.

How can we talk in the future?

I doubt it will happen.

See you later.

Sari

Dear Naomi

May 2, 2011

To: Naomi Levy, Israeli Postal Service
Re: Serious and Strange Defects in Delivering Foreign Mail to My Home

Dear Madam,

Since I wrote to you in April, the postman has apparently decided to compensate me for failing to deliver my mail by delivering pieces of mail addressed to my neighbors at different addresses in Kerem Hateimanim, and also mail addressed to previous occupants of Yehia Kapah 17, who haven't lived here in many years. On the other hand, many pieces of mail addressed to me are still returned to their senders, even though the address and postage are correct.

Attached are photocopies of two pieces of mail sent to me

by Hapoalim Bank, as well as a letter from the American Merrill Lynch company. The three letters were returned to their senders, despite the fact that the address and postage are correct. I have been informed by the bank that additional letters have also been returned to them, and for that reason, the bank refuses to send anything to my house. Additional senders who have informed me of returned mail include Yale University; the Division of Motor Vehicles of the State of New Jersey; and my aunt, who lives in New York, and who is still trying to send me a card for a birthday I celebrated eight months ago.

I request three things:

Please send me, to my home address, every piece of mail addressed to Sari Bashi, Yehia Kapah 17/3, Tel Aviv.

Please refrain from sending me pieces of mail that are addressed to other houses on Yehia Kapah Street or any other street in the Kerem Hateimanim neighborhood.

Please answer the question I asked in my previous letter—is the postal service transferring or allowing, at any phase, my mail to be transferred to the Shin Bet?

I would be grateful for your kind attention and your prompt response.

Very truly yours,
Adv. Sari Bashi

Osama

Loving a Jewish Woman

I stalled for time. I took the long way home from the university. Dinner was a cigarette on the balcony. I turned on the television and then turned it off. Without meaning to, I called Sari's home number but hung up when she answered.

I felt ashamed.

Because I called, or because I hung up?

"Love may tire from too much waiting or maybe grow ill," Mahmoud Darwish, the Palestinian national poet, wrote in one of his later poems.

Mahmoud had a Jewish girlfriend. They say she was a dancer. In his poems, he called her "Rita." He wrote her letters—in Hebrew, of course—during the periods when the military government banned him from leaving the city of Haifa, as part of the restrictions imposed on Palestinian citizens of Israel until 1966. He couldn't travel to Jerusalem to see her. He wrote that he dreamed of drinking tea with her in the evening—I guess because even on the rare occasions when he got a permit, he wasn't allowed to stay past sunset.

They say that after Mahmoud and "Rita" broke up, she joined the Israeli air force. She must have been very young. Some people in Palestine doubt she was real. Years later, she divided her time between Berlin and Tel Aviv. Darwish left Palestine and didn't return for many years.

I wonder what it was like for him, to love a Jewish woman. From his poems, it seems he loved her even after they separated.

"Between Rita and my eyes there is a rifle," Darwish wrote. "Rita's name was a feast in my mouth. Rita's body was a wedding in my blood."

I feel disconnected from the people around me, a foreigner in my own city, where I remain a Gazan, a refugee, and separated from my family, whose way of life is no longer familiar. Darwish has been dead for years, but he reconnects me to the people around me. Sometimes I felt that Sari did too. She would ask questions about friends and family, and describing them to her brought them closer to me.

In the morning, I woke up stretched out on the couch, still wearing the previous day's clothing, with Darwish's book of poetry on the floor next to me.

Sari

May 19, 2011

Response from Israel Post Ltd., Tel Aviv—Central District
Case No. 11/000000
To: Adv. Sari Bashi
Re: Mail Delivery to Your Home Address

Greetings,

Your additional letter was received with thanks.

Further our letter of April 30, 2011, your question about letters addressed to you being transferred to the Shin Bet was referred to the security and operations division of the Israeli Postal Service.

Based on the answer we received from them, I can respond that we have no further information on that matter.

At your service always.

Very truly yours,
Nahara Friedman
Director of Public Inquiries Dept.
Israel Post
Here for Everyone, Everywhere.

Osama

A Goat with Wings Is Still a Goat— Even in the Academy

In a futile attempt to persuade the female students in an introductory course on the history of science that female Palestinian students outperform male Palestinian students, I presented the results of the TIMSS tests and even the matriculation exams taken in high school—the Tawjihi—over the past ten years. Female students outperform male students in both tests. Surprisingly, most of the female students insisted that such claims were false.

"I can tell you that what makes the university different, as an academic institution, is its reliance on findings, research, ideas, debates, and arguments, rather than on guessing. In other words, the goat is not a goat if it has wings," I told them.

The female students laughed, but they continued to press their case without offering any supporting evidence. Disappointed, I addressed one of the male students: "Mohammed, aren't we Palestinian men lucky?"

Even now, I still wonder why these female students—the entire university, it seems—thought that male students were more qualified.

Maybe another debate held in the same context provides an answer. In a different course, the students debated the religious position that a woman is intellectually and religiously inferior. A number of female students offered interpretations of that religious ruling:

"A woman is inferior intellectually because a man's *Shahada* (witness testimony in Islamic law) is worth a *Shahada* statement of two women."

"She is religiously inferior because of the monthly menstrual cycle that doesn't allow her to perform religious commandments such as prayer and fasting."

"But don't you think there's an inherent contradiction in that whole argument?" I asked one of the female students.

"What do you mean, Professor?"

"You are using religion to justify a religious ruling," I answered. She fell silent and seemed to think about it, while a male student in his last semester, young and religious, decided to take up her argument, quoting additional religious texts.

"So," I asked him, "do you mean that your female colleague, sitting there next to you, is intellectually inferior to you?" The question embarrassed him, but another female student came to his rescue by calling out from the other end of the lecture hall, "Of course."

Sari

Arid Jerusalem

JUNE 2011

Hot. The air was dry in Jerusalem. A half year had passed since the massive wildfire in the Carmel Forest of Northern Israel, and Gisha's legal team—three lawyers and a law clerk—were looking for parking outside the Supreme Court. On our way, we passed a firehouse with two brand-new fire trucks, shiny in the morning light. We paused at a crosswalk and waited for a large bus with dark windows to pass.

"That bus is arriving from Beitar Illit," said Hadas, the lawyer who runs the legal department.

"Yeah?" the law clerk asked.

"I had a hearing there once, in Beitar Illit," Hadas continued. "Crazy story. After submitting a High Court petition, we managed to prove that a Palestinian family owned land inside the settlement and should be allowed to access it. But in response, settlers took revenge on the family. One day, they got a bill from the firefighting services for forty thousand shekels, for putting out fires over the course of eight years. We requested the incident reports, and we noticed that every year, around the same time in the spring, a fire broke out, and the family was charged for extinguishing it. I looked at the calendar and saw that it was Lag b'Omer." Lag b'Omer is a spring Jewish holiday during which children light outdoor bonfires.

"No way," I laughed.

"Yeah," Hadas said. "They charged the Palestinian family for every Lag b'Omer bonfire. It took months to get the bill canceled."

We approached the entrance to the Supreme Court. A wide, high-ceiling hallway with a wall made entirely of glass looked out over the Nahlaot neighborhood, where I lived for four years. When I was clerking at the Supreme Court, I would leave the building through the elegant reception hall and spot my apartment through the huge window, enjoying the view after a long day at work.

We walked upstairs, preparing for two scheduled hearings, one for me and one for Hadas. My hearing concerned the state's appeal of a district court verdict requiring the Defense Ministry to turn over a document that calculated the number of calories residents of Gaza would be permitted to consume, as part of a policy that limited the entrance of goods, including food, to the Gaza Strip.

Hadas's hearing concerned "Ihab-in-Love," as we called him in the office, a Palestinian student from the Gaza Strip studying in Belgium, who wanted to enter the West Bank in order to marry his sweetheart, who lived there.

I hadn't been to the Supreme Court in months, and I hadn't argued a case there in years, the consequence of growing Gisha to a staff of twenty, which increased my managerial responsibilities.

Hadas's hearing was scheduled for nine and mine for eleven thirty, but they were both delayed until two thirty, in different courtrooms, which prevented us from supporting each other. Hadas took Noa, the law clerk, to her hearing, a favorable one, in which the justices pressured the state to let Ihab enter the West Bank for two weeks, in order to propose to his sweetheart and sign a marriage contract in the presence of her parents.

After we had each finished our hearing, I approached the uniformed legal officer representing the Israeli military in Hadas's case. The legal officer had to decide whether to follow the justices' recommendation or to submit an update informing the justices that the Defense Ministry insisted on its refusal to allow Ihab to enter the West Bank from Jordan.

"Listen," I said to him. "They already issued an order nisi. If you don't want to get hit with a ruling in our favor on the entire issue, reconsider your position. You know there is no chance he'll remain in the West Bank. He has to return to his studies. In any case, he and his family live in the Gaza Strip. It's not customary for the fiancé to join the family of the fiancée, but rather the opposite."

We reassured the military and the state that Ihab did not want to stay in the West Bank but rather just visit it for two weeks. We submitted his return plane ticket to Belgium from Amman. We submitted a letter from the Belgian university confirming his enrollment. We hinted that he was also willing to deposit a financial bond to guarantee his departure. We didn't argue that he had a right—as a Palestinian—to enter and remain in the West Bank, part of the Palestinian territory but controlled by the Israeli military.

"But every time we make a concession, as a gesture beyond what the law requires, you hold them up before the judges and try to turn them into precedents," the officer said to me. "You're shooting yourselves in the foot. Each time you wave one of those cases in our faces, you discourage us from being generous in the future."

"I personally would be thrilled if you were to reject the justices' recommendation and bring us all back to court, because I think you'll get slapped with a ruling that will serve us well in the future. But we have a client waiting in Amman who needs to get back to Belgium before the end of the summer vacation. He can't wait for a precedent-setting verdict, and so I suggest you consider whether you really want to insist on this one."

As we left the court, the law clerk approached me. "Why didn't you object when the officer said that it's all a gesture, not required by law, and that they have no obligation to let Ihab enter the West Bank?" she asked.

"Why would I argue with him? I'm not going to persuade him."

"So why did you bother talking to him?"

"Because I thought maybe I could convince him that it would be easier for him to give us what we want."

I didn't want to discourage the clerk from thinking the law didn't matter. And if she chose to represent more powerful clients, it would matter. I wanted to explain to her what tactics she should adopt, if she's representing the weaker side. But I didn't know what to say, and I had gotten hungry. I had devoured the sandwich I brought with me hours ago. I invited everyone to stop in Abu Ghosh to eat hummus on our way back to Tel Aviv.

Osama

Eleven Years

So much time has passed. What should I prepare? What should I wear? I need to straighten up the apartment.

I'm going to see my mother in a few hours, after eleven years of being separated by a ninety-minute drive that I could never make, because of the walls and fences and military orders. The Palestinian Authority called my brother Mohammed last week to tell him that after weeks of demanding more and more medical documents and clarifications, Israel approved two requests for travel to the West Bank: for my mother to accompany my sister Hayat for rehabilitation, and for my brother Mohammed to accompany his four-year-old son, Tamer, for treatment for his thalassemia.

The morning flew by, but time also stood still.

And then—the taxi driver called. I climbed the stairs from my ground-floor apartment, built into the slope of the hill, in a sprint. I went outside to the quiet residential street, lined with concrete apartment buildings. The street here was so much wider than in her home in the Jabalya refugee camp, and the buildings must have seemed tall and expansive. She opened the taxi door. We didn't recognize each other for a fraction of a second, and then the pain washed over me. I hate Israel. That's the feeling that overcame me the moment my mother got out of the taxi.

I wanted to burst out crying, but I restrained myself, and I held myself back even more when I saw my sister Hayat, who looked nothing like herself. I rushed to help my mother open Hayat's door. Hayat had suffered a stroke at her home in Libya, and my mother brought her from there to the Gaza Strip and, finally, to my apartment in Ramallah.

It was as if I had leaped twenty years into the future. The static image I'd held of them in my mind was suddenly and abruptly revised. As if I were not me, my mother, Areej, was not my mother, and Hayat was not my sister Hayat. Mohammed brought the suitcases, and Tamer followed behind him. They sat on my sofa and looked around the apartment, taking in the spacious kitchen with a door to the garden, the window nook with a view of the neighbor's lemon tree, the hallway leading to the bathrooms and bedrooms.

I had met Tamer, who has thalassemia, once before, a year ago, when he and Mohammed got a permit to visit Ramallah for treatment. Mohammed had seen my life as a professor, as a secular divorced man, as a resident of Ramallah's bourgeois Masyoun neighborhood. All this was new to my mother, and she was new to me.

My mother described how the Israeli soldier at the Erez checkpoint between Israel and Gaza spoke to her and Hayat, and my hatred for Israel grew. "Get completely undressed," the soldier told Hayat, because she was sitting in a wheelchair that didn't fit into the scanner. I had heard the same story that morning from my friend Salim, who'd also just received visitors from Gaza, including his mother, a cancer patient, who was also in a wheelchair. He apologized for his bad mood at such an early hour, and I didn't know that, at that very moment, my mother and sister were undergoing the same humiliating body search he reported. I brought them glasses of water and boiled more water for coffee.

My mother said, "I'm telling you, they left nothing on her—like the day she was born. She was left with only panties while the soldier checked everything and put that device between her legs."

I put my mother's and Hayat's bags in my bedroom and ignored her protest about taking my room. We drove to the rehabilitation center in Ramallah, and even though we were no longer seeing each other, I kept wanting to say to Sari, "Do you know how much I hate the Israeli part of you? Do you know how much I can't stand your so-very-close friend Josh?"

I was so angry, but as we waited for the appointment, I stepped away to call her. I wanted to talk to her, to cry, and I wanted her to be by my side.

My mother can't walk well, because of pain in the joints of her feet. Still, she pushed Hayat's wheelchair for all three kilometers of the Erez checkpoint between Gaza and Israel. My mother does everything for Hayat, even recites her daily prayers for her. Hayat has lost the ability to speak, other than a nodding "ah," but she can still recite short passages from the Quran. It's funny to see how alert Hayat is during prayer, and how she sometimes refuses to accept my mother's version of the prayers. They argue over the correct words during Hayat's prayer time, my mother using words and Hayat with vehement headshaking and facial expressions, until they resolve the dispute, and Hayat finishes her prayers.

"The hospital is not sure they can help Hayat," I told Sari over the phone. "My mother and Hayat will come back tomorrow for an evaluation."

"Hayat is strong," Sari said. "And your mother is persistent."

Despite the warmth of her words, Sari was anxious to end the conversation. I forgave her.

Sari

His Mother

Is she happy? Warm? Judgmental? Does she pray a lot? I'm trying to imagine her, but only the stereotype comes to mind: a seventy-three-year-old Palestinian woman, hair covered in a hijab, religious, a refugee. I haven't seen Osama for months, but when he asked me to come, to meet his mother, I could think of nothing else.

She is Osama's mother, the woman who held him for the first time in her arms, two months after his father had abandoned her. The mother who sent him to school, filled his schoolbag with books that she couldn't read, because her parents kept her home until they married her off at the age of thirteen. The mother who struggled with her son's mischievousness, his insistence on playing football, on escaping to the sea, and, years later, abandoning religion and the refugee camp. Osama told me about her "clever way" of checking whether he had gone swimming instead of going to school. She would grab his arm and lick it, to taste for the remains of sea salt.

For eleven years, they were separated by ninety kilometers and a policy that allowed travel between Gaza and the West Bank "in exceptional humanitarian cases only."

"She's healthy," Osama told me, when I asked if the journey had been hard for her. Areej Fahed is not a humanitarian case.

I knew how badly Osama had wanted to see her and also how scared he was of visiting her in Gaza. Last year, when Osama traveled to London to defend his dissertation, he had an opportunity to visit her. For the first time in four years, the Rafah Crossing between Gaza and Egypt opened for routine travel. When the Israeli military allowed Osama to leave the West Bank, to travel to London to defend his dissertation, he could have flown from the UK to Egypt and entered Gaza via the Rafah Crossing. I explained that to him, but I also told him what he knows better than me—that no one could know when the rules would change; no one could guarantee that he would be able to exit Gaza.

The temptation was great. His mother. Gaza. The sea. He asked his brothers for advice. Mohammed told him not to come, not to risk it. If the crossing were to close, and he got stuck there, rather than earning a living—giving lectures, conducting research, raising Firas, and sending money to his mother—he would be dependent on his family in Gaza.

The last time Osama had visited Gaza, sixteen years ago, he got stuck when the military refused to issue him an exit permit. A car full of VIPs smuggled him out, but the fear remained. And that was before Firas was born.

Now I had arrived in Ramallah after weeks of staying away, aware this could be my only chance to meet his mother. I sat across from her, eating her *molokhiya*, the leafy green called "Jew's mallow" common in Palestinian cuisine, and hoping she wouldn't notice that I didn't like it—it was too bitter. I smiled and hoped that warmth and friendliness would make up for my silence. My vocabulary in Arabic was too meager to attempt conversation. She examined me as I cleared the dishes, wiped the table, and chopped vegetables for a salad Osama had requested. I imagined her assessing how I would take care of her son. I felt the clumsiness of my movements. Her energetic nature reminded me of my mother. She seemed to be in constant motion.

Indeed, Osama complained, "She doesn't rest for a minute."

Hayat sat in her wheelchair near the table, and Areej fed her forkfuls of salad and spoonfuls of rice, dabbing the corners of her mouth with a napkin. Her hijab slipped down to her shoulders, and I saw that her exposed hair had white roots and dyed-red ends.

I sat across from her and Osama's nephew, who had gotten a second, shorter permit to come with his father. Tamer has a stormy disposition. It's hard for Mohammed to set limits for him, because Mohammed worries about his health, and maybe also because he is so beloved as the eldest, the only boy among three girls, including his triplet sisters. I asked Tamer if he liked his grandmother's food, and in response, he mimicked my accent in Arabic, maybe also my grammatical mistakes.

Osama translated his mother's response for me: "Tamer, that's how she speaks. If you understand her, answer her." She got up and began washing the dishes, forcefully pushing aside Osama, who tried to insist that she rest.

Osama sat to roll a cigarette, and I made a face. "Maybe you can persuade him to stop smoking?" I asked Areej.

"I try, but he doesn't listen to me," she answered, which Osama begrudgingly translated.

"Maybe you can convince him to fast," she said to me. The month of Ramadan was approaching.

"*Kul yom ana batlob min Allah*," I answered, carefully conjugating the sentence ("Every day I ask that of God"). Osama gave me his surprised and indignant look, the look he reserves for drivers who cut him off, but his mother seemed encouraged.

"Maybe you can convert to Islam," she suggested.

"On the condition that Osama also converts to Islam," I told her in English, but Osama refused to translate the reference to his lack of religious devotion.

Osama

My New Mother

"You have to be a little stupid in order to be happy," my mother had said, referring to the apricot festival in the nearby village of Jifna, where people bought shawarma and picked apricots as if they didn't have a care in the world. I had watched her face as Mohammed and I argued about my sister Hayat's care, which angered my mother. "As long as I'm alive, she will stay with me, and I will care for her until her condition improves. After I die, you can do what you want with her." We were debating how to persuade her to let us bring her some kind of paramedical help.

I can't manage the sight of my mother at her age, and in her new shape. Eleven years. When did those lines appear around her mouth? When did her gait slow? Why had she begun to fast on Mondays and Thursdays, outside the month of Ramadan?

Her head and back are bent, and she limps on her left leg. Her hair has gotten thinner and is almost entirely white, except for the ends dyed in henna. When I was a child, she added henna highlights to her black mane of hair. I remember her at weddings, dancing with a clay jug balanced on her head. I knew a strong woman, her back straight, who would return from the market carrying on her head a basket laden with impossible quantities of vegetables and fruit. A woman who was busy all day doing household chores, visiting neighbors, and raising chickens and rabbits in the courtyard outside the two-room house that she and my brothers and sisters and I shared with my aunt and uncle, after the Israeli General Ariel Sharon demolished the house we had lived in since I was born. The woman who taught me how to slaughter chickens and rabbits for food, because in my father's absence, my brothers and I were responsible for tasks usually reserved for men. The woman who yelled at me if I came home late, worried that the Jews would hurt me, that I would run around with the wrong friends, neglect my homework. The woman who sewed our schoolbags from wire clothing hangers and pillowcases and made sure we all finished high school, even though she was never taught to read.

That was the image I had in my head, but I met a different woman, and so many details have evaporated over time. Who are still her friends? How does she get along with my older brother? Does she still cook *fatiyar* (a savory pastry similar to spanakopita), spinach, or Tihal (chicken spleen) with hot red peppers and parsley?

I'm trying to get reacquainted with her, pushing myself to create new memories: She drinks her tea sweet. She likes eating dinner. She is as wise and discerning as I knew and remember her. She likes kebabs. She likes to sleep on a high pillow. She likes to see that she's important to Hayat, even though they scream at each other. She likes exploring Ramallah . . .

Sari

JULY 2011

Hayat's rehabilitation ended without her being rehabilitated. There was no change in her condition, and the hospital gave her no exercises or reason for hope. The doctor examined Tamer and gave him a new prescription. Mohammed wanted to return home to his wife and three daughters.

Mohammed and Osama took Tamer for a last errand in the city, and I stayed home with Hayat and Areej. Hayat sat on the couch, her eyes wide open, as if she were in a perpetual state of surprise. When I spoke to her, she smiled hesitantly or said, "Ah," which is "yes" in Arabic but might have just been a sound that came out, "ah." His mother folded towels and placed spices into the suitcase. I went to the kitchen to pack fruit and water for their trip. I heard a noise and saw Areej dragging a huge suitcase from the bedroom to the living room.

"Areej!" I called and ran to take the suitcase from her. But she had already rested it next to the front door of the apartment.

The boys returned. The taxi driver called to say he was close. Mohammed and Osama brought the suitcases outside, while their mother tried to get Hayat out. The elevator was broken. Like many buildings in hilly Ramallah, this one was built into the slope of a mountain, and Osama's apartment was on the ground floor. The entrance to the street was three floors above us, higher on the hill. Areej cajoled Hayat into climbing the first step. Hayat's eyes grew huge, and she began to make noises of protest, moaning mixed with crying. Areej became annoyed and tried to push her forward. Osama and Mohammed came down the stairs, smiling. Osama removed his mother's hands from Hayat, Hayat relaxed the muscles in her face, and Mohammed took Hayat's shoulder and hand. Osama sent his mother up the stairs and took his place on the other side of Hayat, holding her arm.

"Let's go, my beautiful sister," Mohammed called, and the two of them took Hayat upstairs, half supporting her, half dragging her, laughing and comparing her steps to those of a sleek racehorse. The tension dissipated, and when we reassembled at the entrance to the building, the goodbye hugs began. The taxi driver, a Bedouin man from the Negev, was clearly impatient.

"*Bahibak, Yama,*" Osama told his mother ("I love you, Mama").

After the taxi disappeared at the bend of the road, it was quiet. Osama walked down the stairs, and I followed him as he entered the apartment and went straight to his bedroom. I sat next to him on the bed. He covered his face in his hands and began to cry, the bitter sobs of a child. I wrapped my arms around him.

"I'm sorry," I whispered in his ear. "I'm sorry."

Osama
Nowhere

When I was in London, I attributed my loneliness to the fact that I was outside my country. Now, I can't explain it. I have lived in Ramallah for more than half my life, and I still feel foreign in this city, which I find beautiful. I still feel like I don't really know it. That I don't have friends I can talk to.

"My father lived here forty years, and he had only one friend," Salah, my mechanic, who is also from Gaza, told me to make me feel better. He added, "I know a lot of people, but they're not friends."

I don't fast during Ramadan, but still—no one invited me to iftar, the traditional meal, eaten at sundown, that ends the daily Ramadan fast. An acquaintance, who also doesn't fast, said to me in jest, "I'll invite you if you promise to decline." I now understand better what Nasser and Zuhair in Gaza told me about their Ramadan fast: It's more social than religious.

How should I relate to a city where I'll probably live out my last days, but where I don't feel I belong?

Yesterday I heard someone yell at a kind handyman, fixing a door at the university, "You've become Gazan," because his face and hands were stained with grease and dirt. The handyman laughed and answered, "God forbid," even though I was standing right next to him, and he knew I'm from Gaza.

One of the Palestinian national security officers, also from Gaza, told me about being arrested by Israeli soldiers and then released at a checkpoint far from home as an Israeli-imposed curfew came into effect. "These West Bankers closed the mosques in our face, man, when we couldn't find a place to sleep."

Another said, "One of them refused to give me a cup of water, even though he was watering his garden."

A third said, "These West Bankers are like the Jews. Actually, maybe the Jews are better."

What do you do with a city where you feel disrespected most of the time, and where you always have to defend yourself from people who look at you with hostility, who are ready to abuse you—just because they can?

I'm tired. Very tired. I don't sleep enough. I wake up quickly, rarely managing six hours. A month has passed since my mother returned to Gaza, and it feels like forever. Ninety kilometers from my house to her house. Which used to be my house. I don't know most of my nieces and nephews. My uncles and aunts have died without me saying goodbye. I don't have family or holiday dinners. My childhood friends meet each other without me. I miss the sea. Is all that I have done, all that I have accomplished, worth this loss and this distance?

Sari

The Invitees

Osama and I resumed seeing each other. I'm going back and forth between the life I built in Tel Aviv and the life I am now trying to build in Ramallah, trading the sea for the hills, and the roof of my building on summer nights for the garden in the back of Osama's apartment. I feel excited and scared and still haven't told most of my friends where I go each weekend. Osama and I are back to trying.

One day, Osama called me at work to ask which fruit trees I liked. Which herbs. He needed an answer immediately—the guy from the nursery would be there any minute. We had a moment of crisis: How do you say "plum" in Arabic?

"It's purple on the outside, tastiest when it's also purple inside, best eaten cold . . ." I said hurriedly.

"Yes! I got it!" he said, and he promised to order the right tree.

Osama is planting trees. Osama is trying to prove to me and to himself that he is fighting for happiness. He's building a new life in Ramallah, rediscovering the beauty of its hills, its summer festivals, the lectures at its cultural centers, and the vegetables sold in units of three kilograms at the outdoor produce market in the center of town. He says he has stopped looking for work abroad. He's investing in his life here, with me, insofar as the Israeli military will allow that.

The first time I saw the garden, I couldn't believe it. The wild green weeds were gone. He'd planted neat rows of eggplants, tomatoes, parsley, and basil. The fat sage bush next to the tall, elegant lemon verbena. Peach, plum, and cherry trees. Mostly, I couldn't believe the sight of the gardener, Osama Mustafa Hassan Fahed, watering the trees every morning, buying medicine for the ailing lemon tree, torturing himself over the tiny chili peppers that got burnt in the sun.

Osama is embracing hope.

The house began to fill with my things: Vietnamese coffee and the milk I drink it with, artificial sweetener, body cream, a backpack for long runs, a hand blender for making soup, clothing that I don't bring back to Tel Aviv anymore but would rather leave in the apartment, and Osama washes it during the two or three days a week when I return to my life in Tel Aviv. It pains me that Osama can't join me. I want him to meet my friends, come with me to a dinner or a party, a visit to see Yael and her baby.

And there's the problem of the life I'm supposed to be building in Ramallah. My current challenge—making friends. I know some foreigners in Ramallah, journalists and representatives of international organizations who earn their livelihoods from the Israeli-Palestinian "conflict" before moving on to Nigeria or Thailand or the Czech Republic. James, the Australian friend who taught me to ride a mountain bike, told me that it's easy for him to meet people when he moves to a new place. There's a network of temporarily placed foreigners who open up to each other easily.

"James can come to the dinner," I told Osama. I have been planning this dinner for weeks. It doesn't matter when we do it or what we serve. I'm trying to compose a list of invitees. I'm trying to create a social circle.

"Who is James?" he asked.

"I told you—the Australian guy I know from work, the one I joined for a biking trip."

"Yes, invite him," Osama said.

"What about Samer's friend Tom?" I asked him. "You said he was nice."

"When did I say he was nice?"

"OK, I guess he was the one who said you were nice," I corrected. "But Tom is OK. I'm starting from scratch, Osama. I don't have the luxury of being picky."

"I'm sorry, sweetheart. Invite him."

During a trip back to Tel Aviv, I visited Yael in the evening after work. I asked her if she would come to dinner in Ramallah. "Have you gone crazy?" she said. "I have a daughter."

"So bring her."

"You really have gone crazy!"

"So don't bring her," I said. "Leave her with Amir. I'll take you from Jerusalem to Osama's house. You would be in the car with me the whole time."

"Sweetie, you know that I love you, but there's no way."

"Why not?"

"Because it's dangerous, and I won't endanger myself or my baby."

"It's not dangerous to ride in the car with me without getting out of it until we reach Osama's house."

"Sari, you know it's not like that. And it's not just because of the danger."

"Then what's the real reason?"

"First of all, that is a real reason. It's dangerous. But it's not just that. I wouldn't feel comfortable. I don't go to the occupied territory. I was there only once, ten years ago, when I was working for the Rabin Center, and I had to go to a village near Qalqilya for some project. The feeling was terrible."

"Why?"

"Because, you know. I couldn't look them in the eyes."

We were sitting on the sofa, speaking quietly, because nine-month-old Maayan was sleeping. Yael pulled her hair into a ponytail and wrapped a rubber band around it.

"The situation there is so terrible, and I haven't done all that I could to stop it," she said.

"You don't need to talk to anyone or look anyone in the eyes. Just ride with me in the car until we reach Osama's house."

"Sari, you know how much I love you and want to meet him. But I can't."

I tried my friend Boaz, the actor whom I'd briefly dated years ago. Maybe it was a mistake to ask him in front of his girlfriend, Neta. The three of us sat in a café underneath Neta's parents' apartment in Ramat Hasharon, a new six-story building with a lobby and a gym. Neta didn't say a word, but she didn't take her eyes off Boaz, checking his responses.

"I'm scared," Boaz said.

"I know it sounds scary, but it's really very simple. Drive to Jerusalem and park in Pisgat Ze'ev. I'll pick you both up from there. We'll drive to Ramallah—they won't check us at the checkpoint—and you'll be in the car with me until we reach Osama's house."

"Sari, it's Ramallah . . ."

"It's driving with me in the car to a quiet residential neighborhood, getting out of the car for two minutes to walk into Osama's house, and once there, eating a delicious dinner with him and me, just like you're used to doing at my place in Tel Aviv." I could hear the desperation creep into my voice and hoped they wouldn't notice, because it would undermine the sense of confidence I was trying to convey. Neta turned her gaze toward me with a look of mild hostility. I had noticed some tension between them lately, and clearly this conversation wasn't helping to stabilize their relationship.

"It's important to me, Boaz," I said. "We're a little isolated. We need support."

"There are different ways to express support. I very much support both of you and very much want to meet Osama. But I wouldn't feel comfortable. You yourself said it's illegal."

I arranged a date to meet David for coffee. We had to talk about Gisha, in any event, some issues with the staff and a donor who was dropping out. At the end of the conversation, I invited him. "Do you remember you said you would agree to come to dinner at Osama's?"

"Of course," he said, smiling.

"And you said that Anat would come too, right?"

"Truthfully, I haven't asked her, but I'm sure she would. I'll ask her."

"You could come early, and we could show you around Ramallah, if you want to see the city."

"Sounds interesting. I'll get back to you with dates."

Weeks passed, and he didn't propose dates.

I got a promise for a future visit from an unlikely source: Noa, a lawyer friend, whose father had spent two years in prison for meeting with members of the PLO in the 1970s. She was three years old at the time and wandered between friends' houses with her mother, who had become the sole breadwinner. Noa now spends her professional life getting demonstrators released from jail, while being scrupulous about not providing the authorities with any excuse to arrest her.

Currently eight months pregnant, she told me, "I wouldn't survive the trip from Tel Aviv to Ramallah without stopping at least three times to pee. I also can't come immediately after the baby is born. But give me a year, until my daughter gets a little bigger. I would love to meet him."

I didn't invite Josh, who actually would have come. He ventures to Ramallah occasionally for meetings. And his American accent is helpful.

"We need to talk about Josh," Osama said, when I was back in Ramallah. "I know you love him. And still. I can't host someone who takes part in the occupation."

"I understand," I said. "In your place, I would probably say the same thing. But I'm not in your place. I'm in my place. Josh and Yael are the closest thing to family that I have here."

"We'll think about what to do," Osama said.

"I told Josh what you said—that you wouldn't have spoken to him had you known that he does reserve duty."

"What did he say?"

"He asked, if and when I come to live with you, would he be allowed to visit?"

"What did you tell him?"

"I told him he would always be welcome in my home."

Osama smiled, and I felt relief.

"But it's not my home yet," I said. "Let's wait."

Osama

Dreams Are Free

Summer. Vacation from teaching. I'm revising an essay at home, spending hours in front of the computer. Under pressure from Firas, who had visited me over the weekend and coached me on what to write, I created a Facebook profile in the hope of learning something about his life. Procrastinating, I click "Like" on his posts about cars, Lebanese pop stars, and restaurants in Ramallah. I come across the profile of a friend from Ramallah, whom I haven't seen in years. She had written the following post:

> *A competition for the best proposal for an activity for this weekend. Competition rules: Any proposal, but not sitting in a restaurant or café, because it's the end of the month, and we have already spent our salaries. Not a trip outside Ramallah, because the petrol is too expensive . . . not staying at home with friends and baking a cake, because buying eggs is an unpardonable crime against the chickens . . . not a romantic meeting, because no one can stand each other. And there's no sea, of course, even if we travel . . .*

The last date for receiving entries is tomorrow, close of business.

Go to sleep, I posted in response. *You'll dream that you're in a restaurant, you're traveling outside Ramallah, you're on a romantic date with Brad Pitt on the seashore, and believe me, everything is free.*

The next day, her Facebook page declared me the winner of the competition. I hesitated, and then I called her. It had been months since we'd spoken on the phone—I'd lost touch with her, as I had with most people in Ramallah. We arranged to meet in a café that is the current trendy place to go. I thought it looked exactly like the previous trendy places to go, only they were more generous with the snacks that came with the beers we ordered: peanuts, cubes of salty white cheese, sweet lupine, and cucumber sticks.

"I've missed you, *Abu Firas,*" she said, using the Palestinian convention of nicknaming parents after their children ("Father of Firas"). She refused to let me pick up the tab.

Sari

Trail Run

I gave in. I bought a car. Osama and I decided to try "for real" this time, and I'll have to start driving from Ramallah to Tel Aviv in the mornings. I know there's a way to drive to Tel Aviv via the villages that surround Ramallah to the west, but the Israeli maps don't show the route. I need to find it before I can drive it. I want to get to know the route up close, at the slow pace of a morning run.

For the first time, I dared to run beyond the villages and paths surrounding Ramallah, to the forbidden roads of the settlers.

I left Osama's house on a Friday morning, part of the weekend in Ramallah. Quiet. I stretched my quadriceps, bent and extended my body to wake up my calves, turned on the GPS watch that measures speed and distance, and jogged toward the main road. I crossed lines of stone houses and ran under a jasmine tree, delighting in its intoxicating scent. At the end of the road, I ascended a steep gravel path that curves up and then down to the wadi, the dry riverbed below. At the bottom was a construction site where they had begun to pour the concrete foundation of a building, threatening the almond trees that blossom in winter, the wild deer that skip across the terraces in the early mornings, and the remnants of old stone seasonal agricultural shelters that Osama calls "castles."

Since it was Friday, there was no construction. Large, mangy stray dogs passed me, appearing defeated; they didn't even bother to bark. Buzzards circled overhead, and olive trees lined the slopes of the path.

I reached a narrow, curving paved road about ten meters above the wadi. Osama had warned me that military jeeps sometimes patrol that road, which also leads to the Beit El settlement. I ran in the direction of the village of Ein Qinya, climbing a continuous ascent that wound between the hills. After four kilometers, I turned right, onto the windy road up to the village. In front of me a white sign announced "Ein Qinya," in bright blue letters in Arabic and English. The Israeli army usually doesn't allow Palestinians to mark the names of their towns on main roads used by settlers, but this was an access road between Ramallah and Ein Qinya, and after the army closed off the main road to the west, it had become the village's only exit and entrance.

I passed the first houses and the small school. The red flags of the Popular Front for the Liberation of Palestine adorned its walls. I neared the mosque and the kiosk on the left side, where I sometimes stopped to buy water. I met the stare of a young man getting out of a white truck, until he lowered his gaze. I smiled at the elderly woman washing the stone courtyard in front of her house. "*Sabah elkhair*," I said. "Good morning."

She answered, "*Sabah elnour*."

Instead of continuing straight, as I usually did when I run in the villages, toward the Bedouin encampment near the stream that leads back to the road to Ramallah, I turned left toward the western road that leads to the settlement of Dolev. That road used to lead to Tel Aviv, but it's now blocked on both sides by a yellow metal gate that rests on gray concrete blocks placed on each side of the road, about fifty meters from the last house in the village.

It's an unmanned obstacle. On foot, you can easily step over it.

The road became smoother, well paved, as I climbed up the hill. A sign in Hebrew for "Dolevim River" against a brown background signified an official Israeli nature site. Above, to the right, a barbed-wire fence surrounded the hill, and an electric cable, dotted with sensors, wound around it and surrounded the settlement of Dolev. To my left, down the mountain slope, I noticed a path between the trees. I ran toward it—it was shaded and also might hide me from the residents of the settlement. Running under the protection of the trees, my breath eased. But the path ended without warning in a steep slope, and I had to pick my way through the trees to go back up to the paved road, the one next to the settlement. I ran past the sign "*Ulpana*," the name for a religious school for teenage girls, thinking of the elderly woman in Ein Qinya who poured water on the stones in her courtyard and waved hello to me, wondering if she had ever been here, a place so close and yet so forbidden.

In this quiet expanse, the settlement houses were above me, white with red roofs, spread out in steep rings that surrounded the mountain. I didn't see anyone. I didn't hear anyone. I imagined eyes watching me from behind the fence, from inside the homes, from the other side of the window of the security booth next to the entry gate. I accelerated, ran and ran, but the settlement stretched on and on. Suddenly, at a bend in the road, the wall of trees that had accompanied me on the left side retreated, revealing a spectacular view of exposed hilltops, and below them wide roads stretching westward. On the horizon, I saw the towers of Modi'in, an Israeli city located midway between Tel Aviv and Jerusalem.

Northwest of them, I could also see the skyline of the outskirts of Tel Aviv. I ran down the steep hill, my feet slapping the asphalt. The sun climbed in the sky, and I wanted to reach the junction at the bottom of the hill, to decipher the green interurban sign I saw there and to figure out where I was.

Down the slope of the hill, green plants rounded terraced circles, surrounded by irrigation pipes. Were those grapevines? A strong smell of fertilizer. A car passed me, driven by a thirtysomething woman, wearing a white T-shirt similar to mine, her brown hair tied back into a ponytail.

The sun scorched the asphalt. On the sides of the road were campaign advertisements for central committee elections for the Likud, a right-wing Israeli political party. The candidates' smiling faces accompanied me down the hill. A huge real estate agency sign showed an image of pastoral villas with the caption, "The diamond that is in Dolev—think central Israel, but really central."

I ran toward the sign I had seen from a distance. "Modi'in: 16 kilometers; Tel Aviv: 47 kilometers."

Only forty-seven kilometers to Tel Aviv. Were it not for the checkpoints, I could leave my apartment in Tel Aviv in the morning and run straight to Osama.

I turned in the direction of Beitunia to the steep road on which an occasional Palestinian vehicle turned, a private car or taxi bearing the white or green license plates assigned to Palestinian cars. At the entrance to the road was a red sign: "Entry for Israelis into Area A endangers your lives and is a criminal offense!" Next to it, on a concrete block, someone had sprayed in Hebrew, "Death to the Arabs."

The sun burned high in the sky. I wasn't sure of the way. If I were to get lost, Osama would wonder what happened to me.

Two hundred meters before the top of the hill, before the entrance to the nearest village, I turned back the way I had come, to take the sure way home. Running down the hill from the villages, I am Palestinian. Running up the hill toward Dolev, I'll be a settler.

Ten meters before the junction, on another concrete block, someone had sprayed in Hebrew, "Death to the Jews."

Two teenage boys stood at the bus stop on the main road, wearing white shirts and black pants, ritual fringes dangling from their hips and yarmulkes on their heads. One of them pointed at me. I felt a sudden, overwhelming urge to be in Ein Qinya already, to be the foreigner who crosses their village from time to time, waving hello and buying a drink in the little grocery store. I wanted to return to my wadi, to Osama's house, to a place where I could drink a glass of water.

I ran past the boys, my gaze pointed straight ahead. On the hill leading up to the settlement, heat competed with anxiety in setting the pace of my run. My leg muscles flooded with burning lactic acid buildup that would not clear until I slowed down. I sprinted the last hundred meters before the barrier between Dolev and Ein Qinya, as if crossing a finish line.

"Woof, woof!" A gigantic black dog bared his white teeth, growling, furious, about to make mincemeat out of me. He lunged but was suddenly jerked backward, as an iron chain tied the dog to a large rock across from the first house of Ein Qinya. I passed him, now at a slow jog.

My running watch recorded seventeen kilometers thus far. It was 9:00 a.m., July. I was seven kilometers away from Osama's apartment. Three children played ball in the elderly woman's sparkling clean courtyard. I decided not to ask for a glass of water. Maybe she had seen me arriving from the direction of Dolev. I had been in a place that is off-limits to her, that blocks her access to the main road. How could I ask her for a glass of water?

I ran along the wadi, back to Osama's house. I ran down the stairs and opened the door of the cool apartment, lit with the gentle light of the garden shaded by fruit trees, a soothing light after the blinding sun. Osama was waiting for me. Firas had slept over, and Osama wanted to make us breakfast. I joined him in the kitchen and drank four glasses of water, one after the other. Collapsing into a kitchen chair, I thought about the route I had discovered, a route that would require me to fight, if I wanted to traverse it.

"I ran to the settlement next to Ein Qinya," I told Osama.

"Drink, sweetheart," he said. "And then go take your shower, please."

Osama
Other Israelis

For years, my interactions with Israelis were limited to soldiers. But after Sari entered my life, I started to remember other Israelis I had known.

During one of the periods when Israel closed my university, I worked at a construction site in the Israeli city of Holon. Or was it Bat Yam? In any case, I worked with Moshe and Abdullah. During the lunch break between ten and ten thirty, they would trade stories their grandparents had told them about the pre-1917 period of Ottoman rule over Palestine—the train that used to run from Haifa to Damascus, the rich businessmen who grew oranges, the *Falastin* newspaper in Arabic, and the *Moriah* newspaper in Hebrew.

Another Moshe, an Israeli merchant, used to travel with us by public taxi from Gaza to Ramallah and Jerusalem, before the checkpoints interfered, on his way to Tel Aviv. He would ask the driver to change the radio station that broadcast readings of the Koran to the one that played Farid al-Atrash love songs. He would say, in Arabic, "There's a time for your God, and a time for your heart."

At the end of the workday in Holon, an Israeli boy plays football with us, using a discarded metal can. His laughter fills the air. His mother stands a few meters away, and she's not worried about her son's safety among the "Arab workers."

The Israeli contractor, Shlomo, has no patience for any of us, even for his brother Jackie. Shlomo argues with Moeen, the veteran Palestinian worker, about where to ground the water pipes. He is so impressed by Moeen's abilities that he puts Moeen in charge of supervising the work. Shlomo knows I'm good at chess, and during breaks, each time he beats me, he doesn't hide his excitement.

Shlomo yells at the Israeli worker Dudu, "Dig here . . . nu."

"You don't need to shout, Shlomo. I get it."

"Nu . . . here. Enough, enough. You ruined the pipe. What an idiot."

"But you told me to dig more . . ."

Palestinians and Israelis gossip together about the bosses and the municipal supervisors of Holon, Bat Yam, Jaffa, and Tel Aviv—solidarity among workers over lunch.

As my historian friend Ann Marie says, my sense of geography is messed up. After being trapped for so many years, I can't draw the connections between Holon, Bat Yam, Ein Yahav, Jaffa, and Tel Aviv, where I worked on Israeli construction sites; the West Bank towns of Qalqilya and Tulkarm that I used to be able to visit; and the Ketziot Prison.

I remember now. As the Israeli army kept my university closed, and I spent more time working on Israeli construction sites, the Hebrew in my mouth took over English, the language in which I was supposed to conduct my university studies. I grew almost fluent during my eleven-month prison sentence.

When I hear Sari speaking Hebrew on the phone at my place, or catch fragments of the language in the background when I call her in the middle of her workday, I'm reminded of a picture I saw in Talya and Eli's house in London, of two elderly men—Palestinian and Israeli—under a banner with the slogan "Two states for two peoples."

Sari

Control-F

AUGUST 2, 2011

Nibal, Gisha's research director, comes into my office for our weekly meeting and announces, "In an hour, they'll publish a list of nineteen hundred Gazans in the West Bank whose registered addresses the Israeli military agrees to change."

It was to be another partial list, the continuation of a commitment the Israeli government made six months ago to the British diplomat Tony Blair to allow five thousand Palestinian residents living in the West Bank to officially change their addresses from Gaza to the West Bank, and thus continue to live where they'd been living.

We had submitted Osama's name to the army, but it wasn't included on the first list of approvals published three months ago, numbering three hundred names. In the meantime, Osama and I were busy waging another battle against the army, a small and modest one in the context of the occupation, to allow Osama to leave the West Bank to go on vacation with me in Jordan. A battle for the right to dive. A battle for the right to swim. A battle for the right to wear, in Osama's presence, cute, short summer dresses that I hoped would be acceptable on the tourist beaches of Aqaba.

Josh asked me why we were planning to travel to Jordan rather than somewhere else more interesting, more different, less hot.

"We can't buy plane tickets," I told him, since we still needed a permit for Osama to leave the West Bank. "We'll know only at the last minute if Osama can travel."

The response letter from the army included the following instructions: "The resident should submit a request, via the Palestinian Authority's Civil Affairs Committee, one week before the desired exit date, including the documents that demonstrate the humanitarian need for which exit is required."

I had never requested a travel permit for a vacation. Osama's other trips, for which we fought hard, were for the purpose of study or were approved as part of the court-monitored arrangement. Other Gisha clients traveled when relatives got sick abroad, and even then, the military sometimes approved the request only after the relative had died. On the military's list of priorities, a condolence visit is more humanitarian than a hospital visit, because the severity of an illness can be proven conclusively only in retrospect.

I decided to ignore the demand for humanitarian documents and to submit the request to the Israeli military through the mediation of the Palestinian Authority, the local administrative government that Israel and the PLO set up in 1994. This route would still require me to fight—with Osama, who hated any contact with authorities, Palestinian or Israeli. I approached him on a Saturday morning as he sat in the garden smoking a cigarette. I held the letter in my hand and plastered a huge smile on my face. He had finished watering the trees not long before, so the ground was moist, a rich brown in contrast to the deep green of the cherry tree.

"Do you remember what David told us, that we should happily and proudly embrace the role imposed on us as resisters, people who challenge the consensus?" I placed a chair next to his and sat down. He raised an eyebrow, suspecting he wasn't going to like whatever would follow that preamble.

I continued, "And remember what I told you, that happiness is the best form of resistance? Well, here we have a golden opportunity to practice it!"

I showed him the letter, which cited one of the reasons for restricting Osama from leaving the West Bank for Jordan as "the policy of separation between the Gaza Strip and Judea and Samaria." I translated for Osama "Judea and Samaria," the biblical term for the West Bank.

"Do you think they know that Aqaba is not located inside the Gaza Strip?" I asked. "And that one usually doesn't cross through Gaza in order to reach Jordan from Ramallah?"

He laughed, and I took a deep breath.

"So I'm asking you to go tomorrow to your favorite people, the Civil Affairs Committee of the Palestinian Authority, and ask them to submit a request in your name to the army to coordinate passage via the Allenby Bridge. If the army refuses, we'll take a vacation in the West Bank. Every day, we'll travel to a different place where we can swim. We'll cite their refusal in our court case, to show why they should allow you to change your address, why a temporary staying permit is not enough and prevents you from traveling. And we'll write about it in the *Maqluba* book."

To my surprise, the next day, Osama went to the Palestinian Authority's Civil Affairs Committee and submitted the request. In the meantime, I followed up on the request with the army, trying to get an answer that would determine whether we'd travel to Jordan the following week.

And now Nibal is here, settling into the chair across from my desk and telling me that in another hour Osama might be able to travel whenever he wants, without permits and without the fear that he wouldn't be allowed to return home. I hope Osama doesn't hear about the list before it's published. It's hard enough for one of us to be in suspense.

In the middle of our conversation, Osama calls my cell phone. I return his call after the meeting ends, and as I confirm the rumor he also heard, I see that the news website Ma'an has published the list.

I open the PDF file on the Ma'an website and press Control-F.

"I'm so nervous I can't find the letters on the keyboard," I tell Osama. I try to calm down. My fingers search for the Arabic letters pasted onto the keyboard with stickers to type out Osama's name. Here's the *alif.*

Last night we celebrated Osama's forty-fourth birthday. I traveled the two and a half hours from work to meet him at a restaurant in Ramallah. We sat in the garden, and I allowed myself to take off my jacket and sit across from him in the summer dress I'd bought in Vietnam, a wine-colored sleeveless dress with a low neckline.

"You're so beautiful," he said.

Where the hell did the letter *sine* disappear to? There it is. I type it and then type the second *alif.*

"I made your life difficult, didn't I, sweetheart?" The air in the restaurant's garden was cool and magical. I nodded vigorously.

"I'm sorry. I've stopped being hard on us. Now it's your turn to be hard on me, if you want."

We talked about the apartment, repairs we'd make, a new color of paint, about the years we would need to wait until the young trees would bear fruit. He tried to persuade me to taste the shrimp he ordered, and I found myself trying to explain to him the laws of kashruth observance.

"But it's fish," he protested.

When I realized I didn't know how to say "scales" in Arabic, and he didn't know what it meant in English, the conversation deteriorated into his protests and my laughter, until I decided it was time to break the bad news to him: "You know that if I come to live with you, we'll need three sets of dishes. One set of kosher dairy dishes, one kosher meat set, and the third—for you and Firas to eat whatever you want on them, meaning nonkosher meat."

"How can you justify comprising one-third of the population of the house but demanding two-thirds of the dishes?"

The *mime* is easy to find—a long, narrow line with an elegant half circle at the top. I press it.

We have been good together recently. Actually, we've been great. And because we are making it work, as Osama and Sari, our need to overcome the external threats has become more pressing.

"Sweetheart, it's not fair for you if we can't change my address," he said at the restaurant, after we ordered another round of drinks—wine for me and beer for him. We had agreed that if the Israeli military didn't include him in the lists of people whose addresses they promised to change from Gaza to the West Bank—if he remained trapped in Ramallah—he should leave and look for work in Europe.

"You don't want to leave, and your work is important," Osama had said.

"Let's wait and see. In the coming months, we'll know whether they'll change your address."

I look for the *ta marbuta*. Tiny, it always hides from me on the keyboard, even when my thoughts aren't racing back and forth at a pace that borders on hysteria. The door to my office is open. If his name is on the list, will I manage to stop myself from screaming? I'm searching for my own future there, too, in that PDF file.

I type the *ta marbuta* and press Enter.

The answer appears: "Reader has finished searching the document. No matches were found."

I try again. "Reader has finished searching the document. No matches were found."

"I don't see your name yet, sweetheart," I tell Osama.

I hear him call to Firas: "Baba, pull up the website of the news agency Ma'an."

I ask Osama for his identification number, to search that way, typed it, and hit Enter.

"Reader has finished searching the document. No matches were found."

"Sweetheart, I don't see your name."

In the background, I hear Firas say he had found the website, and then silence.

"No," Osama says.

Again silence, and then Osama says, "Damn them."

"I'm so sorry, sweetheart," I say.

"It's OK."

"It's just one list. And the fact that they published it is a good sign—it means that approvals are being processed, that it's just taking time. You see, the process hasn't been frozen; they are still issuing approvals."

"Yes, sweetheart."

"There's no logic to these lists, and there's no reason to think that you won't be on the next list."

"Yes, sweetheart."

"I'm sorry, Osama. I love you."

"Thank you, sweetheart."

In the office, exuberant voices shout the names of favorite clients who appeared on the list. Monir and Nisreen compare our client list with the list on the Ma'an website. Hadas stands behind their chairs, studying the screen and breaking out into screams every time another familiar name appears.

"Laila Shaheen is on the list!" she calls out, and jokes about the free time she will have, now that so many cases are resolved successfully.

Through the ringing of the telephones, the laughter, and the cries of "*Mabruk* ("Congratulations")!" I hear Monir's voice complain, "It's totally arbitrary. They approved Amal Hamdan, but not her husband."

"There will be additional lists," Monir says, after he finishes updating clients by telephone. "But for those who weren't included, it feels like the end of the world."

I leave the office in the evening and skate down Allenby Street on my Rollerblades. Easy, quick gliding, weaving in and out of the slow pedestrians. I call Osama for the seventh time. He laughs at my jokes and tells me about his plans for dinner, and about the flavor of ice cream that he and Firas will eat with his leftover birthday cake. He says he avoided phone calls from friends checking in, that he preferred not to talk to anyone. Again I tell him I'm sorry. Again he says it's OK.

Then he says, "It's just that this time, for the first time, I allowed myself to hope."

At home I call Josh and tell him about the list. I ask him about a date he had with a woman from the university, who had picked him up at a conference on green engineering. Then I realize I'm crying. Josh interrupts his description of their walk home from the bar.

"I'm sorry," I tell Josh. "I just thought that maybe things would get easier for us."

Osama

Cold Shower

Today I was a tourist, visiting ancient sites, admiring the mystery, the legends and stories they contain. A week earlier, the Israeli army allowed me to leave for a vacation in Jordan. That's also a notable historical event.

At the bus station in the Jordanian city of Karak, I watched a group of young men, Jordanian soldiers, buy bottles of Coca-Cola and board a bus with tinted windows. When I first noticed them—strong, sweaty, vital, carrying huge weapons—for a minute I forgot where I was and thought they were Israeli soldiers.

In the bathroom of our small hotel room, I removed my sweat-drenched shirt while Sari went downstairs to the reception desk to ask for a map of the city. Outside the small window, I could see a warm and full moon, painted almost orange with light. Again my sense of time and space faltered, and I was flooded with memories as vivid as the scenes of an old movie.

In the Ansar 2 prison, the soldier on duty didn't believe my answers to his questions: "You're wearing a kaffiyeh, you're from the Jabalia refugee camp, and you want me to believe that you didn't throw stones?!" He asked me this after I had been standing in the sun the entire day, *mashbuh*, hands tied behind my back and blindfolded, as per an Israeli military practice.

During another arrest, in the wintertime, I became a pawn in a game of flirtation between a male and female soldier. I was standing *mashbuh* in the rain, and the female soldier led me to a kind of shed, as shelter. I think I thanked her. Then the male soldier came and led me back out into the rain. "Enough," she shouted at him in a flirtatious voice and led me back to the shed. He returned, laughing, and led me back out into the rain. She then led me back, and so on . . .

I cursed them both in a voice that no one but me heard.

Usually, I pretended I didn't know Hebrew. During some drive in a military jeep, after I was arrested during a raid at my university, I sat between the driver and a soldier in the passenger seat, and one said to the other in Hebrew, "How about we ask him a question? If he answers yes, I'll hit him, and if he answers no, you'll hit him." They agreed on the rules of the game.

They asked, "Do you smoke?"

I didn't answer.

They both hit me.

In another interrogation, the pretense of not knowing Hebrew actually helped me. The intelligence officer told the plainclothes soldiers, "But don't really do it." And then I understood that they weren't actually going to kill me, even when the barrel of the pistol—or maybe it was a revolver—was in my mouth. I don't know why I believed that. What if the gun fired accidentally? By mistake, just like that, perhaps if I were to stumble because of the blows the soldiers from the special unit had rained upon every part of my body? I remember exactly how the moon looked that night. It was beautiful—until I couldn't see it anymore. I had been awake for seventy-two consecutive hours, swallowed up in successive nights of harsh interrogations.

In the hotel now, I got into the shower.

I had tried to tell her, to tell Sari. Those experiences shaped who I am and what I bring to our relationship. They shape my ability to tolerate risk, to trust her.

"How can you be so confident, in a place you've never been?" I asked her that morning. She moved so easily through Karak. She had planned our Jordanian itinerary and seemed to know where to go at every stop.

"The ground has never been stable beneath my feet," I said, trying to explain the differences. Sari listened. I don't know how much she understood. I didn't manage to say everything.

I let the water flow over me, until I heard her coming back into the room.

I remembered that, because of the deep scars on my face, caused by burns from cigarette lighters that intelligence agents used during one of my arrests, the medical staff at the hospital in Ramallah hesitated to approach me. They thought I was a collaborator who had been beaten nearly to death by the Palestinian "shock forces," who beat or killed Palestinians who collaborated with Israel.

I stepped out of the shower into the dark room, and the white walls shone in the light of the full moon.

Another day of the Ramadan fast had ended. We went to eat dinner.

Sari

Tourists

I ran along the path that wound around a hill on the outskirts of the Jordanian city of Karak, with blue skies and white clouds above me, wide leaves on the sides of the path that looked like lettuce, and on my right, a Bedouin encampment. It was early. Osama was still sleeping when I left the guesthouse, built in the shadow of the Crusader fortress that justified the town's inclusion on the Jordanian tourist map. I had run down one of the steep alleys of the Old City, deserted on a quiet Ramadan morning, and continued toward the agricultural paths that circumvented the hills in ascending and descending rings.

Good morning, Karak. I'm pleased to meet you. I love the transient familiarity and ownership that running gives me over places that don't belong to me. Here, I run up the bend of the mountain, cut through a herd of goats, hear the dog bark, and bend down to pick up a rock. I'm confident I can threaten the dog, teach it a lesson, but then its owner arrives, and I let the rock slip from my hand and call *Sabah Elkhair*, ("good morning" in Arabic) to a middle-aged man, dressed in jeans and a yellowing white button-down shirt. In response, he subdues the dog and stares at me.

I wanted to keep running, but Osama would wake up soon, and we were supposed to visit the fortress and then catch a bus to Amman. And I still had to run through the market to buy us the breakfast we would eat in our room to avoid offending those observing the Ramadan fast.

The path continued, wrapping around the mountain in tempting, ascending circles, but I stopped in front of an olive tree at a bend and turned back the way I came, reluctantly giving up on discovering the rest of the trail. Maybe one day I'll come back.

Last night, before we fell asleep, lying in bed in the simple and clean hotel room, Osama seemed lost in faraway thoughts. To my surprise, he shared some of them with me.

"It's nice here, but I don't feel comfortable," he said. "It's not rational, but I keep expecting the Israeli army to arrest me—for not having a permit, for crossing a checkpoint, for being a young Palestinian man, and I'm not even young anymore."

I wanted to pass my hand over his face, to caress his shoulders, to softly touch the places where they had hurt him.

I ran back toward the hotel, again cutting through the herd of goats, and this time, the defeated dog made do with an agitated growl. After mistakenly running up the wrong hill and ending up in a neighborhood some distance from the hotel, I ran back toward the road, ran up the correct hill, and then stopped at the tiny market to buy bread and tomatoes before sprinting back to the hotel. I found Osama awake, showered, dressed, and standing next to the window, looking for me.

"I'm sorry, sweetheart," I said, searching his face. "Are you angry or worried?"

"Worried," he said in a hoarse voice. "Another ten minutes and I would have gone to the police."

"I'm sorry. The run was beautiful—I left the city and found a path that was endless. I got lost on the way back, and it took time to find an open bakery."

We sat on the bed in the room and ate the bread and tomatoes, which I cut with a Swiss Army knife, as well as cheese and cucumber, and the peaches and plums we had bought the day before. I was impressed by the summer fruits we found in Jordan—they were incredibly sweet and juicy.

"Hey." I got behind Osama on the bed and wrapped my arms around his back. "Are you OK?"

He wiped his hands with the roll of toilet paper we'd taken from the bathroom.

"I'm not sure," he said. "You won't get upset?"

"No," I said, but that wasn't quite true.

"I'm not sure how I feel. I feel uncertain about everything."

I hugged him tightly from behind. "I'm glad you're sharing with me," I said.

Osama twisted around to return a brief hug and then stood. He collected the leftover food and cleaned the knife with a square of toilet paper. We started packing our backpacks.

"Should I tie my hair back or keep it loose?" I asked him and modeled both options. He seemed surprised. We don't have a lot of opportunities to leave the house together. It was the first time I had asked his opinion about my hair or dress.

"It's nice loose," he said shyly, "unless that's too hot for you."

"Where are you from?" the taxi driver outside the hotel asked.

"From Palestine," Osama answered.

"Welcome!" the driver said warmly and then quoted a price that was five times what locals pay. This bargaining drives Osama nuts. He can't understand why the price has to be haggled over. Why not just say how much it costs and be done with it?

In my broken Arabic, I got the taxi driver to halve the price.

"Where is your wife from?" he asked Osama once we were in the taxi.

"America," Osama said.

This trip is supposed to give us a break from being interesting to other people. And also—I told Osama about the signs I had seen in the shops in Petra, when I had visited Jordan two and a half years earlier. They were written in English: "We're sorry, we don't serve dogs or Israelis."

Osama

Diary of a Target

We reached Amman. Sari fell asleep immediately in the small hotel room, and I watched her with envy. How does she do it? I didn't even bother to try to sleep. Memories continued to flood me. I wanted to write.

Starting on March 29, 2002, during the Second Intifada, when the Israeli army began invading the cities in the West Bank, I wrote a kind of journal as Israel reconquered the West Bank, beginning with Ramallah. At that time, I lived near the Muqataa, the office compound of the Palestinian President Yasser Arafat, whom the Israeli army was targeting. I wanted to document what I saw and heard. Writing became to me a kind of act of resistance. The diary was interrupted, first between April 6 and April 11, while I was in detention, and then again after Nisreen and I left our home to stay with friends who lived farther from the shelling.

I responded to the events as they unfolded, and sometimes thoughts and reality got mixed up in my head. Why am I remembering all this now?

MARCH 31, 2002

That soldier holding the gun, viewing us through its sight, must now be thinking, *That man is now smack in the middle of the sight of my gun. Here is his little boy too . . . I miss my Yoav. He must be with his mother now. They're probably going to the beach. I miss them . . . Those two are playing together on the balcony of their apartment. I can hear his son's laughter. But why are they here, violating the curfew?!*

APRIL 2, 2002

Firas is playing next to me. I want to smoke a cigarette, far away from him. How many times were we at the center of the target, and we didn't even know?

"Why did you come here, sweetheart?"

"I'm afraid."

"Should I tell you the fly joke?"

"Yes!"

"Yes or not yes, should I tell you the fly joke?"

"Yes," Firas said hesitantly.

"Yes or not yes, should I tell you the fly joke?"

"No!" Firas giggled.

"No or not no, should I tell you the fly joke?"

"No!"

Does the soldier hear, in his imagination, the laughter of a child?

I hear a burst of gunfire, a scream, and then the sound of crying.

In Amman, the sun began to rise. Why does travel, and being with Sari, bring all this back to me?

In another few hours, we'll return home, each of us through our own border crossing.

Sari

Saving a Life

We returned from Amman. It was the most time we had spent together, and at times Osama was tense, impatient with me. I continued to explore how to be with him in Ramallah, but less confidently. One Saturday morning in August 2011, I left his house early in the morning, dates and a bottle of water hidden in my running backpack. I wore gray pants that covered my knees and a blue dry-fit T-shirt I had gotten from the Tel Aviv Marathon, which I wore inside out to hide the Hebrew lettering. I hadn't yet bought a car but was looking for the path I would have to drive to reach Tel Aviv: the back exit from Ramallah and the adjacent town of Beitunia that leads to the road used by Jewish settlers to drive between settlements and into Israel.

I ran past the affluent homes of the Masyoun neighborhood and crossed the main street toward the industrial zone between wealthy Ramallah and working-class Beitunia. The jasmine trees and sidewalks gave way to a potholed road lined with shuttered metal workshops and mechanics' garages. To the right was a deep wadi. I knew that beyond the wadi, hidden between the hills, was the road I was looking for, the one that I had reached on foot earlier this summer, from the opposite direction, by jumping over the cement barrier between the village of Ein Qinya and the settlement of Dolev. My mission this morning was to find the longer vehicular route to that road. I didn't know where it was, and when I'd asked Osama, he seemed distracted, uninterested. The repetitive simplicity of running, putting one foot in front of the other, reassured me.

Every few minutes, I checked the angle of the sun to make sure I hadn't made a mistake, that I was still running west. Here in the villages, far from the settlements, the army doesn't prevent Palestinians from marking the names of towns. I smiled in relief when I saw the sign in Arabic and English: "Beitunia" to the left and "Ein Arik" to the right. I hadn't made a mistake.

Those observing Ramadan sleep as late as possible, to minimize the hours of fasting. Alone on the winding, deserted road between Beitunia and Ein Arik, I managed to sneak a date and a drink of water from my backpack. When I stopped to urinate on the side of the road, behind a pile of construction debris, I saw a billboard that surprised me with its daring—a model in a sparkling bridal gown featuring deep cleavage and bare shoulders. I could hear Osama's voice in my head: *Why are you thinking in stereotypes?* The modernness of this reassured me. If I'm running, people will know that I'm clearly not fasting, but Osama had told me that Ein Arik has a significant Christian population, and maybe the Muslim residents don't care either.

I reached the small, sleepy village in the curve of the hill, the entrance marked with speed bumps. The main road led me past a big new mosque sporting a narrow minaret that climbed high into the sky and shops—I identified a produce shop and also a small grocery—that were still closed. The houses peered out over me from the hills above. I didn't see anyone, except for worshippers returning from morning prayer, mostly older men who politely, or maybe impolitely, ignored me.

Was it Ein Arik? How would I know? As soon as it began, the village ended. I climbed a steep road, surrounded by fruit trees, that led to another village, or perhaps a continuation of the previous one, with a furniture store at the top and a kind of public taxi stand with a shelter, where an elderly woman waited, holding a little boy's hand.

"Where is Ras Karkar?" I asked, referring to the village that, according to the map, was on the road I was looking for. I couldn't say "the road to Tel Aviv," because for her, that road doesn't lead to Tel Aviv. She was wearing a long, narrow black coat, decorated with black embroidery, and a bright blue-and-purple-flowered hijab on her head.

"Straight and then right," she said.

"Thank you!"

"Are you from Ramallah?"

According to my GPS watch, Ramallah was ten kilometers behind me. People usually don't assume that others have run long distances, but who else would pass through her village running except a woman from Ramallah?

"Yes," I said, waving goodbye.

I left the tiny shopping center and turned right. The familiar steep descent made me smile. I had run part of the way up this road, from the direction of Ein Qinya, on my previous exploratory trip but had turned back early for fear of getting lost. Now I could see there would be a junction below with signs directing drivers to Modi'in and Tel Aviv. This is how I would drive to Tel Aviv. This is how I would get to work in the mornings.

Now I had to return to Ramallah via the shortcut that winds between the Dolev settlement and the village of Ein Qinya, which is closed to vehicles. I turned eastward and climbed the wide road toward the rings of settlement houses at the top of the hill. It was the Jewish Sabbath. The sun burned in the sky. I didn't see another human being. At a bend in the road, I saw the first houses of the settlement. As I passed the entrance gate on my left, I heard a car start and approach me from the direction of Dolev: the settlement's security jeep.

Yesterday, when I decided on this run, I pictured the military watchtower on the hill between Ein Qinya and Dolev. I practiced the answers I would give if a soldier emerged from the tower and questioned me. I had decided I would speak English, be American.

I looked straight ahead, maintaining a constant pace. I heard the noise of the white jeep approaching me. Through the corner of my eye, I saw that its driver was a plump, elderly man, bearded, wearing a yarmulke. I remembered from my religious Jewish elementary school training that the commandment to save a life trumps the prohibition against driving on the Sabbath. I refrained from turning my head, and I didn't slow down. We continued our upward movement for a minute, my gait short on the incline, my body tilted forward, and the jeep alongside me, the sound of gravel exploding under its wheels. Exhaust smoke filled my nostrils.

"Good morning," the security officer said to me in Hebrew, through the open jeep window. I turned my head. He was regarding me from a distance of a meter and a half. His jeep was centered between the white dividing line on the road and the road's shoulder, where I was running.

"Good morning," I answered in Hebrew, flustered, or maybe out of an intuition that the language and accent would reassure him, unlike a "good morning" in English that would leave him unsure of my identity and level of threat.

"Where are you from?"

"Where do I live?" I asked, trying to formulate the right answer.

"Where are you from?" he asked again.

"From Tel Aviv," I said, and I returned my gaze to the road in front of me, thinking of the mistake that young children make: If I close my eyes, no one can see me. We kept climbing the asphalt, my steps short and him driving slowly, his eyes darting back and forth between me and the road in front of him. Suddenly, he accelerated, and his car disappeared around the bend. A minute or two later, it reappeared, passing me on his way back to the settlement.

Had he called the soldiers in the watchtower above? Were there any soldiers in that watchtower?

I continued running, shaking my head to release the tension that had built up in my neck from the effort to avoid turning my head toward the jeep. At the top of the hill, I turned right, in the direction of the old sign still hanging on the gate of the settlement: "To Jerusalem." That road had stopped leading to Jerusalem a long time ago. I continued running on it. The thicket across from the settlement ended, and on my left was the hill with the watchtower that looked out over the exposed road. There were three hundred meters left between me and the concrete barrier, and behind it the village of Ein Qinya. I turned on my MP3 player and listened to a radio program about an artists' protest in Iran. The interviewee, now living in California, described how, at the age of three, he had sung children's songs praising that idealistic revolutionary Ayatollah Khomeini. I heard shouts from above, stopped running, and dared to look at the watchtower. I saw the silhouette of a face pass in the window. Or did I imagine it? I turned off the podcast and continued running at a fast but consistent pace—not running away, just doing speed training. I didn't see anything out of the corner of my eye. Thirty meters until the concrete block separating Ein Qinya from the settlement road. Twenty meters. I looked toward the watchtower and didn't see anyone. I jumped into the road's shoulder, ran around the gate and concrete block, and heard the short, rapid barks of the black dog—that dog who bared his teeth, who was insane with rage, who was desperate to sink his teeth into my flesh, and who was bound with an iron chain to the rock across from the first house in Ein Qinya. I sighed with relief. I made it.

Osama
Ann Marie

I met Ann Marie in 2005, when Nisreen invited her to our home in Ramallah. Since then, she has managed to challenge and confuse me. She was born in South Africa, the daughter of a Black Christian mother and a white Jewish father, was arrested a number of times while fighting the apartheid regime, and after the fall of white rule in South Africa, she ended up in Palestine.

Before I met Ann Marie, my experiences with Jews were limited to soldiers or the construction contractors who employed me. I learned from an early age that Israel is power, Jews are Israel, and that I need to struggle against them. Ann Marie challenged my identification of Jews with Israel and my assumption that Jews are white and against Palestinians. I was reluctant at first because I didn't want to learn from Jews, but I even found myself learning from her something about ourselves, about Palestinians. Ann Marie took me to see the parts of the Ramallah area where the Israeli regime had built the wall. I had heard about it, I knew about it, but I hadn't made the effort to travel there and see for myself. Maybe I was avoiding a painful reality.

As my feelings about Sari became more and more confused, I found myself seeking out Ann Marie's company.

Ann Marie taught me about the history of apartheid and the Holocaust. I was surprised to learn that some of the Jews who came to Palestine were refugees who fled for their lives, and that Ann Marie's father—her white, Jewish father—had lost many relatives in the Holocaust.

Ann Marie feels most at home in the Gaza Strip. She came to Gaza as a doctoral student to study the history of the local authorities there, and she decided to stay in Palestine. Ann Marie has always lived on the margins of society. I think she enjoys that status, not just in South Africa but also in Gaza—the refugee camps must remind her of the townships of her childhood during the apartheid era. Unlike other solidarity activists, Ann Marie allows herself to criticize Palestinians. "The whole world is busy working on Palestine, except for Palestinians," she said after returning to the West Bank from a solidarity conference with the Palestinian people in Johannesburg only to find people in Ramallah obsessed with local political intrigues and devoting their energies to attending summer festivals. She doesn't always manage to hold back her tears when she hears the answers, the stories of people's lives, especially in the Gaza Strip.

Sari
Children

Years ago, when I was still Osama's lawyer, and he was explaining what would be at stake if the Israeli military were to remove him to Gaza, he told me that he loves Firas to the point of drunkenness. His face lights up when Firas is around. I remember the games he played with Tamer, his then-four-year-old nephew who visited from the Gaza Strip. Osama took him on the mechanical horse in the mall in downtown Ramallah, and when the boy expressed wonder at the horse's sudden movement, Osama lifted him up and set him down on the horse over and over again, entirely swept away by the child's joy, by his own joy. As I watched them, I was terrified to decipher the wish that crept into my heart: *I want him to be the father of my children.*

Last night, after weeks in which I felt him slipping away from me, Osama said he wanted to talk. He wanted to tell me about his arrest in the spring of 2002. He told me he sat in his apartment in Ramallah and wrote all morning while the Israeli army invaded as part of a massive military operation, imposing a curfew and conducting mass arrests of teenagers and young men. Just before two in the afternoon, the soldiers entered his apartment. He asked them to take him quickly so that Firas, then four years old, wouldn't see. The soldiers arrested him quickly and quietly, in a kind of grotesque gesture of compassion. Six days later, after he was released, Osama called home, and Nisreen gave Firas the phone.

"Are you my father?" the confused child asked.

As I try to understand what he was trying to tell me, I feel a wave of rage at the world that undermined Osama's sense of security, that's preventing him from trusting the life we would build together. To be honest, I also feel rage toward Osama, who is again retreating from assurances that he wants to try with me, that he's ready.

"What would you do if I told you that I can't bring another child into this world?" he asked me last night.

"I would leave you."

"Just like that? It's so important to you?"

"I don't know if I want children," I told him. "I know that I want the option. But, Osama, the subject of children symbolizes something. You are crazy about children. You are the most devoted father in the world. If you don't want children, it's because you don't trust the world. And irrespective of whether or not we would decide to have children, I need you to be ready to trust the world we would build together."

He didn't respond. I had to admit to myself that the world we would build together would always be fragile, threatened by the people in our maqluba surroundings who don't want to leave space for people like us.

I touched his cheek cautiously. "I don't need to know right now," I said, but he had already begun to retreat into himself, and I couldn't reach him anymore. "Try to reach a decision," I said. "When you do, let me know."

Osama

Jews

Ann Marie struggles with how "the Jews," or Judaism, became a symbol of occupation and oppression for Palestinians. And yet she knows that when Palestinians say, "Jews," they mean the Israeli army. Palestinians, like Israelis and the rest of the world, have trouble distinguishing Jews from the Israeli regime.

"I'll tell you the story of a classmate from my master's program," I said, trying to reassure her. "He was telling me how Israeli soldiers entered the village of Bil'in at the same time Israeli activists arrived to protest, in solidarity with the residents. He told me that 'the Jews came from the North,' referring to the soldiers, and that 'the Israelis came from the South,' meaning the solidarity activists."

Ann Marie smiled.

It was hard for me, too, to see Jews—or actually, Israelis—as ordinary people, not soldiers. As much as I appreciate my conversations with Ann Marie, they disorient me. There are Jews and even Israelis who oppose the occupation. I was active in grassroots resistance—slogans, stone throwing, strikes—during the First Intifada and served time in an Israeli prison for it. Now that I'm an academic, I understand—thanks to Ann Marie—that I haven't done enough to understand the occupation. And maybe my resistance and the resistance of others would be more effective if we understood it better.

And maybe if I understood all that, having a love relationship with Sari would feel less scary.

Sari

Bouazizi

We named the car Bouazizi in honor of the Tunisian fruit seller who ignited himself and the Arab Spring and signified, to us, the yearning for freedom. I bought my Bouazizi from Kfir, the husband of my friend Gila, who was moving to the United States to enroll in a master's degree program. When I mention Gila to Osama, I call her "Umm Alma," meaning "Mother of Alma," after their toddler daughter with whom I love to play football. If Osama forgets who Kfir is, I remind him using the nickname "the Occupation Soldier."

I didn't invent that nickname, and I'm careful not to use it in Kfir's presence. Gila was the one who coined it, on a Friday evening when I came for dinner. She was alone with Alma and Alma's infant brother because Kfir had been called up for military reserve duty. I told Gila that I would go to Ramallah the following day to see Osama, and she told me that Kfir was in the West Bank now, adding, in a tone of relief, that he wasn't serving near Ramallah but rather farther north, guarding settlements near Nablus.

"He hasn't considered refusing?" I asked her.

"No."

"Because he thinks it's better that he be the one standing there, to treat people humanely?"

"No, it's not like that," Gila said. "His perspective is much narrower. He's thinking about the guys serving with him in his unit. He says that if he doesn't go, someone else will have to take his place."

"Have you tried to persuade him?"

"He knows what I think. Yesterday morning I drove him to the meeting point. He wore his uniform. He asked me, 'How do I look?' I told him, 'Like an occupation soldier.'"

When he's not playing the role of an occupation soldier, Kfir plays the role of a devoted father, talented cook, creative interior designer, and all-around trustworthy person. My father always told me that when you buy a used car, the most important question is who the seller is. I bought Kfir's car without driving it, without bringing it to a mechanic, and without checking for liens or an accident history. You can trust Kfir's meticulous care.

Bouazizi is a white 2001 Ford Focus. The windshield boasts stickers from the Israeli baby supply store Shilav and a Hebrew University parking permit from 2006. In the trunk, I found baby clothing, a black sweater, a yarmulke, a red plastic pen, and an Israeli flag—the kind they distribute for free to *Yedioth Ahronoth* (a popular Israeli newspaper) subscribers during the week between Holocaust Memorial Day and Independence Day. I threw all this into the dumpster underneath Kfir's and Gila's apartment, in the Old North neighborhood of Tel Aviv. I scratched away the parking permit and Shilav sticker and left the car parked in their neighborhood, because I hadn't yet insured it.

I felt a wave of anxiety as I began researching insurance policies valid in both Ramallah and Israel and towing services that would come get me in the West Bank. As I tried to explain to Palestinian and Israeli insurance companies—in Arabic, English, and Hebrew—what coverage I needed, the protection I was looking for, I realized how vulnerable I felt. No insurance company would really protect me.

In preparation for my first drive, I studied maps from Google, the

United Nations, and Machsom Watch. I tried to memorize which roads were off-limits to Palestinians (those near settlements) and which roads were off-limits to Israelis (those leading to Palestinian cities), in order to navigate my way from Tel Aviv to Osama's house. I was afraid of getting arrested if I were to arrive at a checkpoint forbidden to Israelis. I was afraid of getting stoned if a Palestinian attacker were to find me on a settler road. I couldn't ask colleagues for help, because I didn't want to tell them where I was going and why. The Israeli maps didn't show the Palestinian roads. The Palestinian maps didn't show the settler roads. The United Nations maps showed all the roads but didn't distinguish between the checkpoints where they inspect the cars carefully and the ones where they don't. I tried to understand where I was allowed to drive and where I was forbidden from driving and where I could pass, even though it was forbidden.

One summer evening, I left the office and drove to Ramallah. Just Bouazizi and me. I passed the traffic jams of Tel Aviv and the airport and got onto Road 443 near Mitzpe Modi'in, a park entrance familiar to me from Friday-morning runs in the Ben Shemen Forest. I continued into the West Bank, driving through a settler checkpoint without even slowing down. The highway stretched forward, and I saw spires of mosques extending upward from the hills on either side. I passed an exit with a sign in Hebrew: "Last exit to Ramallah—no Israeli cars beyond this point!" And then another sign: "Exit prohibited for Israelis!" A wave of panic hit me, as if someone had guessed my plan.

I continued on Road 443, past the settlement of Giv'at Ze'ev, to a new checkpoint that separated a part of the West Bank where Palestinians are supposed to be able to travel from a part of the West Bank where they are forbidden from traveling. The checkpoint was huge and looked like a border crossing. The soldiers waved me on without a word. I found myself on a well-paved road with signs pointing the way to Giv'at Ze'ev, Jerusalem, and the Ofer military base. It was getting dark, and I was afraid to ask, "Is this the way to Ramallah?"

I turned toward the deserted road lined with streetlights that had not been turned on and reached a traffic circle. The separation wall stood in front of me, the concrete overhang of Qalandia. I drove toward it and stopped at the line of cars waiting to cross, under a red sign with Hebrew words: "This road leads to Area A, which is forbidden to Israelis by a general's military order. Entering Area A is a criminal offense and endangers your lives!"

I drove over the speed bumps, in the single lane that leads to Ramallah. On the other side of the checkpoint, soldiers inspected a long line of cars trying to enter Jerusalem. On our side there were no soldiers, just cameras hanging from pillars and watchtowers that looked out over us. I thought of Kfir and wondered whether he had ever served at Qalandia, checking documents and deciding who would pass and who would not. I drove over the last speed bump and turned toward a concrete barrier on my left and a barbed-wire fence on my right. I breathed a sigh of relief to be past the checkpoint. Here, traffic from Jerusalem, Nablus, and Jericho is channeled into a single lane, after the Israeli military closed the alternative routes to create a chokepoint that it could open or close. Drivers are particularly aggressive on this congested stretch of road, where Palestinian police officers are not allowed to enter and Israeli soldiers have no interest in entering. I navigated the route that seemed unfamiliar from my new position in the driver's seat, steering clear of public taxis that cut me off and even drove in the wrong direction, speeding head-on toward me and swerving at the last minute, all to save a few minutes. There were no signs for the turnoff from the center of town toward the Masyoun neighborhood, so who had the right-of-way? Is that narrow road really two-way?

The neighborhood was quiet, with an occasional car returning home. The trip had taken me a little over an hour. Children playing football in the street parted to clear a path for me, and then I watched them resume their game in the rearview mirror. I parked on the street across from Osama's apartment, put on a sweater to cover my bare shoulders in front of the neighbors, and turned off Bouazizi.

Osama

Geography

I had been feeling out of sorts, uncertain. On a weekend in which Sari stayed in Tel Aviv, Ann Marie invited me over for a healthy lunch. "What happened?" I asked. She'd never cooked a meal for me.

"We'll chat," she said, "and then we'll drive to the villages of Al Jib and Bir Nabala."

She laughed when I asked where Bir Nabala is. Turns out it's a village on the outskirts of Ramallah, just a few kilometers from my apartment, but together with two other villages, it's entirely surrounded by the separation wall. "I think I'm the only non-Palestinian in the world who understands what is going on here," she said, referring to my confused geography.

We drove past fields littered with junk cars—the green farmlands of the Qalandia village were divided into two parts by the separation wall, reducing them to storage spaces for Israeli cars that Palestinians scrapped for spare parts. We turned onto a newly paved road, funded by the United States development agency. We entered Bir Nabala through a narrow tunnel that ran underneath the wall, which at that point was a ten-meter-high concrete structure. Ann Marie knew that for years I hadn't dared go to the villages, where the Israeli army sometimes erects flying checkpoints, because, according to the Israeli military's records, I was supposed to be living in Gaza. Now I had a month left until the expiration of the temporary staying permit that Sari had gotten me, and I could explore a bit outside Ramallah.

Ann Marie drove slowly over the potholed roads and told me the history of the place. It looked just like Ramallah looked to me in 2002, during the massive invasion: quiet and full of destruction. Cats leapt in and out of the dumpsters, looking in vain for something to satisfy their hunger. I was flooded with a sense of horror, fear and death waiting in ambush.

Ann Marie parked the car at a dead end, and we got out. Small dogs approached us, looking for food. No one was there, except for us—Ann Marie, the dogs and me, and the smell of burned garbage. I turned back toward the car, and Ann Marie read what was left of a sign: "Welcome to Bir Nabala." Right across from it was the wall.

"I've never been here," I said. It was four kilometers from my home as the crow flies, but my car can't fly over the wall.

"You know, Osama, I'm trying to understand your sense of geography—how you see the world—but I can't."

Ann Marie's Arabic, with her South African accent, is amusing, but it's also a little hard to understand what she means sometimes. "When the Israelis would still come here, you would see a lot of things written in Hebrew. Now there's nothing."

She meant signs for certain places, like mechanics' garages and carpentry shops, I think.

"So the entrance to Bir Nabala used to be here."

"Yes, and when they finished opening the *merkam haim* road, they closed this entrance."

I remembered something that Sari said to me when we met in Aqaba after arriving from two different routes: "We traveled south in order to come north."

"What does *merkam haim* mean?"

"*Merkam* is fabric, and *haim* is life. It's the name they give the alternative roads they opened to allow some semblance of life for Palestinians, after they closed them off from the main roads."

"How did they put those two nouns together?"

"As Orwell said, newspeak." The "Fabric of Life" road was the tunnel underneath the wall that allowed village residents to exit the enclave toward the city of Ramallah. At the checkpoint between the village of Al Jib and the colony Something-Ze'ev, I think, Ann Marie tried to show me the closure on a UN map. Choking back tears, she said, "This whole land has become *Palestinianfrei*" ("Free of Palestinians"). She took two photos of the checkpoint.

I kept silent and studied her face. Why had she spoken in German?

She once told me that, on her father's side of the family, among those who didn't perish in the Holocaust, she has relatives in Jerusalem or Haifa, but she lost touch with them after a series of particularly caustic political discussions. Just once, when the son of a beloved uncle died, she attended the funeral.

On the way out of the village, in Arabic that sounded almost local, she said, "My heart breaks when people call me and ask me to get them a visa to South Africa." She choked back tears and summoned something that resembled a smile, then continued, "They're trying to escape the apartheid here."

Tomorrow Ann Marie will travel to Cape Town to visit her relatives. There, too, she'll transgress boundaries. I kissed her.

"Such is the world," I told her. "Despite its cruelty, it is beautiful, thanks to you."

Sari

Conversation in the Garden

We were sitting outside, in the garden. It was the end of August, but the night air was already cool. Osama lit a cigarette and moved his chair, trying to make it so the wind would stop blowing the smoke in my direction.

"The smoke always blows toward you; it doesn't matter where I sit," he said.

"Maybe it's a sign that you should stop smoking."

"Maybe."

Because of the vacation for Eid al-Fitr, the Muslim holiday that marks the end of Ramadan, Osama had time to make a nice dinner. I arrived late from work after getting caught in the holiday traffic, and everything was ready, the table set and the wineglasses waiting to be filled. We ate spinach in tomato-and-hot-pepper sauce, salad, and bread. He had also defrosted the leftover chicken in mole sauce that I had made earlier in the month and insisted that I finish it.

"It's kosher!" he said. We cleared the table and sat outside in the garden. The night air was cool and pleasant. I drank tea and looked out at the hill on the other side of the street, enjoying the dreamlike quality of Ramallah on summer nights.

"I want to ask you something, even though I think I know the answer," Osama said.

"Yes?"

"About the possibility of leaving this area. For you."

"I don't want to leave. You know that. But if we can't change your address, then yes, you have to leave. I mean, I think you would want to leave, and you would be right. Under no circumstances should you go back to being trapped. If we build a life together, and we're not able to change your address, I'm ready to consider leaving. But not tomorrow. We need more time. In the coming months, we'll know more about whether the army will change your address and also—we'll have more time together."

"That's what I thought you would say." He dragged on his cigarette and inhaled the smoke. I waited, afraid of what would come next. The last few months had been exhilarating, rehearsing our life together. But Osama's dark moods seemed to come more frequently, even though he was gentler with me when they did come.

"I wanted to suggest something," he said. "I wanted to suggest that we see each other once a week so I can have space to think. To give me time." He searched my face.

"It's just a suggestion," he said hurriedly. "I'm checking with you; I'm sharing with you."

I shrugged and took a sip of tea. A mosquito landed on my calf, and I crushed it with my palm.

A month ago, he wanted me to come live with him, asked me if I liked the apartment. He would call in the middle of the day, send text messages full of yearning. He brought me back from the cusp of getting over him, said he would fight for our relationship, asked me to give him another chance. A month ago, we were talking about how we would raise a child in our maqluba world, how we would talk to him about identity, religion, and language. "Maybe it would be better to have a girl," I said. Osama would go nuts for a girl, and maybe it would be easier, because each of our upside-down societies makes fewer demands for girls to embody and defend national ideals, including through the use of violence.

I tried to stay calm. I tried not to get angry. I tried not to cry.

"I can think about it," I told him. "I will think about it." My stomach dropped. "But, Osama, we can reach a point in the relationship where we are hurting each other too much for it to work. Even the greatest love can be killed by too much pain."

PART TWO

Recovery

Sari

Hello, My Name Is Sari

We broke up. For good. I know that it's for good, because today, September 4, 2011, they published another list of people whose addresses the military agrees to change from Gaza to the West Bank. Osama's name was not on the list. I didn't call him.

I predicted this the day before yesterday as we ate a breakfast of vegetable omelets and tahini and wrapped up the things ex-lovers pretend to be able to wrap up. I packed my hair dryer and running backpack. I put my clothing in a plastic grocery store bag. I wiped down the countertop.

"If they publish another list of address changes, and your name is on it, know that I am thinking of you, and that I'm happy for you," I told him over the breakfast table. "And if they publish another list, and your name isn't on it, know that I am thinking of you, and that I am hurting for you. But in any case, I won't call you."

And now, just two days later, they published a list.

There were cries of joy from the room where the intake coordinators sat. The name of an old and beloved client, Ahmed Hadad, was on the list. Hadas screamed, and Rinat ran into the room. After he made it back to his carpentry shop in Tulkarm, Ahmad built a wooden table and had it delivered to Yasmin, the intake coordinator who maintained telephone contact with him during the two years in which we tried to get him back to his family in Tulkarm, after he had been deported to Gaza.

"But it's my job!" Yasmin had protested over the phone, after the table arrived at her house, intricately designed, solid and tangible.

"You don't understand," Ahmad had told her. "No one else listened to me the way you listened to me."

I scanned the Osamas on the list. Thanks to the military's methods of psychological torture, I'm learning the order of the Arabic alphabet. I found four Osamas, but my Osama was not one of them. And anyway, he's not my Osama anymore.

"Did you put lemon in the tahini?" Osama had asked that morning two days ago, scooping up the remainder of the tahini with the Iraqi pitas that I like, except in Ramallah they don't call them Iraqi pitas, but rather Taboon bread.

"I also added garlic and salt," I had told him, eating hungrily. "I was lazy; I didn't bring parsley from the garden." I had run in the hills that morning, slowly climbing up toward the blue sky and the sparse clouds, until I reached the new residential neighborhood the Palestinian Authority was building on the hill on the other side of the wadi, which Osama called "Salam Fayyad's settlement," after the Palestinian-American businessman who had been tapped by the US government to be the Palestinian technocrat prime minister. That run was good training, continuous climbing. I bid farewell to the hilly, beautiful, complicated landscape; said goodbye to the roads on the other side of the mountain that I had navigated and the ones that I would not reach, to the village residents who'd gotten used to seeing me cut through their neighborhoods, and to the hilly roads that had strengthened my muscles and my aerobic fitness, even though I hadn't done speed training for months. Two days later, on the flat boardwalk in Tel Aviv, I would be surprised by my speed.

"I want to try to keep writing the book," I told Osama, who had sat across from me and ate a lot less than I did. "We decided one of the topics of the book is a love story, which ends now." My voice was stable, but the tears flowed with a force I couldn't control. "But there are also other topics, and we haven't finished writing about them. I want to try to keep writing, and you are welcome to do the same, but if you do, I'll ask you not to put your writing into the Dropbox. Maybe we can talk in six months and see where we stand with the writing." I didn't want to get little notifications that a file had been added or edited in the Dropbox. I needed to close that window into Osama's life.

I don't think I'm looking for an excuse to stay in touch with him. I understand that it would be too painful. We tried to build a life together as human beings, as a man and a woman, as Osama and Sari, and in the end, we failed for all the ordinary reasons that people fail and break up, and for all the reasons unique to us, Osama and Sari. I see that as a kind of victory over the occupation and the roles that its participants tried to assign us: occupiers and occupied. We managed to create a nonspace space in which we could love, build a relationship, and ultimately fail and dismantle everything on our own merits.

"I want you to have a happy life," Osama said. "I hope to meet your children someday." I wanted to hit him.

"You have David's telephone number, right?" I asked. Osama nodded. The tears spilled with greater force into large drops that landed on the remains of the omelet and the very tiny puddle of tahini left on the plate, because it really had come out delicious.

"Please be in direct contact with David about your legal case. He'll pass the tasks on to me. I'll keep writing the letters, but he'll be the one to talk to you."

"There's no need. I'll manage."

"Are you willing to listen to me?" I nearly shouted, with explosive aggression that surprised both of us. My voice broke, and he nodded that yes, he was willing to listen to me. "If you don't stay in touch with David, you'll prevent me from resolving the ethical problem that arose when I fell in love with you and allowed my feelings to deprive you of Gisha's legal representation. I tried to resolve the problem by finding you good-quality alternative representation, meaning David. If you refuse to accept it, you're re-creating my ethical problem."

"OK," Osama said.

And now, three days later, I'm back in Tel Aviv, writing a letter to the military that David will sign, asking for another temporary permit to allow Osama to remain in his house, which almost became our house. I request that they expedite the application to change his address, because how many more times can I search in vain for his name on the lists?

And now I'm writing another *Maqluba* chapter.

What was I thinking? How can I publish the book if we're not together? Who holds the copyright on a love story? On the occupation? On the story of another person's life, which I tried to tell out of sheer love for him?

I don't know and don't want to know if Osama is also continuing to write the *Maqluba* book.

I have stopped trying to find a place for myself as an Israeli in Palestinian society, which is occupied by Israel. Now I'm trying to refind my place in Israel, which is occupying Palestine. And I'm still trying to arouse empathy and maybe also spark critical questions and doubts among our nonexistent community of readers, Israeli and Palestinian.

Hello, my name is Sari. And I am continuing to write the *Maqluba* book.

I'm documenting the end of the love that tried to find a place in Palestine, in Israel, in London, and in Jordan. In Gaza, Iraq, and New Jersey. A love between a seafarer and a trail runner, who, as in the story of the fish and the bird, loved and loved each other, but couldn't find a place where they could build a home.

He loved me in each of the three languages: *Ya Hilweh, ya Habibti, ya Omri, ya Hubi, Hamuda sheli, Ahuvati, Love, Sweetheart, Runner, Bahibek, Ani ohev otakh, Mushtaq, I miss you, I love you, I live you, Bahib ismek.* And I tasted my love for him in all the languages and all the accents. I loved him with a force that I couldn't express in words, but I feel it so strongly now, in the stream of tears flowing to form a saltwater sea he could cross to find his way back to me. *Osama Fahed, Ghazawi Ibn Areej, Saken elbaher, Hubi, Habibi, Sea Dweller, Baby, Darling, Hamoud sheli, Ahuv sheli,* the person I wanted to spend my life with, whom I now have to box up into the dry category of "my ex."

Osama
Liberty

Sari's birthday passed a few days ago. I wanted to call her, to feel her presence, her joy, her love. And at the same time, the old fears, the ones that made me push her away from me, flooded my brain, like demons in an animated movie. I remembered that night in 2002, when Ariel Sharon, then Israeli prime minister, threatened to bomb Palestinian President Yasser Arafat's compound. Our apartment on the fourth floor was a few hundred meters from the compound. In the middle of the night, I carried Firas, then four years old, in my arms. All the neighbors were awake. We brought the children to an apartment on the ground floor, hoping Israel would not shell our building, that it would be precise in attacking the compound.

Today I finished teaching and came back home to the television announcing that the Israeli soldier Gilad Shalit had left the Gaza Strip, and a few hundred prisoners, released from Israeli prisons, entered it. Shalit had been held for six years, and negotiations for his release in exchange for Palestinian political prisoners had finally yielded an agreement.

One thousand Palestinian prisoners would be released from Israeli prison directly into the huge prison of the Gaza Strip. I didn't understand why one of their prisoners was "worth" a thousand of ours.

And I felt ashamed. I couldn't remember the name of even one of our thousand prisoners about to be freed, but we all knew Shalit's name, first and last.

I watched a broadcast of the interview with Gilad Shalit by an Egyptian broadcaster, who took pity on him. "He's actually very tired," she said. I almost forgot that Gilad was an Israeli soldier who was ordered to bomb Gaza. Had he taken part in the murder of the al-Samouni family? How did he feel during his years of captivity?

Despite everything, go home in peace, Gilad. You and all the captives.

Sari

Counting the Days

In the midst of my mourning over the breakup with Osama, my father came for one of his visits to Israel. My mood is fragile, and I'm worried about my interactions with him. At 7:00 a.m., I'm in Yarkon Park, at the foot of Performance Hill, getting ready for a "Mercedes" session, as a coach with whom I had trained called it. Like the automobile symbol with three spokes that lead to the same center point, I was to run up and down: sprint uphill with maximum speed on one of the three paths that leads to the summit and slowly run down a second path, then run back up the third path, and so on. I gathered my strength and decided to do just three repetitions that morning. I'll exert 80 percent effort, enough to feel the emptiness and exhaustion each time I reach the summit, but not enough to experience a gag reflex, the result of lactic acid accumulation in my muscles and a sign that I had pushed myself to the limit.

I was trying to go easy on myself. I looked up at the flock of green parakeets that had settled onto my running path, the offspring of a pair of birds imported from Africa that escaped from the pet shop in Ramat Gan and multiplied in the free environment of the park, at least that's the story Tel Avivians tell. The pounding of my footsteps will soon disperse them. A group of bike riders, their lean bodies aerodynamic on their narrow bicycles, rode laps around the hill. I hesitated, searching within myself for reserves of strength, until I chose the source of support I would focus on in order to climb the hill: my friend Gila, the previous owner of Bouazizi, who had sent me an encouraging email that morning in response to my update:

"The car is fine," I wrote. "But I'm going to sell it. I don't need it anymore—we broke up."

"Oh, Sarileh," she'd written. "You will love again."

The tears sprang to my eyes, and I let them fall, rinsing away another layer of sadness. A month and a half have passed, but I still burst into tears without warning. If I'm alone, I don't stop myself.

I wiped the mucus from my nose and throat and wiped my hands on the fabric of my running shorts. I took a deep breath and charged up the hill.

The television broadcasts of Gilad Shalit's release continued all day. It was a celebration of national fortitude, while he seemed so pale, so skinny, so overwhelmed. The fat politicians seemed corrupt next to him, shaking hands, saluting and hugging him. When I saw the military uniform in which they dressed him, I felt betrayed. For five years they talked about "our son" and "our boy." Now they remind us that he was a young man given weapons and sent to fight.

At the end of the day, I got a phone call from Sweden—Abir, the former researcher at Gisha who's originally from Gaza, called to share her joy with me about the prisoner exchange. Her voice was full of optimism and faith.

"Sari, it's so great that he's going home! He and all the prisoners! You see, even our and your crazy politicians can do something good when they want to!"

It's impossible to anticipate Abir's optimism, and I don't recommend trying to do so. During the wars in Gaza, she sounded hopeless, virtually suicidal, but she also had moments of naive faith that all would be made right. I heard her voice clearly over the telephone from faraway and frigid Sweden.

"You know, it's like a holiday today in Gaza," she said.

I asked her if she knew any of the prisoners who were being released, and she said she had studied with one of them at university. She remembered the day—more than twenty years ago—when he hid on campus because the soldiers were searching for him, and later that day, he was arrested.

"His mother—and Shalit's mother—will be so happy!" Abir said.

In the evening, I went to my Aunt Aziza and Uncle Shafiq's house. Shafiq was my father's eldest brother. It was day two of my father's twenty-one-day visit. The silence between us remained our primary strategy for keeping the peace. I was afraid that if I spoke, I would lose control, so I sentenced myself to silence. My father's brother Reuven also came to dinner with his Ashkenazi wife, Batya, and their two sons, who were just a few years younger than me. Aziza and Shafiq's children can't stand Batya, not because she's Ashkenazi but because she's stupid. Reuven is smart and well-read but awkward. He married in his forties, after living in the United States for a decade, and he still reads newspapers and history books avidly. I kissed Reuven and Batya, and then I escaped to the kitchen to help Aziza while the others stayed in the living room, glued to the huge, loud television screen. From the refrigerator, Aziza took out kubbeh in okra sauce, white rice, salad, tahini, green beans, and store-bought schnitzel. She didn't even heat the food properly, but rather made do with a go-round in the microwave as a symbolic gesture. Her disdain for Batya was reflected in the menu, and she didn't bother to set the table. When I went to the screened-in porch to set out the plates of food, I saw that the tablecloth was stained. Ten years ago, when my brother, Samuel (who at the time was known as Jacob), came for a rare visit, she had prepared two kinds of kubbeh, t'bit, stuffed grape leaves, sambusak, red rice, white rice, chicken patties, eggplant and meat stew, stuffed tomatoes, and chicken in soy sauce. My brother, known for speaking in understatement, pronounced it the best meal he'd ever eaten. You can tell where you stand with Aziza based on the menu.

"In America, people live really far away from each other, right?" Batya asked, joining me in the kitchen.

"Sometimes," I said.

"How far away do they live from each other?" she asked.

"It depends," I said.

My father joined us in the kitchen and asked if he could help. In his presence, Batya eased up on me and directed her questions about America to my father.

"Families don't eat together in America the way we do here, right?" she asked him.

I sacrificed him guiltlessly. It was his brother who had married Batya. Let him bear the burden for a change.

When we were called to the table, those sitting in the living room refused to turn off the TV until we turned on the second TV on the porch, and for a moment, both televisions broadcast together at full volume. Pathos-laden reports from volunteers at the "Release Shalit" headquarters echoed from both sides of the house, and pictures of Gilad Shalit flashed on the screens—the shy boy before the capture and the skinny, pale man who returned home. My cousin Alon picked up a serving spoon with one kubbeh, meat wrapped in a semolina pocket, and two pieces of okra swimming in the soup.

"What's that?" asked Amir, his younger brother.

"Iraqi kubbeh."

Aziza felt pity for the boys, I knew, as Batya's cooking was inedible, and on the rare occasions when they visited, she would try to ply them with something tasty.

"In America, do you eat a big meal for lunch?" Batya asked my father.

"Sometimes," he said.

"Because on TV they show big dinners, with lots of meat."

"Yes," my father said.

"Here, we eat light things for dinner, like yogurt or an omelet, you know, but not meat," Batya explained.

"I know," replied my father, who had lived in Tel Aviv from the age of nine. He loved Reuven and was patient with Batya for his sake.

A picture of Gilad Shalit stumbling on the steps of an army base after his release flickered on the TV. The picture switched to the victory arena in Gaza City, where freed prisoners were climbing a huge stage that had been erected in a central square. The green flags associated with the Hamas faction flapped next to Palestinian flags.

"Why did you bring us the Arabs? Why?" Batya screamed suddenly, waving her hands at the television.

I let the spoon and fork fall to my plate and quickly pushed back my chair. My father, who was sitting next to me on the porch, pulled his chair forward, startled, to let me pass. I walked through the living room and out of the house.

"Where are you going, Sari?" Aziza called after me.

"I'll be right back," I said from the other side of the screen door.

I will not fight with them. I will not fight with them.

The evening was cool and pleasant. Autumn. I walked outside barefoot, and the solid contact of the sidewalk under my feet calmed me. I looked around. It's a shame they built those towers on the other side of the highway, beyond the low-rise houses. If I look in the other direction, toward the neighborhood, I can still pretend that Kiryat Ono is a small and quiet village, as it was in the 1950s, when Aziza and Shafiq bought the tiny shack that became their house. They'd left Iraq as teenagers without their parents—Shafiq was from Baghdad and Aziza from Basra—and were introduced by relatives. They spoke Arabic to their children, and my cousins knew it well but answered in Hebrew. Aziza still read novels in Arabic, when she could find them. I always imagined that Osama would enjoy meeting them, a fantasy that was impossible even before we broke up.

I reentered the house.

"Did you close the door all the way?" Aziza asked.

"Yes," I answered. My father moved his chair closer to the table to let me reach my own chair. My green beans were still resting on my plate. They were delicious—light and refreshing.

When we finished eating, again I escaped to the kitchen, washed dishes, and promised Aziza that I would make sure Reuven's sons took the leftover kubbeh home.

"But they never take things home; they're too shy. And what am I supposed to do with nine kubbehs?"

"I'll make sure they take it."

"How?"

"Don't worry."

"Then maybe get them to take the white rice too?"

"Now you've gone too far," I told her. "I can only speak for the kubbeh. If you try to push the rice, too, you'll ruin the whole deal."

I put the container of kubbeh next to Alon, who had gone with the others to sit in front of the TV in the living room. I informed him that he would take it home, that there would be no arguing with me, that people force things on me too.

The television broadcasted footage from the prisoner release near the Beitunia checkpoint in the West Bank. My running path was behind the hill and the industrial zone that you could see on the horizon. A Channel 2 reporter was interviewing the prisoners, some of whom were quite elderly. The camera panned to a demonstration near the checkpoint.

"We will continue the legacy of suicide!" one of the demonstrators shouted.

Batya opened a new battlefront by saying, "That's the difference between us and them."

I set my glass of water on the table.

"They have no humanity. Their mentality is . . ."

This time no one seemed to notice me leaving. The evening air was pleasant and cool, and the smells of the neighbors' cooking wafted toward me. I steadied my breathing.

When my father told me, three months ago, that he was coming for a visit, I decided that if Osama and I were still together, I would tell my father about us. I would invite my father to meet Osama, even though I knew he would never agree to come to the West Bank. When I was still fantasizing about Osama and me staying together, I had assumed I would stop coming to family meals in Kiryat Ono, because Osama wouldn't be able to join. I assumed I would visit Shafiq and Aziza alone from time to time, midweek, that I would sit with them for a bit and come home with containers of kichri, an Iraqi red lentil and rice dish, chicken patties and stuffed vegetables that Aziza would give me, and share them with Osama. Osama had spared me that conversation with my father.

I returned to the house again, to my chair in the living room. Aziza served tea. The reporter continued broadcasting from downtown Ramallah, from the square where the public taxi used to drop me off, on my way to Osama's apartment. I felt the remnants of longing well up inside. This sadness has so many layers.

The camera switched to Hamas leader Khaled Mashaal's speech declaring victory over the Zionist enemy.

"It's a shame they didn't kill him," Aziza said. When the broadcast returned to the demonstration in Beitunia, Aziza chanted along with the demonstrators, in Arabic: "*Asha'ab yurid tahrir il-ard!*" ("The people want to liberate the land!")

"As if we're not here," she added in Hebrew.

I drank tea while my stomach contracted. I hoped for some minor racist comment from Batya that would give me an excuse to leave the house again, but her previous outbursts seemed to have satisfied her. She was busy interrogating my father about his wife. Was she still working, and at what age do women retire in America? Because in Israel, it's sixty-two.

I considered taking up smoking. Considered how that would amuse and horrify Osama. When smokers excuse themselves and step outside, no one wonders why.

Osama

Today, October 22, 2011, the Palestinian president and leader of the Fatah faction, known by his nickname Abu Mazen, flew to Cairo and promised the military ruler of Egypt, General Mohamed Tantawi, that he would end the factional split with Hamas. No one believed him, but the internet flooded with jokes about Hamas.

A Hamas police officer and a motorist:

Do you have a license?

Yes.

Do you have insurance?

Yes.

Are you in a state of purity before prayer?

No.

I'm writing you a traffic ticket.

I can't stop thinking. Thinking about you. I want to call, to apologize and also to reproach you. Why did you bring us, me, to this situation?

Why did you let me break up with you? Why, for God's sake, didn't you fight for me?

Breaking news: The price of women's headscarves and men's traditional robes has risen, while the price of razor blades has plummeted.

I love you. Am I wrong? I remember your vitality, your smile, your energy, and I yearn for you. But under no circumstances will I call you. I'm afraid you'll cry and refuse to talk to me. I'm thinking of coming to you, but I'm afraid you'll refuse to talk to me even then, or maybe you're traveling.

I want to see your apartment, see you in your space. Do you love me?

Do I love you because you are positive, stubborn, you swim against the tide, you are athletic, you love the sea, you're modest, you're different? I miss who I am with you, braver, more open. I miss the questions you ask about the people around us, the world you open up to me.

Hamas announced a ban on wearing undershirts and underwear, because they drink arak (the word "drink" in Arabic also means "to absorb sweat").

I need to mature or to be a little more ready—that's what I tell myself every time I think of you, am about to call. I need to be able to control my fears so that they don't lead me to retreat within myself and leave you far behind.

"If you love her, leave her alone so that she won't suffer with you," Josh told me, when I wrote to him to ask his advice. I'm trying to tell myself the same thing. And still I have to fight not to call you. But I'll submit a request for a permit to go inside (inside the Green Line, the internationally recognized borders of Israel). If I could just see you, talk to you, even though I don't know what I'd say.

An important announcement for the few Fatah people left in Gaza: In Habash, there is property whose seizure won't cause injustice to anyone. We call on you to immigrate there! (When Muslims in the city of Mecca were oppressed, the Prophet Mohammed called on them to immigrate to Habash, now Ethiopia, where a Christian king ruled who protected Muslims. Hamas took control of Gaza from its rival faction, Fatah.)

I won't travel abroad. Is that a good enough reason for you to come back?

I agree to have just one child, a girl. I'll let you pick the name, though there are certain names I prefer . . .

Sari

Iraqi Memorial

I know I should stop approaching situations by imagining how Osama would respond to them—it has been a month and a half, and I'm healing, calming down, recovering—but Osama really would have enjoyed the Iraqi memorial service I attended today, the anniversary of the death of Aziza's sister's son.

I thought about Osama when I saw the picture of the mother, now ninety-three years old, and the son who died in a military training accident fifty-two years ago. The photograph was taken in 1949, when they were still living in Basra. They sat in the photo studio, a young woman of stupefying beauty and her seven-year-old son, already the only surviving member of her family, after the death of her husband and daughter, each from a different illness. Ten years later, the mother and son moved to Israel, and the boy finished his secondary studies at the *Hadassim* government boarding school. "Very well-reputed school," Aziza told me. "Moshe Dayan's son studied there." The boy was drafted into the army and promptly died in a bizarre training accident involving a tent, a rope, and an unidentified weapon.

On the back of the photograph, the name of the studio, "Style," was printed in English. Judging by the ferocity with which she embraced her son, it looked like the young mother, even then, was terrified of losing the boy who had become her whole world.

The mother in the photograph was Rivka, Aziza's eldest sister, and she sat, withered and hard of hearing, on a padded chair in the living room of her apartment in Ramat Gan, a walker by her side, wearing a brown-and-white dress that exposed the reddish spots on her legs. She had trouble recognizing the guests who obeyed her instructions to come every year, to remember her child who, had he lived, would have been sixty-nine years old.

"I'm the daughter of Joseph, Shafiq's brother," I shouted at Rivka in Hebrew. I said it to reassure her, so she would know that she wasn't supposed to recognize me. She said, "What?" in Hebrew, and then, I think, "*Min?*" which is "who" in Arabic. I took a chance on the similarity between the Palestinian Arabic I was learning in 2011 and the Iraqi Arabic that Rivka spoke in the 1920s and shouted my family relationship at her in Arabic: "*Ana bint Joseph! Akhu Shafiq! Shafiq joz Aziza!*"

Olga, the Ashkenazi wife of one of the nephews, explained to me why Rivka still didn't respond to me. "It won't help," Olga told me. "She doesn't understand English."

But the wrinkled beauty queen smiled and offered me food. Dinner was on hold because we still hadn't assembled the quorum of ten men required to say Kaddish, the Jewish prayer for the dead. The men who filled the room—nephews, brothers, brothers-in-law—removed wrinkled yarmulkes from their pockets and placed them on their heads uncomfortably. There were only nine of them, none of them knew the prayer, and the food was getting cold.

"She's ninety-three and still cooks?" I asked Aziza.

"She taught her caregiver to cook," Aziza explained, pointing to a fortysomething woman of Filipina origin who was turning over the pot of t'bit, the Iraqi-Jewish dish of chicken stuffed with rice and then cooked in rice, onto a huge platter. The caregiver placed it on the table in the garden, which was already full of trays covered in tinfoil: kubbeh, rice, fish with eggplant, pickled cabbage and turnips, and stir-fried vegetables in coconut milk with rice noodles, a gesture to the caregiver's home cuisine.

"You made food for a hundred people!" the Ashkenazi wives of Rivka's nephews complained, seemingly genuinely concerned. I never understood why large quantities of food threaten them. And anyway, it didn't look to me to be too much food. But then again, I had resumed training intensely for an ultramarathon, and my concept of how much was reasonable to eat had been revised upward.

Aziza brought dishes from the kitchen, and I marveled at the lightness of her step. She had passed her eightieth birthday but still wore black spandex pants and big gold earrings.

I wondered how the memorial service would have looked in Iraq. I bet that there, too, they would have drunk Coca-Cola and eaten dates. Maybe without the vegetables in coconut milk.

I tried to get Osama out of my head. It was only through him that I began to look at my family history differently. Through Osama's eyes, I noticed the Arab-ness that had been suppressed and rebranded as Eastern-ness or Spanish-ness, the terms used in Israel to refer to Arab Jews. But the Arab-ness was hiding in plain sight, patiently waiting to be noticed in the names, food, language, and family photos. For centuries, my family and Osama's family had been Ottoman citizens of the Levant, sharing broadly similar circumstances, until 1948 propelled them toward such different outcomes.

That reframing of my family history was something I could keep with me, and one day it would stop reminding me of Osama.

Osama
Fayyad

I called a friend who works in the Palestinian NGO sector to make plans to meet. She didn't answer, and I left a message on her voicemail. I felt so lonely. It had been two months since I ended my love relationship with Sari. I had swallowed my pride and emailed two of Sari's friends, Josh and Yael, and each told me not to reach out to her.

Ten minutes later, my friend texted me back: "Meeting with Fayyad." The Palestinian prime minister, who was far more popular with the Americans and Israelis than with us. I laughed and texted, "Laughed out loud. Thanks for answering me while meeting with the prime minister."

I was surprised and flattered when she responded again two minutes later: "You are more important to me than this banker."

Sari

Staff Enrichment

Once every two months, we hold a ninety-minute workshop for "staff enrichment." Our office manager brings in a film about a relevant issue or a speaker, often one who works in social change for another cause, or at an environmental protection organization, maybe to remind us there's injustice outside of Gaza too.

Today the film topic was close to home: the military justice system in the West Bank and Gaza, with interviews of gray-haired, retired officers and judges about how they enforced military law in the recent past. The interviews are interspersed with footage from the 1980s of Palestinian men in detention cells: waiting in line, blindfolded, or sitting at defendants' tables at trials held on military bases.

They are so young. The camera pauses on one of them, mustached but with the face of a boy. He reminds me of a photograph I had seen of Osama when he was twenty: long hair, black mustache, a young student making his way from the Jabalia refugee camp in Gaza to the university in the West Bank.

Is that what he has become to me? A historical relic that I associate with the First Intifada?

The retired Supreme Court justice tells the camera that he felt comfortable ruling on cases of administrative detention because the person must be dangerous and the detention has to be approved, but in his opinion, it's not right that the detainee has no opportunity to view the allegations against him. I remembered a conversation I had with Yael, in advance of my planned move to the West Bank, which I canceled when Osama broke up with me.

"At least by moving to Ramallah, you're saving yourself from the enlightenment of northern Tel Aviv," she had said.

During my clerkship at the Supreme Court, in the library there, I occasionally ran into this retired justice I'm watching talk into the camera. His secretary helped me when the printer in my judge's chambers jammed.

It's impossible to straddle so many worlds, identifying with the oppressed and living as the oppressor, fighting for people who are trapped and enjoying a life of quiet privilege among the pubs and boardwalk of Tel Aviv. But in Tel Aviv there is the sea, in Tel Aviv I have friends, and in Tel Aviv I learned to run long distances. I'll relearn how to live in Tel Aviv.

Osama

Hope

I arrive home from the university at five thirty, tired and not in the mood to cook. I open the refrigerator and take out a container of hummus. I fry eggs and put them on a plate. I turn on the television and start to eat. After a few bites, I push the plate away without getting up from the couch. I light a cigarette and flick through channels, my eyes half closed, looking for some mindless film.

At the department meeting today, we approved the final student grades, and seeing that I'd given more than one student a failing grade in my intro to the history of science course, a colleague told me, "You're going to earn yourself a bad reputation." I've known this colleague for years, and I thought he would respect the integrity of my academic standards and understand my willingness to create friction and discord in order to maintain them.

Am I too hard on the students? We complain that they don't read the material, don't prepare for classes, don't do anything to advance their own education. But at the end of each semester, we pass all the students, mostly with high marks. "How can that be?" I asked today at the meeting to validate the grades. No one wanted to talk about it. Many of my colleagues work second jobs, and even those who see how much academic standards have deteriorated over the years seem to have given up trying to reverse course. I felt my colleagues' discomfort and realized how distanced I am from other people, even at the university where I so love to teach. I've become a dissident here too.

"If you love her, let her be," Josh wrote me in an email I read in the morning, before leaving for work. I lost hope every time I thought of his guidance, which included a reminder that I had hurt her badly. Hope returns when I think of Mahmoud Darwish, whose poetry I've been reading before bed. I train myself not to lose hope, because, Darwish wrote, hope is not "material and is not an idea. It's a talent." I try to become infected with Darwish's illness of hope and, like him, to feel "some kind of happiness," even if "its source is wrapped in uncertainty."

I miss Sari.

Tense. Ready. Fearful. I can't let things end like this. I'm walking a fine line. I need to do something.

Sari

Insomnia

I can't sleep, and I don't know how to deal with insomnia. For as long as I can remember, I have been blessed with an incredible talent for sleeping. Seconds after my head hits the pillow, I plunge into a deep and healing slumber. Osama, who suffers from chronic insomnia, who struggles to succumb to sleep, used to go crazy watching how easy it was for me.

"But you fell asleep in the middle of the conversation!" he would complain the next morning, after I woke up with a musty taste on my unbrushed teeth, still wearing my bra and work blouse, an earring crushed between my ear and the pillow. I would have a vague recollection of being in some conversation with Osama and abandoning it in the middle of one of his sentences. Sometimes I would fall asleep in the middle of my own sentence and then wake up moments later, startled, recalling words I had said in a stream of consciousness, associations linked to one another only in the language of dreams. I would apologize in a sleepy voice, adjust my hold on Osama's chest or back, and plunge again into a happy slumber.

Long runs intensified my delight in sleeping. On days when I trained hard, Osama would wake me from sleeping on the couch, beg me to come with him to the bedroom, help me get up, and guide me to bed, insisting that I at least take off my pants. The exhaustion in my muscles enhanced the total surrender to sweet and ready sleep.

Osama, in contrast, would wake after just three or four hours of sleep; go to the living room to watch television, read, or write; give up on falling back asleep; and make a cup of coffee. After the alarm clock dragged me out of bed for a morning run, I would find him sleeping on the couch, a news program playing on TV, and the evidence of his nightly ordeal strewn across the coffee table: an article about semantic communication among science researchers in the nineteenth century, a book of poetry by Mahmoud Darwish, a half-full bowl of sweet lupine, a legume eaten as a snack in Palestine, a second bowl with the shells of the lupine, and a mug of tea papered on the bottom with a thin layer of dried-up mint leaves.

"Poor thing," I would say to him after returning from my run to find him in the kitchen, washing dishes, his eyes bloodshot. "What time did you get out of bed, sweetheart? How long did you manage to sleep?"

Now, as if I were trying to join him, to adopt his torment as my own, I wake in the middle of the night after three or four hours of sleep, surprised to discover that the dawn is still far away. This insomnia confuses me. I blame the mosquitoes that have moved into my apartment for autumn and go to the store to buy a refill bottle for the electric mosquito repellant. I turn on the fan and point it straight at myself, at my battle arena with the buzzing monsters, hoping to make their environment unwelcoming, but the cool breeze also chases away my sleep, a good friend whose betrayal I'm struggling to come to terms with.

A sudden yearning catches me off guard: In New Jersey, where I spent my childhood, the mosquitoes have already gone into hibernation. It's cool there in October.

Soon I will resume living. Soon I will rise from the grief I've allowed myself to cling to. I'll rejoin the world, life, happiness, connection with others, and love. Without him.

In the first weeks after we broke up, I couldn't stop sleeping to escape the pain of consciousness. My friend sleep protected me. But then I began to dream: I'm in Ramallah, riding a public taxi, but I don't know where to get off. Or I see Osama at a work event and am disoriented by the happiness that wells up inside me, afraid I'm being pulled back to the starting point and that a fresh pain of separation will knock me off my feet again. Now I'm running away from dreams, or maybe I'm staying awake to cling to the feeling of being in love with him. Maybe it's pain that wakes me at two in the morning, the sound of the fan in my ears, the voice of a partygoer from the street wafting in through the open window, my body tense in anticipation of the mosquito buzzing, and my heart filled with terror for the moment when I will declare the end of my mourning, the moment when I will let go of Osama.

Osama

To Sari

My sweetheart, do you remember that you wrote in the *Maqluba* book about the nonspace space, the no-room room we created, you and me, in order to share our lives inside it, and as a way of putting distance between ourselves and our crazy reality? Now I'm returning to that space alone, inhabiting it by myself, after a long and bitter struggle with that reality, a struggle that failed.

Sari, when I called you today, you told me that you are writing the end of our love story, and that made me very sad. I went out for my daily walk. I watched three little boys playing football in the street, oblivious to the cars or any other danger. I decided that you are free to end the love story whenever and however you want. But I will return to the nonspace space of the beginning of our relationship. I will return to it as a different person.

I really didn't know that our reality—Israeli and Palestinian—was so ugly.

I really didn't know that the occupation is so extraordinarily successful. I don't know any of your friends, I never visited you in your apartment, and I never kissed you there, by the sea.

I miss your nephews, Menachem and Haim.

I long to be in your office, your apartment, your street, to be in your space.

Your voice, your love, your sharpness, your stubbornness, your pain.

I really didn't expect that I would love you so much.

Sari

NOVEMBER 2011

After the breakup seemed final, after I made it past the searing phase of the grief, after I decided to rise from the *shiva* (in Hebrew, "seven," for the seven-day mourning period after the death of a first-degree relative) that I decreed upon myself, a shiva that lasted two and a half months, and to resume living—he called. He said he wanted to try again. Said that he hadn't given all he had to give the last time, that now he was ready, that we would build a life together and have two children, if I wanted, that this time it would be different.

I listened to his voice in all three languages—*Bahibek*; "I love you"; *Ani ohev otakh.* I heard him say my name from that deep place in his throat—the low, rich, familiar voice—filled with poetry and sensuality and curiosity and love of life. The voice that connects me to him instantly by a thread that binds the two of us, a thread that pulls me out of my bedroom in Tel Aviv—Friday evening as I'm sitting on the floor, my back to the wall, the telephone in my hand—and snaps me toward him, to his house in Ramallah, the house that will become our house. That's what he's promising.

"We had this conversation in June," I said, referring to the last time I went back to him after he broke up with me, the time that we said would be our last chance.

"This time it's different," he said. "I need you. I love you. I live you."

I tried to gain control over my voice, stabilize my breathing. The space heater pushed hot air into my wet, raw face. I could go to him. See him. Touch him. Feel his love envelop me with its dizzying force, a force met by the power of my own love for him. A crazy love, a love that knows no boundaries. A love that changed my life, changed who I am. A love that even two and a half months of mourning have not managed to temper, that I realize clearly, from the tears flowing like a stream that has just been replenished with fresh, sweet, winter rains.

"I can't, Osama." The pain seared my stomach, which he used to caress gently, a smile on his face as, at my request, he pronounced the word "stomach" in Arabic: *Baten. Batnek.*

"I need to heal," I told him. "I need to move on."

Osama

DECEMBER 2011

Ann Marie said she would meet with Sari later today. I couldn't get her friends to advocate on my behalf, so I'm sending my friends as emissaries, hoping to soften her resistance. Maybe a few days ago I would have felt some optimism about it, but not anymore.

Josh didn't reply to my last email or telephone messages asking him to talk to Sari for me, and I saw that, too, as a sign that it's done, over.

In his poem "State of Siege," Mahmoud Darwish writes: "We do what prisoners do. We do what the unemployed do. We sow hope."

Darwish left Palestine and didn't come back for twenty-five years. Not because of the one he called Rita or fear of having children. He submitted a request to travel to Moscow for university studies. For years, the Israeli authorities had persecuted him, arrested him, barred him from leaving Haifa, harassed him. And then, suddenly, he got a permit to travel. The message was "go and don't come back." He went and didn't come back.

I didn't have Darwish's courage. The Israeli army allowed me to travel to university studies in London. Maybe in my case, too, they had an ulterior motive: We don't object; go in peace, hoping that I would decide not to return to being trapped in Ramallah. They push people into a corner and then suddenly open a tiny window, as if they are offering a choice. If I had Darwish's courage, and if I didn't have Firas, maybe I also wouldn't have come back.

Sari

Weight-Loss Diet

In the first weeks of the mourning period, I actually ate pretty well. I enjoyed imagining vitamins and antioxidants healing my body. Broccoli with garlic, brown rice, fruit. I reconstructed the foods that Osama and I had prepared together, this time with less cooking oil—spinach, okra, beans. I also cooked Gazan fish, fried with hot peppers, onion, garlic, sweet peppers, and the fish spice we bought in the market in Nablus's Old City, in the shop that looked like a cave, laden with coarse fabric sacks overflowing with red, orange, yellow, and brown powders. I found a few insects that must have hatched from eggs in the spice—it had been sitting in my kitchen throughout the summer—but I insisted on tasting of that winter day when we walked through the narrow alleys of Nablus together. Later, in the service taxi back to Ramallah, I fell asleep, my head on Osama's shoulder. I didn't wake up even when the car stopped for inspection at the checkpoint.

"They didn't check ID cards?" I asked Osama when I woke up in Birzeit, ten minutes from Ramallah, my head heavy from sleep and my stomach full from the hummus we ate in Nablus.

"No, they barely looked inside," he said and caressed my hair.

"Is it OK that I fall asleep like this?" I was still trying to decipher the West Bank's social codes.

"It's OK," he said.

I plucked the bugs out of the jar and sprinkled the powder on the fish, trying to conjure up the feeling of Osama's fingers placing my head, which had slipped, back onto his shoulder, allowing me to continue sleeping until we arrived home.

But after Osama called me, the grief returned, even surpassing its initial force, overwhelming me with no advance warning and creating anxiety that contracted my stomach and prevented me from eating. I tried to eat light things—salad, a cheese sandwich, grapefruit. I didn't know if the convulsions in my stomach were from anxiety or hunger. After one or two bites, I would feel nauseated. I drank a lot of cinnamon tea—cinnamon has curative properties—and I also tried to drink water. During training runs, I felt weak, empty, and I trained less frequently and less intensely. One day, I stood in the kitchen, making a cup of tea, and I felt like I was going to faint. The pain lashed at me over and over again—now also pain over Osama's pain, Osama's regrets, Osama insisting, Osama refusing to give up, promising me the same things he'd promised in the past, after previous breakups, promises he couldn't fulfill. The sobbing battered me, wrinkled my face, drained my body of liquid and salt, tore apart my insides, and imposed a weight-loss diet on me.

"What, you stopped eating?" asked one of the runners at a race I attended to accompany a friend. He pointed to my legs, exposed in my running shorts and apparently skinny.

"I'm inspired by the cottage cheese protest," I told him, referring to the wave of social protests that broke out in Israel in 2011, sparked by protests against the price of cottage cheese. "I'm waging a consumer boycott of all the food companies." It was a burden to have to communicate with the outside world.

I'll go back to sitting shiva, I thought to myself. I'll reconfine myself to the house. I'll drink hot cocoa instead of cinnamon tea because cocoa has calories.

Osama

Beer with Ann Marie

Ann Marie surprised me with a visit. She admitted, with a short laugh, that it was her first social meeting thus far this month, and the month was almost over.

"You don't have to visit me because you feel sorry for me," I told her.

"Who says I'm coming for you?" she asked. "You're not the only one who hasn't managed to belong anywhere."

We drank cold beers and talked.

"I saw my friend Christina during my trip to the township," she said. Ann Marie had grown up on the outskirts of Cape Town, in an area intended for nonwhites. "I allowed myself to tell her about you."

"Did she have any advice?" I asked.

Ann Marie laughed. "I guess I wasn't being very charitable about your behavior, because she jumped to your defense," Ann Marie said. "She told me that I shouldn't think you're always in the wrong, because Sari runs long distances.'"

"What did she mean?" I asked.

"I think she was hinting that you are both stubborn."

At the end of the conversation, she said, "I'll talk to Sari in another two months, if she'll allow me." Her first conversation with Sari had been cordial, she said, but went nowhere. Sari told her that she needed to move on.

"Of course," I said.

We exchanged kisses, said farewell, hope to meet again before the end of the year, maybe we'll even celebrate together. I wanted to ask but didn't: "What do you think about inviting Sari?"

Sari

Morning After All

December 21, the shortest day of the year, and the sun still won't rise for a while. My knee is injured from running, but I'll try to do speed training today. I have been resting it for a week, and the break from running is driving me nuts.

When Osama asked to get back together, he messed up the end of the story for me. I refused. He sent Ann Marie to talk to me. She seemed embarrassed but said I should understand how much the political situation affected Osama's ability to feel safe, to trust me. I felt embarrassed, too, but I refused. He had his brother Mohammed call me from Gaza to plead Osama's case in Arabic, English, and even Russian. I refused. He sent Suha to talk to me.

"I know he hurt you, but he's changed," she promised me. "I wouldn't come to you otherwise." I refused.

He spoke to Josh and asked him to mediate. Josh told him to let me be, to let me recover, and in the last few weeks, Osama has left me alone. I haven't heard from him or his agents.

But my calm has been ruptured. I wanted the breakup—and its recovery—to happen quietly. I didn't want drama. Not in the *Maqluba* book—this is not a romance novel—and not between Osama and me. I dreamt of spending quiet evenings with him: making dinner, drinking tea in the garden, nagging him about his cigarettes, and if Firas were home, watching television together. I wanted to drink coffee with Osama in the dim light of morning after my run, before leaving for work, and to plan the evening we would spend together, and the weekends, the mythical dinner to which, in the end, I invited no one.

And if we couldn't hold on to all that—I wanted the calm of the breakup, the serene sadness and pain that heal with time.

It has been almost four months, and my heart is spinning more dizzily than on the day we broke up.

A few minutes before six in the morning, and outside there's still no sign of the dawn. I tried to summon up the strength for a speed-training session to empty my head of negative thoughts, my body of heavy materials, to release myself into movement, into the physical difficulty, into the longed-for clarity that eludes me during the day but appears sometimes at the limits of my physical capacity—at the end of the interval, when I'm panting and it hurts, and I will collapse, I will faint, I will vomit. I will fill my lungs with air. I will smile to myself because I've managed to reach a distilled moment of presence and consciousness, to know exactly what I need, where I am, and where I am going.

Osama

Made-to-Order Illness

"So what illness do you want?" Sa'ed asked me.

I burst out laughing, mixed with tears that I tried to conceal. "Heart disease or bone cancer would work," I said. "AIDS is also OK."

"I swear, I don't know what we're doing. We're jinxing ourselves," Sa'ed responded sadly.

Sa'ed was from the West Bank and decided to propose marriage to Rama, a woman from Gaza whom he'd gotten to know through video conversations. They had to figure out where to get married and how. Once it became clear that the Israeli military would not allow Sa'ed to travel to Gaza or Rama to travel to the West Bank, the couple traveled abroad to get married. But they weren't allowed to come home together to the West Bank so that Rama could live with Sa'ed, according to the custom that the bride comes to live with the groom's family. The Israeli army doesn't allow travel between Gaza and the West Bank.

For an entire year, Sa'ed and Rama have been trying to be together.

Sa'ed tried everything to bring her to the West Bank, and Rama has tried to leave Gaza by any means, legal or illegal.

"As you know," he told me, with a mischievous smile, "I am ill with a serious heart condition for which I needed to travel to Jerusalem, so I asked for a permit for Rama to accompany me. *Yil'an dinhom* (a curse in Arabic; literally: "May their religion be cursed."). They approved my permit but refused hers."

"*Yil'an dinhom,*" I cursed them on his behalf. I expressed condolences for his pain and then tried to move the conversation in the direction I wanted it to go. "Listen, they asked me for a lot of documents in order to get a permit to enter Israel. Can you help me get a medical report?"

He didn't ask why I wanted a permit—if I, too, was in love. Maybe he was being polite, and maybe he thought it better not to know the reason for my request. He opened his email to show me the paperwork that would get him to Jerusalem: a medical report and a doctor's appointment.

"So, for the medical report, you need a name, ID number, and date of birth, right?" I said.

"Right. OK, so what illness do you want?"

"I'm open to suggestions."

The next day, Sa'ed told me he'd called his aunt, who knew everybody, to make the arrangements.

"I thought of a great illness. What do you think?" he said and then disclosed his suggestion.

"Heart failure is excellent," I said. "I prefer an illness that warrants three days in Israel with a companion."

"No problem."

Sari

Interval

I ran along the Charles Clore boardwalk between Tel Aviv and Jaffa, starting from the northern side, running one kilometer as fast as I could, past the Manta Ray restaurant, the Irgun Museum, the fishermen casting their rods above the railing—and stopped. Filled my lungs with air. One minute to recover. A second minute to prepare for the next interval: running back to my starting point. Six times, six kilometers. The wind was strong, but I pushed myself to maintain a consistent pace of three minutes and fifty seconds per kilometer. I fought the urge to start too quickly and to continue too slowly. I practiced restraint in the beginning and effort, exertion, in the middle. Control. Awareness. For the last minute of each interval, I pushed as hard as I could, charging forward, unrestrained. I'm pushing. I'm running. My muscles are burning, and I can't breathe, and that woman with the dog is staring at me, and I stop. Bend over, gag. Fill my lungs with air. I did it. I had managed another session of interval training, and I felt better than I had before I started out this morning.

I began the slow run home, the air pure and the visibility clear and sharp. Behind me, the sea grew more distant and then disappeared. I was also putting distance between myself and Osama, honing my body to recover from him.

Osama

Medical Report

I called the phone number Sa'ed had given me, for a doctor he said would help, for a fee. I was surprised by how openly the doctor spoke with someone he had never met.

"My name is Osama. You heard about me from Sa'ed."

"Welcome. How can I help you?"

"I think Sa'ed told you that I need a medical report."

"OK, sure. Come to my clinic."

"I would, Doctor, but I don't suffer from a specific problem."

"You mean, you want a fictitious medical report."

I was shocked. I hesitated, then said, "That's correct, Doctor."

"OK. How do you want me to send it to you?"

"Um, email?"

"Yes," he said easily. "Early next week."

Weeks later, I called the doctor again to tell him that I hadn't received the report yet.

"I'm sorry. What do you want it to say?"

"Write whatever you want: I'm blind, urgently in need of an operation, at risk of losing my sight, anything, Doctor."

"No problem."

A few days later, I received the following medical report, with the heading "Detached Retina—Urgent":

To: (the name of the hospital)

A case of Rt retinal detachment need urgent surgical repair (Pars Planna Vitrectomy).

As soon as possible.

And then the name and the doctor's signature, with the date.

I took a deep breath. The documentation of this medical situation would allow me to submit a permit to the Israeli authorities. I needed the permit to enter Israel not to get treatment for my eye, not out of longing for Jerusalem, not with the intention of blowing myself up, and not even to see the sea. All I wanted was to see Sari and to apologize to her.

Sari

Medical Exemption

It was my weekly meeting with Hadas, the director of the legal department at Gisha, and we laughed at the military's new initiative. The military authorities said they would agree to change people's addresses from Gaza to the West Bank. In order to process the change, people had to first be present in Gaza and then travel to the West Bank. But while they were happy to issue permits to let Palestinians reenter Gaza, they refused to issue permits to let Palestinians travel to the West Bank. We deliberated how to word our letter objecting to the procedure, when suddenly Hadas stopped laughing.

"You know, my son is being conscripted in six months," she said. I knew Roi as a charming, introverted boy, warm and cynical, like his mother.

"You poor thing."

"He'll bring the uniform home. A weapon too. I'll have to embrace him—I will embrace him. I'll have to launder his uniform, visit him at the base, bring him care packages."

"What position does he want in the army?"

"He doesn't know. He just keeps saying he wants combat duty."

"Maybe he'll have some minor accident at home. Maybe some small but disabling injury?" I managed to squeeze a tiny smile out of her.

"You know that in the Middle Ages, Jews in Europe would lightly maim their sons to get them out of military conscription." Hadas had earned a PhD in history.

"Go for it!"

"No chance," she said. "He has a profile of ninety-seven. He doesn't even wear glasses."

"You raised a healthy child."

Had Osama and I stayed together, I would not have had to worry about my children being conscripted. The military doesn't conscript the children of Palestinians from Gaza.

It's been four months. The sobbing still takes hold of me sometimes without warning. Actually—every day or two. Osama's name still hasn't appeared on the lists of those whom the soldiers in uniform agree to recognize as residents of the West Bank.

Osama

Conversation with Myself

Good morning. I don't know where to start. I noticed you didn't sleep very well last night. And I heard you swearing in English. How about you stop writing, send Firas to school, finish writing, and then take a hot bath before going to the university? There's no need to rush to get to work this morning. Don't lose faith. She loves you.

I'm not sure how . . . how she could allow herself to enter my life, break into my world, and then disappear like that.

Calm down, Osama . . . enough of those tears, Osama.

What right did she have to do that? Because she can? She thinks she can come and go whenever she pleases, and that I'm stuck here and will never move?

Don't think like that, Osama.

Because she's American, Israeli, Jewish, she has freedom of movement. She's taking advantage . . .

Osama, enough! Stop! You're taking advantage of your situation to arouse sympathy. Listen to me for a minute: Take a shower and go to the university. Why did you call her?

I'm not sure . . . to hear her voice. She was also so very sad. But she was firm. "I'm in front of the office. I don't want to collapse. I have to go." And she hung up the phone. But she was full of softness, as usual. Her voice was warm, enveloping, understanding.

I'm searching for hope in every little detail. Sometimes I find it, and sometimes I lose it. She asked me not to call her. I promised.

Sari

Arabic Studies

I brought volume II of my Arabic-language book to the basement of the clinic and signed into the imaging department. I was waiting to undergo a biopsy, a reminder of my family history of breast cancer, a history that dictates a cycle of monitoring, examinations, and—thus far, for me—false alarms. In our family, the women don't die of cancer, but they undergo screenings, tissue analysis, and at a certain age, the decision to cut and mutilate.

"It's almost certainly benign," the doctor wrote in the referral for the biopsy, and I believed her. I imagined Osama's voice, rich with a tinge of laughter, reassuring me on the other side of the telephone. When we were still planning our lives together, I wondered how I would go about my medical care. Would I go to Israel, where I'm entitled to access the public clinics, or Ramallah, where Osama would be able to accompany me to examinations like this one? He once explained that his health insurance from the university would cover me if we married, but only if the ceremony were conducted by a religious official.

As I waited, I opened the book and absorbed myself in the language study I'd resumed recently. Without the commute from Ramallah, I had time in the mornings, before running and work, to throw myself into studying Arabic. I would wake up at 5:00 a.m. or even 4:30 a.m.—in any event, I'd started going to sleep by 9:30 p.m.—and sit at the kitchen table, the muted dawn starting to illuminate the street as I made coffee and reviewed lessons in spoken Arabic, completing the homework I had neglected while taking the Arabic course I'd started when I began traveling to Ramallah to see Osama.

I fell in love again with learning the language, taking the time to read, practice, study its structure, and wonder over and over again at the similarity with Hebrew.

I recalled a Saturday afternoon months ago, when Osama and I were still together. While I prepared bulgur kubbeh (Iraqi fried dumpling of bulgur grain stuffed with meat and onions), and Osama dispensed advice about the texture of the dough, he also gave me a language lesson. As I rolled the kubbeh, anxious they wouldn't come out as good as Aziza's, we talked about calendars—Hijri, Hebrew, Gregorian—and went through the names of each month in Hebrew and Arabic, marveling at the similarity of the languages.

"*Tishreh*," I offered, citing the Hebrew name for the first month of the year.

"*Tishrin!*" Osama responded with the Arabic parallel.

"*Heshvan*."

"No, *Tishrin* Number Two."

"That's original. *Kislev*."

"*Kanun*."

"No good. *Tevet?*"

"*Kanun* Number Two."

"What, they didn't have enough money for another name? *Shvat*," I offered.

"*Shbat!*"

"*Adar*."

"*Aadaar!*"

"*Nisan.*"

"*Nisaan!*"

"*Iyar.*"

"*Aayar!*"

Only after we broke up, in the month of *Elul*, *Eylul*, I resumed studying Arabic from books and listened to the conversations in the CD that came with the textbook. I started with the beginners' volume to solidify the fundamentals I'd skipped while practicing with Arabic speakers in Ramallah who hadn't had the consideration to limit their conversation with me to the vocabulary of volume I.

"Sari Bashi?" the medical assistant called. I entered a room with dim lights, where the doctor and nurse waited, and they asked for the consent form. Before I sign, I told them, I wanted an explanation of the stages of the biopsy and the risks of complications.

"I already explained to you last week," the doctor said. A woman in her forties or fifties, very pretty, she wore a fitted blue-gray cotton dress and orange tights, a bright orange scarf around her neck.

"You didn't mention complications."

"Because the chances are very remote," she said, with an impatien sigh. "If I had two left—I mean, really left—hands, then I could mis the area and puncture your chest. That's the only serious possible co plication. I have conducted thousands of biopsies and have yet to o that."

"And the stages of the procedure?"

"We inject a local anesthetic using a needle. Then w nsert a very fine needle to remove a number of cells for analysis. ll get the results in a week to ten days, from your doctor."

"And I can't play sports?"

"I explained to you last week," she said, b wed the pace of her speech and also softened her tone. "We don't mend exerting yourself today and ask you to avoid getting th vet. Tomorrow you can do whatever you want."

I returned to the table where I n the week before, when

she conducted the ultrasound and lingered on the right breast. Now the doctor connected the ultrasound equipment that would guide her during the operation. The nurse spread clear gel on my breast. There was a hum of electric equipment, an almost calming background noise. Each time I felt the tears well up, I focused on conjugating the Arabic verbs in the first verbal stem, second pattern, the ones that always confuse me.

Ana Batlob.

Inta Bitutlob.

Inti Bitutlobi.

I get confused in the second-person feminine, where the *shva* vowel migrates to the second root letter. The book says that in some regions, Arabic speakers leave the *shva* vowel in the first root letter, like the parallel pattern in Hebrew, but I'm trying to use the more common form of spoken Arabic to maximize the chances of people understanding me.

"Now I'll insert the needle with the local anesthetic. You'll feel a stab. It will hurt for a few moments."

I'm almost certain that the conjugation of the verb *katab* ("to write," and it's *katav* in Hebrew), present tense, is different in the workbook than in the main volume, and that's why I'm confused right now. Do you conjugate it using the third pattern, like *yitrek*, ("to abandon") or in the simpler pattern of the verb *fatah* ("to open," and it's *patakh* in Hebrew)? I revie d in my head conversations I'd had in Arabic with Osama to try to re mber. "I want to write about your Aunt Aziza," he'd said to me in slo careful Arabic. How did he correct the verb *katab* in the notes I wou leave him in the morning, when I left the house before he woke up i der to get to work on time?

"The anes a is spreading over the area now. Do you feel that I'm stabbing you

"I'm not sure, d. "It might be the memory of the first stab."

I heard the sou a stapler firing a staple into a thick stack of papers.

"During the biops use a device that will fire small rounds.

That's how it sounds. You'll feel as if you are getting hit with a mild blow. We will do that a number of times." The doctor pointed to the device the nurse held, but I turned my head in the opposite direction, toward the wall.

"Like piercing an ear," I said.

"It's similar."

Yesterday I met with a colleague from the Gaza Strip who'd come for a rare visit to Israel to participate in a training on desalinization. In 2007 and 2008, we had maintained daily contact, when the restrictions on bringing fuel into Gaza disrupted the water supply and sewage treatment. We filed a Supreme Court petition against the restrictions and took affidavits from this colleague about the impact of the resulting electricity shortage on water wells and treatment plants. He was a precise man, an engineer by training, but also sensitive. During the war in 2008–2009, he gave me information about the extent of the fuel shortage, to support our attempts to try to get the Israeli military to allow fuel supplies to the water wells. His apartment was close to the Ministry of Interior, which was periodically bombed, and he kept moving with his family from one relative's house to another, trying to find a safe place. One day, during a report on the amount of diesel reserves Gazans had for drinking-water wells, he burst into tears. He apologized, saying he was trying to help the residents who depended on the water system, but his children were terrified, and he was struggling to calm them an himself down.

At our Gisha office in Tel Aviv, it was a beautiful day outside ith a clear December sky. Abir, our field researcher in Gaza, whos ouse was near the sea, was praying for rain, because during the war, loudy days, the poor visibility disrupted the naval bombardment neigh-borhood. We were working under a state of emergenc I spent both the days and the nights in my office. Looking at Aviv sky-line outside the window, I imagined the engineer in s house, the sound of the bombings, whose echoes I heard ov hone, ringing in his ears as he gave me a report on the functio the water wells in Gaza City and monitored the proximity of the explosions, wondering if they would reach his house.

Now, two years later, we sat in a Thai restaurant in Herzliya, in the high-tech area. He ordered a Caesar salad and refused my entreaties and those of the waitress to order a main course, a Thai dish.

"I want something light," he said. "I'm trying to lose ten kilograms." He pinched a roll of paunch underneath his blazer and smiled. "I didn't use to have this."

The doctor said, "Now a shot—you will feel a mild blow."

Trak! The sound of a stapler firing a staple.

Huwe butlob, I say to myself and then correct that: Better to say *biyutlob*. Both forms are acceptable, but the second emphasizes the structure of the pattern in the present tense so that I'll conjugate it correctly from other points of view as well.

I gave my Gazan colleague medical equipment to bring to Tamer, Osama's nephew, who has thalassemia. The equipment includes kits for checking iron levels in the blood and a replacement belt for supporting the thigh bones. When Tamer visited Ramallah and bought the first belt, we called it "the karate belt" and took pictures of ourselves inflicting imaginary kicks and punches on each other. Last week, over the phone, I told Mohammed, Osama's charming little brother, that I would divide the equipment into two packages in order to avoid burdening the engineer, and that I would send the second half with an employee from international organization entering Gaza. Mohammed had stopped t ng to persuade me to talk to Osama, but his voice and laugh were th me as Osama's.

hat's your relationship to them?" the owner of the Israeli medical s y company asked me over the phone when I asked him for a discou

"I'n od friend of the family," I said.

The placed the ultrasound wand on the shelf.

"We'r ," she said, and all at once I lost my grip on the verbs *yitrek* and

"Don't cry," the doctor said and turned her back to wash her hands at the sink. I heard in her voice discomfort but also compassion. "It's almost certainly benign."

I collected my bra and shirt from the chair in the corner of the room. As I dressed, I thought, *This is what it feels like to move on.*

Osama

A Report, an Appointment, and a Treatment Summary

In order to get an entry permit to Israel for medical care, "You need a medical report, an appointment from the hospital, and a treatment summary," the head of the Gaza department in the Civil Affairs Office told me.

"OK. Would it be better if I just ask for an ordinary entry permit?" I asked hopefully.

"No, that won't work. They don't give nonmedical permits to Gaza residents," he said dryly.

"Thank you."

"You're welcome."

When my colleague Jaber, who lives in Jerusalem, arrived with the confirmation of the appointment at the hospital in Jerusalem, I called my friend Suha for advice.

"Ironically," I told her, "I have a medical report that says I need a serious operation in my right eye, but my appointment is for an orthopedist, and I don't have a summary of the treatment that justifies the referral."

I read what the Israeli doctor wrote in the appointment confirmation: "The hospital administration confirms that the patient Osama Fahed, ID number xxx, has an appointment at the orthopedic department on xxx, for one day, and he'll need to be accompanied by a companion."

I laughed. "My options are to get a new medical report that matches the medical appointment (for example, a broken bone or spinal cord paralysis); to get a medical appointment that matches the medical report (but the eye hospital might scrutinize the request, and the Israeli authorities might find out—hah, as if they don't know!); or to call the eye hospital and hope they understand the situation. Or to travel to Tel Aviv without a permit."

"Don't even think of that last option," my brother Mohammed warned, when I called him for advice too. "Your address is Gaza, and if you get caught, you won't leave Gaza for a year, or forever. My brother, is there any disease you have not exhausted?" Mohammed laughed.

"I'm ready for any illness and any treatment, but I need them to match up," I said with a sigh.

"Don't worry, Abu Firas. We'll figure it out," he said, and promised to call me back.

The besieged Gazans in Gaza are determined to help the besieged Gazans in the West Bank.

A half hour later, Mohammed called me back. "There is very good news. Very, very good."

"Did you get me another medical report?" I asked.

"Much better. Sari called me and said she'll talk to you this week."

I hadn't considered that possibility.

"Are you serious?!" My heart soared, but I was still worried. How would I find her? What did she want to say to me?

Sari

Advice from David

The day after my biopsy, I went for a long Friday-morning run in the forest. I met David later in a Tel Aviv coffee shop, after he finished a morning of meetings with clients and reviewing documents he hadn't had time to read during the week. The café was busy—waitresses brought elaborate "Israeli breakfasts" to tables of fashionable twentysomethings chattering loudly, and mothers sipped cappuccinos while their babies slept in strollers next to them.

I told David about Osama's wooing attempts, including recruiting everyone close to us for his campaign of persuasion, and the huge framed painting that arrived at my office, wrapped in brown paper.

"He must have commissioned it based on a photograph from the Tel Aviv Marathon," I told David with what I hoped sounded like casual disdain. "It's a meter high, a picture of me with my hands clenched, one of my legs in the air, a blue running cap on my head, and the race number seventy-seven pinned to my chest."

"You left his area, and he can't reach you because of the borders," David said.

"It has nothing to do with borders. I refuse to see him, and I wouldn't agree to see him if he were in Tel Aviv either."

"Yes, but he's not in Tel Aviv, and he can't reach you," David said, taking a bite of his sandwich. "What did you do with the painting?"

"I hid it behind my closet. Still wrapped in the brown paper. I'm still alive; it would be weird to hang a framed portrait of myself in the apartment."

Since the breakup, I had become dependent on these meetings with David. At first I would cry, and David would pass me napkins and regard me with his penetrating gaze, ask questions and listen. Sometimes I asked him questions about how he decided to marry his wife—they raised together three sons who were now in their twenties and thirties—and what alternative paths his life might have taken.

That day, I spoke nonstop, explaining, arguing with myself, telling David how idiotic the idea of going back to Osama would be.

"Give it another chance," David said.

I was shocked. "But last time, and also the time before that, I gave him one last chance, and each time he went back on his promise to have kids."

"So give him another one last chance."

"Why?"

"People make all kinds of choices in life. Not everyone loves that strongly."

"And if I give him another one last chance, and he changes his mind again and decides that he doesn't want kids, and then again regrets it and asks me for another chance, will you tell me to go back to him again?"

"No," David said. "If he changes his mind again, I'll tell you to move on."

Osama

JANUARY 2012

It's overwhelming to have Sari here, in my apartment, after four months, sitting next to me. I tried so hard to look at her, to smell her, without her noticing.

Sari didn't even comment on her photographs that I had hung in the apartment: her with her work friends, us together in Aqaba, and her with her nephews in New York. She asked to speak first.

"We need to talk honestly," she said. "Like adults, with respect and integrity."

"OK!" I said, thrilled to hear her say anything, to hear her voice.

"I'm really, really angry," she said. "You throw me away when you want to and then bring me back when you want to. How can I trust you? I don't trust you."

"You're right," I said.

"I think it's the end this time. There's no reason for us to see each other again. I already decided that I'm not getting back together with you."

"I'm sorry, Sari. I—"

"Will you let me finish?" she screamed.

I did let her finish, but when she stopped speaking, and I tried to say something, she yelled at me again.

"You're not listening! You do whatever you want, and you don't care how it affects me!"

I thought to myself, *I'm finally seeing her express anger at what I do.* I always thought she was a rock. The way she grasps what happened between us pains me, to the point where I myself wanted to tell her not to get back together with me.

When she calmed down a little, she said in a childish voice, "I'm hungry."

I fried two fish, and Sari prepared salad.

We talked about the house, about Ramallah, and my work. "What would you tell people at the university about us?" she asked.

"If the choice is between them and you, Sari, I choose you." I was telling the truth.

At 10:30 p.m., she said she wanted to go back to Tel Aviv. I vehemently refused. The streets are too dangerous because of the army and the settlers, and also "our" boys who might open fire on her car. She insisted. I implored her.

"Are you afraid of the army, or do you want me to stay?"

"Both. But I want you. I want you to stay."

I couldn't fall asleep. She managed to sleep a little.

When her alarm clock rang at 4:30 a.m., I asked her if we could speak in Hebrew.

"*Ani ohev otakh,*" I said, tasting the words on my mouth. "*I love you.*"

"*Ani adayin koeset,*" she said, testing me. "*I'm still angry.*"

"*Ani yode'a.*" "*I know.*" She was surprised, impressed.

I tried to postpone her leaving as long as possible. When she finally insisted, I thanked her for the visit.

"Please think first of yourself and only afterward of me," I said to her.

I love you, I wanted to say but was afraid of her reaction.

She said, "I'm ready to do one hundred percent of the pregnancy and birth, but twenty-five percent of the child-rearing."

I didn't tell her, but I've already chosen a name for our baby daughter: *Noor*. "Light" in Arabic.

I wondered if landlords would agree to rent us an apartment in Al-Bireh, a larger but more conservative city than Ramallah. Would the Palestinian Authority allow an Israeli to buy apartments in the West Bank? I prefer to live in Ramallah. Between 150 and 200 square meters would be perfect.

"Do you have time for me to show you the new housing complex they're building in Ein Musbah?" I asked, trying one last time to delay her departure.

Without warning, she screamed at me: "I want you to know that there are consequences to the things you do. I didn't realize how angry I was until I saw you."

Before she left the house, she said, "Is it OK if I use your toothbrush?"

I almost cried with happiness.

Sari

Exceptional Humanitarian Case

He called me Saturday night, a few hours after I returned home from visiting him, the second visit since I agreed to see him again. This one was easier, and I missed him after I left.

"Hayat died," he said. His voice was choked, distant.

The next day, I traveled to him, telling the staff I was taking a vacation day. I wrote a letter to the military asking to allow Osama to travel to Gaza and gave it to David for his signature. Lately, the army has considered the death of a first-degree relative to be an "exceptional humanitarian case" that is grounds for getting an entry permit into Israel, for the purpose of traveling from the West Bank to Gaza.

I asked Osama's brother Mohammed to send me a copy of the death certificate and began to nudge Roi, the officer in charge of public affairs in the Civil Administration. I spoke nicely and complimented him on his professionalism, in the hope that the request would be granted.

Osama

FEBRUARY 11, 2012

When my eldest brother, Omar, called, he said, "Let me say it to you directly: You know that our lives are in the hands of God. May God grant you the years he took from Hayat, your sister."

"No," I said, choking up.

"There is no wisdom and no strength except what God gives us," Omar said, and he insisted that I repeat the saying to make sure I was OK. I repeated it but understood nothing. How could this happen?

"How is Mama?" I asked.

"Thank God, she is OK," Omar said.

Friends from Gaza called to express condolences—Walid, from the university, whom I hadn't seen for seventeen years. Ali, with whom I'd spent years working on construction sites in Israel. Abed, who studied with me at the UNRWA school and was already a grandfather.

"We haven't seen you for seventeen years. We miss you . . . I swear, everyone is waiting for you . . . We don't think it's a good idea for you to come to Gaza . . . Those Jews, you can't trust them, even if they say they'll let you return . . . Be careful. Don't go . . . Don't do anything stupid."

Sari

I brought semolina kubbeh that I had in the freezer, and while Osama went on an errand with Firas, I prepared the soup with the beets I had bought in the vegetable shop near Manara Square, where the bus from Jerusalem dropped me off. Firas went to his mother's house, and Osama and I ate red kubbeh soup. When he caressed my face, I felt his joy at being close to me, mixed with his grief over the death of his sister.

In the evening, friends came over. Osama served them coffee and dates, as is the custom when someone dies, he explained to me. He introduced me proudly but also with some bashfulness. It was my first time meeting them. The guests smoked, smiled uncomfortably, and asked about the hoped-for visit to Gaza.

"Inshallah," Osama said, and surprised me by taking my hand in front of all of them. They looked away.

The next day, still waiting for an answer from the military, we went to the center of town because Osama wanted to buy a present for David, to thank him. I called Roi again. "The funeral was yesterday," I told him. "But you know, now there are three days of mourning."

"He's barred for security reasons," Roi said. "The matter was sent to the Shin Bet to be handled, and I'm waiting for an answer."

At noon, I returned to the office in Tel Aviv. Roi called at three o'clock. "When does he want to travel?"

"Now," I said.

"He needs to reach Erez Crossing no later than nineteen hundred sharp. Are you sure he'll make it?"

I called Osama on the other line and asked what he thought.

"Now!" he shouted.

Osama

Seventeen Years

Usually, people measure distance in kilometers or miles. I measure it in years.

When I got out of the taxi, a pack of teenagers and children welcomed me, apparently my nieces and nephews. I recognized only the oldest, Eden and Arij, university students who were little girls when I left Gaza. I asked the others to speak so that I could try to identify them by their voices, familiar to me from telephone conversations. I guessed right for three of them.

"Do you want to come to the mourning tent first?" my brother Mohammed asked me.

"I want to see Mama."

I found her in Omar's apartment, sitting on the floor surrounded by women. She rose to meet me at the door. I held back my emotions as best I could when she embraced me and started to cry.

Many of my female relatives had become more religious and avoided shaking my hand, out of heightened standards of gender segregation. I wasn't offended. I noticed my sister-in-law Renad and offered her my hand. Instead of shaking it, she put her hand on her heart and smiled. I said to her, "You don't want to shake my hand? Then take this." I touched her lightly on her cheek and immediately left the room. I heard her laughing behind me. I met Salam, Mohammed's wife, for the first time.

Omar cried bitterly. We kept our arms tightly wrapped around each other for about five minutes. This sparked a protest from Renad, who later said to him, laughing, "It's been years since you hugged me the way you hugged Osama!"

I sat in the mourning tent with male relatives and friends who came to pay their respects. We drank coffee and embraced visitors. I'd forgotten how mild the weather is in Gaza, even in winter.

Mohammed told me that Hayat had been fading for months. In the last three days of her life, she became very weak. Mohammed had tried to tempt her with her favorite foods so that she would get stronger. On her last day, she didn't eat anything. A week after her death, Mohammed forgot and went to her bed to offer her a piece of chocolate.

I couldn't hold back my tears. I remember the *basbousa*, the syrup-drenched semolina cake she used to make for us when we were little. I remembered the Singer sewing machine she used to operate with her foot, sewing piecework to earn money to give my mother, and how she'd light the kerosene lamp in winter and stand over me to make sure I did my homework.

Goodbye, my precious Hayat.

Sari

Sociological Research

The student is twenty-eight, pretty, with long brown hair and big black eyes. She thanks me again for my willingness to be interviewed for her research—a thesis about non-Zionist immigrants from Anglo-Saxon countries. I gave her a short smile, one that displayed my impatience. It's two in the afternoon. I have meetings after my interview with her, and I haven't yet eaten lunch.

"How long ago did you make aliyah to Israel?" she asked, using the Hebrew verb for Jewish immigration to Israel that means "to ascend."

"I came here in 1997," I said.

"Did you come here with a program or a youth group?"

"No."

"What made you decide to make aliyah?"

"I didn't decide to make aliyah. I didn't ascend anything. I had Israeli citizenship through my father, who grew up here."

"So you didn't get financial benefits, special provisions for Jewish immigrants?"'

"There were all kinds of benefits, but you needed money to take advantage of them—a customs discount if you bought a car, subsidies for a mortgage if you bought a house. I think I got a few benefits on my income tax."

"But you decided to come here to live," she said.

"No. I got a Fulbright fellowship to do research on ethnic identity for young Israelis of Ethiopian descent. I did research for a year and then stayed to work."

I felt mild hostility, as I often do when people ask me about "aliyah." I realized I would not have time to chop vegetables for a salad and eat it before my next meeting. She was asking the wrong questions, but I was too busy and too hungry to want to help her.

I was taking out on her my annoyance at questions to which, in my fifteen years living in Israel, I have yet to find a good answer: "Why did you decide to make aliyah?" Or worse, my annoyance at comments like "Good for you, for deciding to make aliyah!" As if I came here to fulfill some ideological dictate. As if I'm doing someone a favor by being here.

It's hard for me to accept the admiration of proud Israelis, which is based on an error. It's also hard for me to accept the admiration of proud Palestinians, which is based on a different error.

"You're from America?" they ask me in shops in Ramallah. "Welcome! How is Palestine?"

As if I were a foreigner who came to Ramallah as a gesture of solidarity with the Palestinian people. As if I weren't an Israeli trying to get something—someone—who happened to be in Palestine.

The student is still waiting for my answer. There are twenty minutes remaining of the time I promised her.

Maybe it has something to do with my father. I came to Israel at the age at which my father left it. In the first year, my father would get excited when I told him over the phone that I had hiked in Sde Boker, had bought sambusak from Abulafia, or had gone to see Shafiq and Aziza for Friday-night dinner.

"Yes, yes, we used to hike in that wadi, too, during vacations from the Technion," he would say to me. I felt closer to him during the years I lived in Jerusalem than during the years in which we both lived in New Jersey, in the same house or no more than three miles away from each other.

Maybe I was looking for him in the desert, where he worked on a farm; in my grandmother's small, dark apartment near the sea; or in the food that Aziza would prepare for family meals. There, far away from him, I collected material to fill the silences between us.

Or maybe I was just a twenty-one-year-old woman, an outsider by nature, who had a chance to travel to a different place.

"I was curious," I finally said. "My father grew up here, and I wanted to see where and how."

Osama

Gaza: Jokes and Pain

Every day, guests came to see us—friends and family. I got reacquainted with my eldest brother, Omar, and my sister Sanaa. I met my nieces and nephews. I went with my brother Mohammed and my cousin to watch Spain play Croatia in a big courtyard with a large screen in the middle. I like to watch Gazans watch football: cursing when a player misses a goal, sighing with pleasure and smiling and making rude comments when a picture of a girl or woman appears on the screen.

I slept in my mother's new apartment, the one they built after I left Gaza. In the 1970s, the Israeli army demolished our house and all the other nearby houses as part of an operation to make it easier for them to surveil the area. The Palestinian Authority later restored the land to my family, and my brothers built a concrete building with three apartments in it, one for each brother and his family and a two-room apartment for my mother. In each 110-square-meter apartment, my brothers divided the rooms to allow their sons to sleep separately from their daughters. The buildings in that part of the camp are built

1 meter apart from each other, bringing your neighbor's living room very close to yours.

My mother insisted on sleeping in the living room and giving me her bed. We talked a lot, mostly about the neighbors and my childhood.

"Do you remember Umm Mahmoud?" my mother asked.

"The one who looked a lot like you?"

"Yes. Well, one day, when she was young and recently married, she went outside to sweep the ground in front of her house, wearing a dress with no sleeves." Gaza had become more conservative in recent years, but even thirty years ago, it was unusual for a woman to leave her house dressed like that. "My older brother, *Khalo* Hamdi, came that day from Rafah for a visit, and he thought she was me." My Uncle Hamdi had always been very religious.

"Was he angry?"

"Furious. I kept saying, 'I swear, my brother, it wasn't me!' I had to give him her name, and the name of her parents and her husband's family, and he checked it out with relatives before letting me off the hook." My mother, like most women in Gaza, had always been dependent on male relatives, all the more so when my father left, and she moved in with my uncles.

"Whatever happened to Umm Ahmed?" I asked my mother. I remembered her as a kind but strange lady. She'd adopted a street cat and would feed it every day. Forty days after it died, she made a feast of maftoul, a Palestinian wheat dish, a custom that usually honors the memory of human beings, not cats.

"She died five years ago, *Allah yirhamha* ("may God have mercy on her")." My mother winked at me. "But her cats didn't bring us maftoul."

When my brother Mohammed joined us for breakfast one morning, I heard my mother tease him as she had when he was a child. "Abu Yusef used to say we have three monkeys in this neighborhood." By monkeys he meant troublemakers. "The monkey of *Dar* ("family") Rahma, the monkey of *Dar* Fahed (referring to my brother), and our monkey."

"And you," my mother said, turning to me, "they always said about you, '*Raso zai ras khalo.*'" "His head is stubborn like his uncle's head."

I asked my mother about a childhood memory—that after Israel destroyed our house in Jabalia, we didn't go immediately to live with my aunt but went first to live in the Bureij refugee camp. I remembered crying, and I wasn't sure how long we stayed there. I asked my mother for details, but she said she didn't remember, or maybe she didn't want to talk about it.

I also told my mother something I'd never told her, because at the time I was afraid I'd get into trouble. My father visited us around 1975, when I was in third grade, and he brought the woman he'd taken as a second wife in Egypt, together with their two young daughters. I said something that made his new wife angry, and she pinched me hard and painfully on my side.

"I didn't know that," my mother said. "But I'm not surprised." During that visit, my mother said his second wife kept coming into the kitchen to check up on her.

"She wanted to make sure I didn't try to poison the food," my mother said.

"Did you?" I asked.

"I couldn't," my mother answered. "There were children eating too. When your father arrived, he greeted me formally and asked, 'How are you, Umm Omar?' As if five years hadn't passed, as if we hadn't brought five children into the world."

She told me that when my father left to return to Egypt, I was the only one of my siblings who didn't cry.

"Are you still angry at him?" I asked her.

"God should go easy on him, my child," she said. "Let him rest in peace."

"Abu Firas has aged. His hair has thinned and turned gray," I heard often from others who were gray-haired like me.

My memory returned to me in Gaza, like many other things—laughter, my loud voice. I joked with people in the street and smiled to everyone I walked past.

"*Jee, Wallak, Jee!* You'll get us arrested!" the fortysomething man said to the horse he was trying to get to pull a wagon from the beach to the street. *Jee* is "move" in Arabic slang. He had piled onto the wagon, without permission, impossible quantities of sand—and the horse couldn't pull it from the soft ground to the paved road. Clicking his tongue and checking behind him to make sure the police hadn't come, the man hit the horse over and over again, shouting, "*Jee! Jee!*" My nephew and I offered to push the wagon from the sand, out of compassion for the horse, but the owner refused. "Don't bother, my brothers. He'll manage; he's just making a scene."

Hamas has controlled the interior of Gaza for the last three and half years, and Israel has imposed a tight closure on it. The economy is collapsing. Young people, especially young women, have no work. The pain, the nerves, and the feeling of fear and mistrust were evident in the chaos and traffic in the streets. Drivers shouted and honked at each other and at pedestrians. People moved in a rush and talked very loudly, screaming at each other across the street. Everything is very loud, inside and outside. Gazans laugh most of the time, but they tell jokes so furiously, it's as if they're afraid of what might happen if they stopped laughing even for a moment.

And so many of their jokes are raunchy. My family is like many in Gaza who have become stricter in enforcing gender segregation, having some female relatives cover their faces as well as their hair, and fasting outside of Ramadan. I don't know how Gazans resolve the apparent contradiction, but despite how devout they have become, sexuality drips from their jokes, directly and indirectly.

A tailor asks his customer how wide to sew his pants between the thighs: "If you don't mind, Uncle, tell me—when it's erect, do you place it on the right side or the left?"

The customer answers, "If it becomes erect, I'll put it on my head."

In Arabic, "to put on my head" is a term of deep respect.

A man didn't like the food his wife cooked for him. He wrote a note: "It's not enough to do good work; you need to do your work perfectly." He posted it in the kitchen. The next day, his wife removed the note from the kitchen and posted it above their bed.

Gazans candidly admit that they don't want the Hamas regime and openly criticize its actions and leadership, especially Abu al-Abed, the nickname for Hamas leader Ismail Haniyeh.

"All I want is for them to let me rule Gaza for one day," said the angry taxi driver who drove us from Rafah to Jabalia. "I swear, I'll kill anyone who goes to the mosque! After they wounded my brother-in-law and people tried to administer first aid, they came and fired thirty-eight shots at the first responders and gouged out my brother-in-law's eyes." He cursed Abu Mazen for not routing Hamas out of the government in Gaza.

Toward the end of the visit, I took my twenty-two-year-old nephew to visit my uncle's house, where my mother and siblings and I had moved after our first house in Jabalia was demolished. We walked on new roads that had been paved with asphalt, and I saw more and more houses made of concrete rather than exposed building blocks. Only the market in the center of the camp was as I remembered—noisy, very dirty, and full of life.

I didn't want to knock on the door of the house, which was now occupied by other people. My uncle died a long time ago, and my aunt had gone to live with her daughter in Egypt. I examined the house from the outside, concrete blocks with an asbestos roof. I could see the interior clearly in my memory: On the right was the kitchen and bathroom. There were two rooms on the left—the first where my uncle and aunt slept, and the second for my mother, my two brothers and two sisters, and me, on mattresses that we spread on the floor at night. We'd give our old clothing to a man in the market who would weave them into rugs and sell them back to us, and we spread those colorful rugs on the floor for sitting. In the corner was a stack of gray plastic chairs that we offered guests. We ate on a plastic tarp that we'd spread on the floor, putting a large main dish of lentils or *molokhiya* in the middle, next to smaller dishes for salad and bread. Later, we used a short, plastic table, around which we sat on the woven rugs. When my eldest brother got married, we built another room for him, his wife, and their baby, Eden, the last of whom is now graduating from university.

I stood outside the house as it started to get dark. I imagined I could hear the voices of my childhood from inside the house—my mother, Omar, Sanaa, Mohammed, and Hayat. I felt shaken, unsettled, like something had hit me on the head. I felt like I was about to vomit.

I knocked on the door of the across-the-street neighbor, the one whose hand had been paralyzed by a stroke decades ago. He recognized me, and we drank coffee together. I wanted to talk to other neighbors, but I was afraid to knock on more doors, afraid I would find people changed or afraid of my reaction if they had stayed the same. I wanted to run away from there, and I wanted to stay.

On my seventh and last day, I had a choking feeling when I said goodbye to my mother. I was afraid this might be the last time I would see her. When would I be allowed to enter Gaza again?

"*Bahibek, ya Mama* ("I love you, Mama")," I said, and boarded a public taxi headed to the Erez checkpoint.

Sari

Noises of the Carmel Market

NO LONGER EARLY MORNING

FEBRUARY 2012

Sixty-five kilometers from Tel Aviv to Erez Crossing. A clear winter day, blue skies. I wore a new gray woolen dress, narrowly tailored, flattering, I think.

After getting through the morning traffic jams and the graveled, pockmarked access road to Erez Crossing, I stopped in a small parking lot. Ten Bedouin taxi drivers watched me get out of the car that I'd borrowed back the day before from Josh.

At the top of the hill, behind the fence and the revolving gate, was a large building that served as a kind of arrival hall. Five minutes passed. He came out of the hall, dragging a suitcase on wheels, his figure narrow. When he embraced me for the first time three weeks ago, I felt how thin he had grown. It's still hard when he touches me. I feel the betrayal of trust in my body, which grows tense in his embrace.

When he saw me, his face became the open, happy face of a boy. He walked more quickly, and I ran toward the fence. "You're not allowed to go there!" one of the taxi drivers shouted at me. The revolving gate ejected Osama and his suitcase, and I hugged him. We had until seven in the evening, the hour at which his entry permit to Israel would expire. I took his hand and led him to the car.

One of the drivers called out a sentence in Arabic that I didn't understand. Osama translated: "Take care of that woman. She loves you very much."

Osama

Majdal

While Sari drove, I took a deep breath, entranced by the huge open highway, by the feeling of freedom. We passed roads signs in Hebrew, and I suddenly realized I had no idea where I was or where the car was going. This wasn't the way to Ramallah. I looked at Sari, puzzled, as we approached a junction with a traffic light, and she turned on her left-turn signal.

"How about a little adventure before we drive home?"

We drove north for another sixteen kilometers, until we reached the city that's now called Ashkelon. I started to realize what Sari meant by the word "adventure." She knew that before the Naqba, the Palestinian catastrophe of 1948, there was a Palestinian city here called Majdal, where my mother was born and raised until, at the age of eight, she fled south with her family to the Jabalia refugee camp.

We drove through neighborhoods that looked as if they had been built in the 1970s, past a department store and a huge pharmacy called Super-Pharm. Past men dressed in the garb worn by religious Jews, women of Ethiopian descent, an old woman with a kerchief on her head—so many different kinds of people. We drove toward the beach, and I asked Sari to stop so I could call my mother.

"Mama," I said, trying to stabilize my voice. "What do you want to see in Majdal?"

I thought she would be caught off guard, but my mother began to issue a series of orderly instructions, as if she were describing a picture that was crystal clear in her head: "The olive press; the sheikh's tomb; when you reach the big white houses, turn right at the Ghaban coffee shop."

"Mama, I'm near the sea. Can you be more specific?"

"No, it's not near the sea."

We left the car in a parking lot and continued on foot for an hour. Sari would occasionally ask a passerby how to get to the places my mother asked us to see. No one, not even the elderly people, understood what we wanted. We found no trace of my mother's memories.

I felt a sense of loss and also fear of disappointing my mother, but she accepted our failure with understanding. "Send regards to Sari, sweetheart," my mother said over the phone.

We walked to the edge of the sea. The sky was tinted an impossible blue. I held Sari close to me. The wind blew her hair, tickled my nose. I looked south, toward the Gaza Strip. My permit was valid until 7:00 p.m., and I wanted more and more.

"Are you OK?" she asked.

"More than OK." I felt whiplashed by all this travel, all these new things, and by Sari's presence.

"Do you want to drive to Tel Aviv?"

Sari

Tel Aviv

I couldn't stop talking, as if insisting on trying to cram my entire life into the bubble of Osama's several hours on my home turf.

"There, in the red building, that's where my office is."

"My father grew up here and played football there."

"This is the apartment where I used to live."

"This is Rothschild Boulevard, where they set up the protest tents for the social protests, along this whole road."

"This is a chocolate restaurant: chocolate soup, chocolate pizza, chocolate fountains."

"Here they held the demonstration in solidarity with the prisoner Khader Adnan."

"This is the sea. I run in this direction along the boardwalk and continue east toward the park."

We sat in a hummus restaurant in the Carmel Market, two hundred meters from my apartment. I felt dizzy, like universes were colliding or actually meeting, coming together in a strange harmony. A window opened into a life that could never be—a, sweet, searing, insane fantasy. Osama and me, running errands in the market on a Friday, walking along the pavilion in Nahalat Binyamin, going down to the beach to watch the sunset. I wanted to show him everything, tell him about everything. Only after we finished eating did I dare to ask if he wanted to come to my apartment.

"I talk to you from there," I said, pointing to the balcony above. "And the noise of the cars that you hear is from this street, when they pack up the market in the evenings."

I felt excited, confused, happy. Osama walked ahead of me on the narrow stairway. It was as if his body filled the entire space.

Osama

The Refrigerator

At first I couldn't make out anything, as if my eyes couldn't focus. Slowly, the walls and furnishings took shape. The apartment was smaller than I had anticipated, narrow, with simple furniture. Flooded with light.

Suddenly, I saw it and smiled, feeling relieved, as if I were meeting an old friend.

"That's the refrigerator?"

"Yes," Sari laughed and showed me the chair where she sat during our video calls between Tel Aviv and Ramallah. She showed me the kitchen table where she put the computer, with one corner of the refrigerator in view behind her head.

I wanted to touch her there, in her apartment, there, in her space. I drew her close to me and felt her surrender to my embrace completely, as I hadn't felt her do for a long time. I didn't need anything, just to be there with her, between the four walls of her apartment, the noise of the market surrounding us, in a place so foreign and yet so familiar.

Sari packed clothing to take with her. She locked the door of the apartment. We asked a passerby to photograph us in front of 17 Yehia Kapah Street. She took my hand, and we walked down the street together toward the car.

Sari

A Farewell Half Portion

By the time I opened my eyes, the Carmel Market was already awake. I was stretched out on the sofa, surrounded by cartons and dust and the corpses of cockroaches that I found behind each piece of furniture that I moved. From the open window came a slightly cool early-morning breeze. Friday, April 6, 2012. The last day of the lease on my apartment in a tiny, two-story building in the Kerem Hateimanim neighborhood of Tel Aviv.

For the first time in a month, I had slept in my apartment, in order to finish packing. I consulted with Osama over the phone. "Should I take the shelves off the walls? Maybe I should try to bring the bed frame after all? It's a shame to throw it away."

I looked out the window. Friday belongs to the Carmel Market. Below, in the picturesque alley that had been my street for the past four years, men moved from one end to the other, unloading vegetables and taking glasses of tea from the tray of a short, elderly waiter who passed among them. Outside one of the hummus restaurants, a young man diced onion on a cutting board, a huge pot of chickpeas resting under the table.

I searched for the free Russian-language newspapers I had taken from the kiosk the night before. Not much left to pack. Three kitchen cabinets of plates and cups, one meat and two dairy.

Just before 9:00 a.m., I went outside for a break, to the little coffee shop on the corner. I had never drunk coffee there—it was so close to the house, I never needed to—but in summer I would hear the owner singing through the open window of my balcony. He had been a cantor and opera singer in his youth, and on Fridays, he greeted customers with Italian arias and tunes from Day of Atonement prayers. He was plump, with a potbelly that protruded over the belt of his jeans, and he had thinning gray hair. His singing was crystalline, precise, emotional, and sensuous.

"There's a concert at one o'clock," he told me as he whipped milk for my cappuccino. He must have recognized me by sight—that woman who glides by his coffee shop on Rollerblades every morning—and he seemed curious, engaging me in conversation despite the customers waiting behind me in line.

"I'll come," I lied, because by one o'clock I was supposed to have cleared the apartment for the new tenants.

How could I have not entered his café even once in four years? A young couple sat at a high table on the tiny patio that faced the alley leading to the market. I felt a pang: Osama and I would never drink coffee here together.

I brought a falafel sandwich back home and sat down to rest on the steps outside my apartment. Across from me was the green leafy tree that I would look at from my window nook, almost part of the apartment's furniture, my quiet corner in the old section of Tel Aviv, protected from the modern towers of the newer neighborhoods, dotted with low-rise buildings and small enough that the people who lived and worked in the neighborhood knew me by sight.

I had run out of newspapers for packing the previous night, and I left the apartment to hunt for more. Two very old, very thin men had been sitting on old armchairs placed outside in the alley. At my request, they collected newspapers from an ancient car parked next to them.

"Where are you moving to?" asked the shorter man, even shorter than me.

"Jerusalem," I improvised.

"Will you still travel to work every day?" he asked. They were used to seeing me in work clothes, leaving the house in the morning on Rollerblades, skating up in the direction of the market. On rainy days, when I wore boots and walked rather than glided, carrying an umbrella, they would join the neighborhood's masculine chorus in asking, "Where are your skates today?"

"Yeah, the commute is not that bad," I said.

"My son moved to Ofra, in Judea and Samaria. But he left his job in Tel Aviv. He hated the commute."

"I understand him; it's far," I said. "I'm also moving to that area."

Osama would have been reassured by the Arab-ness of the neighborhood. He would have said that, despite everything, Israelis and Palestinians are similar. "Like in Ramallah," he said to me once, when I complained about the neighbor downstairs who kept telling me not to carry such heavy bags, to dress more warmly in the rain, and to have children already because I wasn't getting any younger, and I'm mistaken if I think a career can make up for not having children. But I think the veteran residents of Kerem Hateimanim are unique, flexible, resilient. They belong only to themselves.

There, on the steps of the building, a half-eaten falafel sandwich in my hand, the tree branches within my sight, I started to cry. I had made my peace with leaving the apartment, the neighborhood, and Tel Aviv, and I was hopeful that Osama and I could make it work together, but only in that moment did I realize I was also leaving behind my life as a single woman, with all the things I had not yet done and maybe would never do.

PART THREE

The Rules of Love

Osama

SPRING 2012

Today, at the end of my class, I lingered to organize my papers. I looked at the students rising from their chairs to leave the lecture hall. The noise, their laughter, the sense of release from the discipline of the class—I find it all fascinating.

Teaching works its magic on me like the hormones coursing silently through my body. I feel excitement when I meet the students, tremendous energy when I enter the lecture hall, and I dance for joy when the students start to discuss and debate. I swell with pride when they reject the limitations of society and of the university. When a student disagrees with me, the world is mine.

Sanaa came to class armed with three articles she'd found to support her argument from the previous class. Basel enhanced his presentation with photos, images, and inspiring quotations, and the entire class applauded. Nur listened patiently to my lecture, raised her hand, and then said, politely, "But why should we agree with you?"

Bashar, Hala, Su'ad, Samar, Asil, Mohammed, both of the Alyas, both of the Rawanis, Al-Ayat, Hassan, Nur, Basel, Mahmoud, Sanaa: I've learned from all of them and feel proud that they are my students.

After the classroom emptied out, and the students' voices disappeared down the hallway, a text message arrived from the real estate agent wondering if I were available at 6:00 p.m. to see the apartment with the garden in the new building in the Tireh neighborhood. Sari wrote that she wouldn't get back from her work in Tel Aviv before 6:30 p.m., and the real estate agent agreed to meet then. The apartment was close to the university, in a quiet area. I hoped Sari would like it.

Sari

Crossing Sides

The road was empty but for a lone car on its way from Ramallah to Tel Aviv. The settlers don't drive on Saturday, the Sabbath, and they also give Palestinian workers the day off. I drove along the winding road, slowed before the speed bumps, opened the window, and stopped at the checkpoint. In front of me stood a smiling soldier, about twenty years old, plump and attractive, with light brown hair and the remnants of adolescent acne on her face.

"Good morning," she said.

"Good morning," I answered, knowing she was checking my accent, which, together with my appearance and clothing, would allow me to cross the checkpoint without displaying my ID card.

There was a time when I would have considered my successful passing of the accent test as an accomplishment. That was in the late 1990s, when I lived in Jerusalem upon my arrival in Israel and was taking a Hebrew-language course at the Hebrew University on Mount Scopus. I hadn't spoken Hebrew since my days of "holy studies" at a religious

Jewish elementary school in the United States. After a week of the language course, I didn't feel as if I were learning a language but rather recalling it. The lessons in the classrooms on Mount Scopus scraped away the layers of dust that had settled on my Hebrew, liberated it to fill my throat as I bought groceries at the supermarket, boarded the bus, and, later, as a journalist, interviewed politicians.

Within a few short months, I found myself living my life in a language that I hadn't known I spoke. The connection was strong. I began to enjoy my new Israeli identity. I felt a sense of success each time people initiated conversations with me in Hebrew, spoke to me easily, and assumed I belonged. I enjoyed the transition to Hebrew-speaking Sari, a Jerusalemite, with two identities.

I worked hard to polish my Hebrew-language skills. I chose my first apartment in Jerusalem because the roommate didn't speak English. I read the newspaper every morning, using a dictionary. That summer, I taught myself to touch-type in Hebrew. When I volunteered in the Supreme Court during summer vacations from law school, I made friends with the Israeli clerks applying to study programs in the United States, and I offered to correct their English on the applications, in exchange for them proofreading the law memorandums I wrote in Hebrew.

I guess I very much wanted to belong, and I seem to have succeeded. See, the soldier is waving me on with "Good Sabbath."

"Good Sabbath," I answered, tears in my throat. I looked at her face, not her weapon, as if hungry for a conversation in Hebrew, even with her. She seemed nice, someone I would enjoy meeting at a dinner, maybe the cousin of a friend. She was more or less the age I had been when I arrived in Jerusalem fifteen years earlier.

I closed the window, guided Bouazizi slowly over the speed bumps, and put distance between myself and the checkpoint. I'm driving to a meeting in Tel Aviv, and in the evening, I'll return to my home in Ramallah. I have crossed to the other side.

Osama

Good Things

When she leaves the house, I ask myself, *What should I do now? Tend the garden? Prepare food? Make more room in the closet for her clothing? Or maybe just surrender to this childlike feeling, let my imagination transport me far away. Keep playing.*

I feel happy, adventurous, full of laughter. In my head, I'm humming the words *happy with an unseen something*, and of course they are Darwish's words.

That taxi driver at the Erez checkpoint said, "Take care of that woman. She loves you very much."

Sari is sharing my home.

Now I need to deal with the authorities, to get the authorizations I need for a work trip to London. On the Israeli side, I need a staying permit for the West Bank so that I can leave and also come back. On the Jordanian side, I need a "no objection" letter in order to enter Jordan, a kind of special visa for Gazans. Sari will ask David to submit the request, and she thinks I'll manage to get permission. And I realized something incredible: The Rafah Crossing between Gaza and Egypt is open, a quirk of the political transitions in Egypt, meaning I can get into Gaza. Have the regional politics gone entirely mad, all the authorities suddenly conspiring to work for my benefit?

Because I couldn't resist this rare opportunity, I won't return to Ramallah straight away from London. I'll fly to Amman, continue to El-Arish, and then travel to Gaza. And Sari will be waiting for me when I return.

Sari

Access Criminal

Osama prepared a simple dinner of salad and fava beans while I showered and then stood at the entrance to the small balcony and looked out at the wadi below. Even though it was already May, the air was cold. Olive and fig trees dotted the agricultural terraces. I looked at the expanse of sky and felt Osama's arms embrace me from behind.

"Close the door," he said. "The food is ready."

We ate, and I felt pleasure at the quiet easiness of having dinner together.

Before bed, I sent David an email—he remained supportive and encouraging of me and Osama, and I wanted to speak with him about my living in Ramallah. I was worried about possible implications for Gisha's reputation.

I grew anxious the next day when David didn't respond. I was worried that David was worried about my move to Ramallah, concerned that the executive director of Gisha, which means "access" in Hebrew, is breaking the law that regulates and prohibits access. Late the next day, I called him.

"I don't have a choice," I said to him.

"You can request a permit," David said.

"That's just on paper," I said.

David is a criminal defense lawyer by profession and a sociologist by nature. He penetrates the hearts of the defendants, the judges, the detectives, and the prosecutors. He scrutinizes their motivations. But as deeply as he understands human beings and the systems they create, David doesn't understand that there is no permit that can regulate my life with Osama. Even if the army were to give me a temporary permit, it wouldn't be continuously renewed. And what would I do when they refuse to let me enter Ramallah? Move out?

"You chose to be a lawyer," he said.

I fought a sense of guilt. We agreed to talk in person. I worried that my conduct was endangering the organization and that I was disappointing David. As a defense to use during the meeting with him, to demonstrate why compliance with the law was impossible, I made a mental list of the laws that affect my life with Osama:

Prevention of Infiltration Law (Crimes and Jurisdiction), 5714-1954: Osama's mother is forbidden to return to her house in Ashkelon.

Order Closing the Area (Gaza Strip and Northern Sinai) (No. 1), 5727-1967: Osama's father is forbidden to return to his family in the Jabalia refugee camp.

Order Regarding Closed Areas (West Bank Area) (No. 34), 5727-1967: Osama is forbidden to live in his house in Ramallah.

Citizenship and Entry to Israel Law (Temporary Order), 5763-2003: Osama is forbidden to live with Sari in Tel Aviv.

Declaration Regarding Closing an Area (Prohibition on Entry and Presence) (Israelis) (Area A), 5761-2000: Sari is forbidden to live with Osama in Ramallah.

Years ago, when I tried to explain to Osama one of the military procedures relevant to his case, he said, "Those are your laws, not ours." For Palestinians, it's impossible not to break the law, because everything is illegal. And because everything is illegal, most of the laws are not enforced, because you can't really outlaw living. So every Palestinian, by virtue of being Palestinian, lives in a state of perpetual criminality. For its part, the military makes do with selective enforcement, knowing that it can't enforce all its laws, all the time, but that the threat of enforcement deters people from protesting or rebelling.

By moving to Ramallah, I went from being a lawyer to being a criminal defendant. For seven years, I was meticulous in running Gisha according to the most scrupulous standards. Every shekel was accounted for, every comma of every legal provision observed. But I can't observe the commas of the military order that forbids Israeli citizens from entering the city of Ramallah because they have placed my love outside the bounds of the law, and that's a law I have chosen to break.

Osama

Entering Gaza

At the small Maraka airport in Amman, I made the mistake of asking the Jordanian border official to speak to me politely, to stop shouting, "Stand there!" and "Give me your passport!" or at least to moderate his tone. The world turned upside down. They took me to a side room for a "conversation": *Where are you going? Who do you know in Gaza? How long will you be in Egypt? What's your job? How much is your salary? Which mosque do you attend? Where does your family live?*

The conversation ended a few short minutes before the plane took off, and I raced to the gate. We were forty-eight passengers on the small Palestinian Airlines plane. When it hit turbulence, the passenger next to me said, "I should never have taken this flight."

One of the two flight attendants immediately replied, "You should be proud to fly Palestinian Airlines!"

We landed at a small airport in El-Arish, where Egyptian soldiers met us. As soon as our feet touched solid ground, the other passengers and I were happy about Palestinian Airlines, and I took out my phone to photograph the plane. An Egyptian soldier stopped me, saying we were on a military base and photography was prohibited.

They brought us to a large hall with a bathroom. It was hot and dirty. Airport workers brought our suitcases. Egyptian army officers took our passports. An hour passed, and they didn't give them back. I understood that we were being detained. They told us a bus would take us to Rafah Crossing. Another three hours passed. There were families, children, elderly people in the group. Finally, the bus arrived, and I realized we were Very Important Persons: Two military jeeps accompanied us to Rafah Crossing, one in front and the second behind.

As soon as we reached the Palestinian side, I noticed the order, the cleanliness, the air-conditioning, and the speed of the security procedures. A Hamas officer looked at my passport and asked, "You're coming from Ramallah? What do you do there?"

"I teach at a university. I'm coming to visit my family."

"Welcome to Gaza," he said, waving me through without stamping my passport.

Seven in the morning, the sounds of the sea, seashells, snails, breakfast on the beach, fishermen casting their nets, trainee lifeguards still drowsy with sleep, people sitting under sun umbrellas, and everywhere, children shouting. Colorful kites fill the air. The hawkers call out, "Fried sweet potato, hot corn, sweet lupine, sunflower seeds, coffee, tea." I think there were more than ten people for each square meter of sand. When I looked left and right, I couldn't see the end of the crowds. I had to ask people to let me pass.

During the day, the beach is mostly filled with men and teenage boys, and they are shouting. The children on the beach shout each time a wave approaches. As with the falafel in Gaza, which you learn to eat by biting at the sides that aren't too crispy, the children approach the water delicately, letting it wash over them from wave to wave. Mechanized tourist boats take a few passengers on short trips in the sea for three shekels each. The Palestinian flag flies next to the FC Barcelona flag. The women swim fully clothed, with pants and shirts, covered with a jalabia. Salam, Mohammed's wife, wasn't the only one who kept the veil over her face as she entered the water. People in Gaza were always traditional, but I saw in my family, too, how their relationship to religion has changed, become stricter.

A donkey pulled the Al-Halab ice cream cart while its owner called into the loudspeaker, "Listen to me . . . listen to me . . . God is one, my friends. Who lost a child? God forbid, don't leave them alone or forget them like that. Who forgot his change from the million shekels he gave me? For God's sake, let me earn a living—my father will kick me out of the house if I come home with merchandise. Get in line, children. There's enough for everyone to buy. Don't worry."

We could hear the faraway boom of Israeli warships firing at the fishing boats, but it didn't detract from the determination of the people of Gaza to enjoy the sea that day. One of the children responded to the shelling with a smile. "*Aqsa, Aqsa*," meaning the Al-Aqsa mosque in Jerusalem, a symbol of Palestinian national aspirations. Hamad, my nephew, was busy observing the warships and the fishermen's response, darting away in small boats to come closer to the shore. The Israeli navy limits the distance from which fishermen are allowed to fish off the coast.

I stayed in the water until nine in the evening. How beautiful the sea is. Memories of childhood, of summer vacations with my grandmother and the huge steaming dishes of eggplant, tomato, and zucchini, roasted with olive oil and special to Gaza's south, that she used to make for us. I will get reacquainted with Gaza.

Sari

Closing the Gate

While I was talking to Menachem, my six-year-old nephew, on Skype, he heard a ping from my cell phone and asked, "What's that noise?"

"It's from my telephone. It means I got a message."

"Why does it make a noise?"

"So that I'll know I got a message."

"What does the message say?"

"Do you want me to read it now?"

"Yes."

It was from Osama, apologizing for his mood during our last conversation.

It had been three weeks since Osama had traveled to Gaza and visited relatives, classmates from high school, colleagues from his work at Israeli construction sites, and cellmates from his time in Israeli prison. And then, in June 2012, a few days before his planned trip back to Ramallah, Egypt closed the border, citing security concerns in the run-up to its presidential election. His nightmares and his anxieties came true.

"Sweetheart," I told Menachem, "it's a message from a friend of mine who feels sad."

"Why is he sad? What's his problem?"

"He traveled to visit his family, and now he wants to go back home, but he can't. He's sad because he wants to come home."

"But why can't he go home? Did he crash his car?"

"No, sweetheart. It's kind of a complicated story. When you travel very far, to another country, there's something called a border. It's like a big gate that has to be opened so that you can go in and out. My friend traveled to visit his family, but when he wanted to return home, they closed the gate. Since then, they reopened it, but every day they only let a few people pass through, and so it will take a long time before he can go back home."

"So why doesn't he just keep visiting his family until they open the gate?"

"That's a great idea, Menachem. You're right. I'll tell him."

When Osama and I spoke in the evening, I could hear the voices of his nieces and nephews, probably Mohammed's children, in the background. I informed Osama that in his absence I had taken over half his closet, which was now our closet.

"What about your closet?"

"It's still mine. There's my closet, and there's our closet."

We tried to plan: We could purchase a new plane ticket from El-Arish to Amman, renew coordination with the Israeli military for him to cross the Allenby Bridge between Jordan and the West Bank, make an appointment to talk to the Jordanian intelligence agents who had told Osama to come see them when he returned to Jordan on his way back to the West Bank. Because he was born in Gaza, he needed their permission to transit through Jordan. In the meantime, people in Gaza are firing rockets on Israel, and people in Israel are bombing Gaza. There are no bomb shelters in Gaza. I just said the stupid sentence: "Take care of yourself."

"Tell me if this is too much for you, sweetheart," he said. "Because I'm struggling."

"I'm OK," I said. "And I'm waiting for you."

During the first two weeks of his visit, I stayed with friends in Tel Aviv, but wandering from home to home only exacerbated my sense of upheaval, so I returned to our rented apartment in Ramallah. I was trying to become more independent there. I called Osama three times a day: Where is that place for washing cars on the way to Beitunia? How do I refill the card for the electricity meter? Can I go by myself to Sareyyet Ramallah to watch the football game? Will other women be there?

In my daily routine, I consistently failed to implement my resolution to be honest about my identity. At the gas station, the fuel attendant heard my accent, smiled broadly, and asked where I was from. I told him that I live in Ramallah, but he asked a second time.

"*Min Amrika*," I told him ("From America").

It was a partial truth, but with my poor Arabic vocabulary, in the fifteen-second interaction of getting back the car key and paying three hundred shekels for a full tank, I didn't know how to make my answer more complete.

Osama

How Do I Feel

I want to see her, embrace her, hear her voice. I miss her temperament, full of humor and irony. We talk every day, and it makes me miss her more, although our conversations restore me to myself for a period of time, like aspirin for a headache.

"How do you feel about Gaza this time, Osama?"

"Mixed feelings, Sari. I don't know. Happy and sad together. This is my childhood, but there is also the oppression here. Pain and anger everywhere, despite the laughter and jokes. It's like people can't let more than a minute pass without telling a joke, as if they're afraid of what else might fill the silence."

I told her about Fakher, who works for Hamas. He's a nice young man with a handsome face. I think she would like him. "There are no honest governments," he told me with a smile. One of his relatives sells bootleg tobacco from a small two-wheeled cart on one of the streets in the camp. Hamas's anti-smuggling authority confiscated his property. They told him he had to pay three shekels for every packet of tobacco, because the price of some kinds of tobacco is officially three shekels. He decided to go to the depot where his cart was, hoping to at least get the cart back, but there they told him he would have to pay a two-hundred-shekel fine for unauthorized use of a public space for commerce. "But the price of a new cart is two hundred," he told them. They didn't relent. He cursed the authorities under his breath at the gate of the depot, and he called Fakher to ask for help. The next day, Fakher joined him at the center, but the authorities told him the cart had already been sent to the district depot or to the prosecutor. Fakher burst out laughing.

I asked him what would happen if the cart owner were to set himself on fire, like Mohammed Bouazizi, the Tunisian fruit seller who set himself on fire and instigated the uprisings in Tunisia and across the Middle East. Fakher smiled and answered, "Hamas would pour more fuel on the fire."

I feel as if I am in prison again. Choked, nervous, depressed, and I can't shake those feelings. I thought about going to the sea, to swim, but I was afraid my mother would worry about me. I need to control myself in front of my family. They have been trapped for years, and I can't stand it even for a month.

Sari

Ruined Peaches

The day after Osama was supposed to have returned, I took "Gaza" to be washed. That was the name we gave his car, and it had taken on a layer of dust and bird feces in the three weeks since its owner abandoned it for the real Gaza. Osama called while I was waiting for the teenagers in rubber boots to finish lathering the car. From the way he said hello, I knew he would inform me of another delay.

"Please, my sister," I heard, and turned around to see one of the teenagers offer me a black plastic chair so that I could sit.

"Thank you very much," I said. I told Osama to whom I was speaking, and when he said, "Nice," I could hear the smile in his voice as he imagined a silly detail of the life that he yearned to return to.

"How much is it supposed to cost?" I asked Osama.

"Twenty."

"But I don't want them to clean the interior."

"Then maybe twelve. Ask them."

They wanted twenty even though they didn't clean the interior, but

I didn't have the energy to protest. I brought Gaza back home and took Bouazizi to Tel Aviv, feeling restless, uneasy.

"There's no point crying over milk that hasn't yet spilled," Josh told me when I confided my fears. We were sitting at his kitchen table, the temporary home I had assumed to save myself the commute between my work and our empty apartment in Ramallah. "You don't know if the army will make it difficult for him to cross into the West Bank."

I let him reassure me.

The following day, I returned to Ramallah to prepare the house again for Osama's return. That day was his second failed attempt to leave Gaza via Rafah Crossing, but they promised he would be able to cross the next day. "Gaza" had accumulated a new layer of dust, and I cleaned it with a rag and window-cleaning spray. During my last stay in the apartment, before I realized how long the delay would be, I had filled the kitchen with double portions of every item of food and beverage for which Osama had ever expressed interest. As if I were trying to buy and cook all the things we hadn't been able to eat together during our extended days of separation.

Now I stacked food into the freezer: soup, bread. The peaches, I guess, are a lost cause.

Osama
Ticket Out

You wait for Egypt to open Rafah Crossing and then reserve a date with the Hamas Ministry of Interior. That's the easy part, although I waited in line for three hours until the employee gave me a ticket with a date and a number. Only later did I realize that the ticket was just to enter Abu Yusuf al-Najjar Hall in Khan Yunis, from which you then have to take a bus to Rafah Crossing.

You have to leave Gaza City very early to reach the hall by 8:00 a.m. via public taxi. The hall appears to be a converted basketball court. It's full of people. There is endless screaming of children, and the elderly people in line for the restroom sigh loudly. Cigarette smoke fills the air. Police shout orders. Clerks call out bus numbers, and if your card matches the number, you're allowed to join the line. Construction workers drill into concrete, fixing some gate inside the hall.

A man standing next to me who had a ticket with the same bus number as mine told me that his brother, who held a senior position within Hamas, would come to collect him. A few hours later, a man dressed in military uniform led him out of the hall.

Finally, I boarded the bus. At Rafah Crossing, a group of us waited in line for hours to cross to the Egyptian side. An officer approached and told us that the crossing was closed, that we should return the following day. We turned to go when suddenly a new group of people arrived and were ushered through. "But they just got here!" we protested. The officers didn't respond.

Sari

Military Service

When I dialed the number of the public inquiries officer in the IDF Command, Judea and Samaria region, I heard the voice of a young soldier talking to her friend. I listened to her describe the party she had gone to on her weekend off until she finished her conversation and asked what I wanted.

"Listen, I don't deal with all those applications to enter Israel and stuff," she said in response.

"It's not an application to enter Israel; it's a request to cross through Allenby."

"Allenby Street in Tel Aviv?"

"Allenby Bridge between Jordan and the West Bank. You coordinated his passage via Allenby Bridge, but he needs to change the return date."

"But I don't deal with applications to enter Israel," she repeated.

"He doesn't want to enter Israel; he wants to enter the West Bank."

"Wait, you just said he wants to enter, right?"

"Not Israel. He wants to cross the Allenby Bridge located between Jordan and Jericho. His address is listed in Gaza, so he needs coordination."

"Listen, I don't deal with all those applications from Palestinians, but if you call in a half hour, I'll transfer you."

"With whom should I speak in a half hour?"

"With me. I'm alone here today."

"But who's responsible for this request?"

"I'll transfer you."

"And what's your name?"

"Shira, but I don't deal with those things."

While I waited at my desk at Gisha, I did administrative tasks that didn't require concentration: listing taxi receipts for reimbursement, confirming the bank transfer of staff salaries, approving the order for a new computer server.

At 1:15 p.m., I called again.

"Hi, Shira. This is Sari again. Can you transfer me?"

"Sure, no problem."

"Who are you transferring me to?"

"To Chen. Bye!"

Chen was the newish officer in charge of public inquiries.

Tal, not Chen, answered the phone, and he seemed troubled by the complexity of my request.

"I'm afraid that if it's not settled now, there will be no one to talk to tomorrow," I said.

"Yes, I understand," he said. "Umm . . . can you call again in five minutes? I'll make some inquiries."

At 1:25 p.m., I called again.

"Did you get a chance to check?" I asked Tal.

"Yes, but now Chen arrived. Can you call in ten minutes, when he finishes? He's busy now."

"No problem."

My stomach was tied in knots. At 1:36 p.m., I called.

"Chen is on the phone right now," Tal said. "Can you call in five minutes?"

1:42 p.m.

"Where does he live?" Chen asked.

"His address is listed in Gaza, but he lives in Ramallah. He has a staying permit valid through September. You already coordinated his crossing for the twenty-second of the month, and he was supposed to return on the twenty-second, but—"

"Why are you calling us?" Chen asked. "Why doesn't he contact the Palestinian liaison office in Ramallah?"

"He's out of the country."

"He can call them by phone. That's the administrative procedure."

"You coordinated his exit—"

"I did that above and beyond what I needed to do, but I already told David that you don't need me for every step of the way."

"I understand what you are saying, and we'll coordinate with the Palestinian Authority going forward, but he needs to return tomorrow."

"He needed to return on the twenty-second, which is the date we coordinated for him. But OK, I'll take care of it. Not now, because I have one or two other things that I need to do."

"Thank you very much, Chen. How should I get the confirmation?"

"I'll call David's office. But not now."

"Thank you very much, Chen."

I calmed down. Hosni, our field researcher from Gaza, came into my office. He had gotten a rare permit to come to Tel Aviv for work meetings. He brought me a present, a huge painting that an artist had painted in Gaza, my portrait. Hosni had given her a photo from my Facebook page. I seemed to be collecting portraits of myself, gifted by men from Gaza.

"Fidaa is a really talented painter," Hosni said. "She got an order for a hundred paintings of Nazareth, based on old photographs. She asked me to help get them to a client in Nazareth, and as a present, she offered to give me a painting."

His voice was calm and calming. I had known him for seven years, since he became the organization's first client when we tried to help him reach his studies at Bethlehem University, in the occupational therapy department. We failed, and he and his classmates finished their degrees through remote video classes and guest lecturers who came to Gaza. After he didn't find work as an occupational therapist, he applied for a job with us.

When Hosni asked how I was, I told him what I had told the staff and board members a few weeks earlier: "I moved to Ramallah." In response to the surprise on his face, I said, "Yeah, I know. My partner is Palestinian—actually, from the Gaza Strip—and I moved in with him."

"I didn't know," Hosni said. Like the other staff members I'd told, he was surprised and curious. It was also a rare time in which I shared something about my personal life with the staff.

"I didn't say anything until now, because it's complicated. Some people don't like for Israelis to be with Palestinians and Palestinians to be with Israelis. And the law bars Israelis from living in Ramallah. It could hurt the NGO."

"I hadn't thought of that."

"Under the law, Osama is not allowed to be in Tel Aviv, and I'm not allowed to be in Ramallah. It's a kind of civil disobedience."

"So you won't be in Tel Aviv tomorrow? Because I understood that we're meeting at Hadas's house in the evening."

"I really want to come," I told Hosni. "Under any other circumstances I would come. But my partner has been visiting Gaza, and he's supposed to come back tomorrow. I haven't seen him for a month, and he has been trying to get back home for a while. Otherwise, I would come."

"I hope it works out for you," Hosni said. "It would be nice if it did."

After Hosni left the room, I wondered what to do with the portrait. I was too embarrassed to show it to the staff. Maybe I would file it behind my closet at home, next to the apology portrait that Osama gave me?

2:45 p.m. The phone rang: Shoshi, David's secretary.

"Chen called me," she said, and I could hear the worry in her voice. "Did you talk to him?"

"An hour ago."

"Well, he called now and said that he won't coordinate Osama's return tomorrow, that Osama needs to call the Palestinian liaison office. He said it's very serious that Osama didn't come back on the twenty-second, and that he won't coordinate an alternative date for him. And I can't reach David on the phone."

"I'll talk to Chen," I told her.

"I'm not coordinating for him," Chen said at 2:50 p.m. "Let him call the Palestinian liaison office."

"But the Palestinian liaison doesn't make decisions—you make the decisions."

"I helped him beyond what my job required, and I coordinated for him the last time. I didn't have to do that. And then Mr. Fahed decided not to return on the twenty-second. So let him wait. It's not my job."

"But, Chen, the Judea and Samaria legal advisor's office referred us to you."

"It's not their job either."

"But they sent us your phone number and told us to contact you."

"The last time, I decided to provide service above and beyond what was necessary. The resident is supposed to contact the Palestinian liaison office. I explained that to David, but I coordinated it anyway, and then Mr. Fahed decided he didn't feel like coming back. When I asked Shoshi why he hadn't returned on the twenty-second, do you know what she said? 'Good question.' Yes, it really is a good question. Let him follow the accepted administrative procedure."

"Chen, he'll arrive tomorrow at the border, Friday, and there will be no one to talk to."

"Tell him not to come until he gets approval to cross. He decided not to return on the twenty-second. Let him return on Saturday, on Sunday. Let him wait for an answer from the Palestinian liaison. I'm not coordinating for him."

I imagined Osama, exhausted from his daily vigil on each of the last three days at the meeting point for traveling through Rafah Crossing, from waiting six hours at Rafah Crossing, from the flight to Jordan, and from homesickness. I could hear his voice on our phone conversation a day earlier as he returned to his mother's house from Rafah Crossing, hoarsely saying how much he wanted to see Firas and me that weekend and to watch the final Europe Cup football game together. I imagined him wandering around the noisy, hot city of Amman, waiting for approval to come home.

"Chen, I understand you. The message is received—"

"I'm not doing this, God forbid, to send a message, Sari. You and I receive service from Yes and Hot, right?" he said, referring to the Israeli cable television companies. "And we expect a standard level of service—that takes into account the limitations of the system and the needs of other customers. And here, we gave you service above and beyond what one could expect, and you want more. It's infuriating. I won't coordinate for him."

I collected myself, trying to banish fears of permanent exile for Osama. My breathing was still uneven. I sent a text message to Osama: *Hey, sweetheart, I need you please to call Nabil to try to approve your return tomorrow. It's important, my love. The army doesn't want to approve it.*

The salads I had prepared and put in the refrigerator would spoil. The chicken I had defrosted wouldn't last. I'll need to buy a new basket of cherries. I'll be able to attend the work party tomorrow night at Hadas's house after all, and that's important, because I'm the executive director.

At 3:01 p.m., David called. During our conversation, a text message arrived from Osama saying that Nabil told him to come to the border crossing tomorrow, as usual. And also: *I love you.* I didn't detect any worry in his short message.

"I think we should wait," David said. "If they don't let him cross tomorrow, we'll call Chen on his cell phone." I didn't say this to David, but on further reflection, it seemed good that Chen directed his outrage at the "temerity" of our asking to recoordinate Osama's return on short notice. He threatened to delay Osama's return home, not to thwart it.

For the first time in the seven years during which Gisha had existed and I had been its executive director, I burst into tears in the middle of the workday. My door was closed, but you could see me through the window that faces the hallway. I lifted the phone receiver and pressed it to my ear, pretending that I was talking on the phone so that no one would knock. I slowed the flow of tears enough to get past the office manager's desk on my way outside.

Downstairs, in the noisy street, I called Yael.

"At some point, I'll be able to see the humor in this," I told her. "The military officer was polite and took the trouble of educating me, explaining to me, for seven minutes, what good customer service is." I stood on the corner, south Tel Aviv in the afternoon, a printing factory in front of me, and behind me the noisy turnoff to the old road to Petah Tivka, the one that everyone used until they built Route 4. I faced a huge potted tree at the entrance to a building, as if I were pouring my heart out to its leaves. The tears spilled and spilled. "But when you're afraid your partner won't come home tomorrow, it's less funny," I told Yael. Two women passed by and slowed, looking at me until I waved at them that I was OK, keep walking.

"It really is outrageous that Osama didn't feel like coming home on time," Yael said sarcastically, repeating Chen's words. Her voice softened, and she added, "Honey, you need to share this with him. You're a couple; you're not supposed to go through this alone."

"Yeah, but he's there, trying to deal with the Egyptians and get home, and that's enough pressure for now."

"Yes," she said. "I guess neither the Egyptians nor Hot nor Yes would give you customer service as good as the service you get from the Israeli army."

Osama

Pat down

Finally on the Egyptian side, after four hours in a crowded, smoke-filled hall, not knowing if and when it would end. I noticed the other travelers inserting ten-pound Egyptian notes into the pages of their passports to persuade the border guards to expedite them. We boarded the bus and rode to the military airport in El-Arish. There, the soldiers asked me for a paper stamped by the Egyptian authorities at Rafah. I told them the documents in my hand were all they had given me at the crossing. I waited outside, in the sun, while a soldier took my passport inside and disappeared. Maybe because I hadn't slipped money into my passport for him? I was terrified they'd send me back to Gaza, but after a half hour, the soldier returned and let me enter the building. After they checked the luggage, the security officer patted me down, passing his hands over every part of my body—everywhere, including between my legs. Even now, long after the incident, I still feel disgust, humiliation, and a strong desire to punch him. I didn't say a word. Then we flew to Amman.

In Amman, the Jordanian security officials told me to wait. I don't remember how long I waited. An officer came to me and, as usual, asked me if I planned to stay in Jordan. As usual, I gave him the answer he wanted to hear: "I am going to the bridge now."

Sari

Jericho

Bouazizi was waiting for me in the parking lot of the train station in Modi'in. The fuel tank was full. I drove toward Jericho, my passport in my handbag. If they don't let Osama enter the West Bank, I'll drive north and meet him in Jordan, via the border crossing in Beit She'an.

Again, the impossible transition between Tel Aviv and the West Bank. This time I kept driving on Road 443 toward Jerusalem and the descent to the Dead Sea. The car headlights illuminated the Bedouin encampments on the sides of the road. I smiled at the Palestinian policemen at the entrance to the city of Jericho, and they waved me on without asking questions.

And then, as if nothing had happened, the tension dissipated. My body became limp, weak. On my telephone screen, there was a message from Osama: "Are you on your way, sweetheart? I just crossed the Israeli side."

Osama

Caffeine

For the first few days after my return, I thought it was just a release of tension, working through the fear that I wouldn't be able to return home. But I started to feel distant from Sari. We continued looking at apartments to buy, but the houses depressed me. The water and sewage infrastructure were rickety, the real estate agents lied, and the finishing work was sloppy. I didn't have patience for Sari's endless questions about the neighborhood, the neighbors, the prices. I got an email from a colleague about a position that had become available in a Swedish university. I forced myself to delete it.

I watched Sari as she slept. When I first met her, she was young, dressed in a black shirt and black pants. Petite frame. Thin. I saw her as sad, shy, although later I realized that what I saw as sadness was intense concentration in her work. Even while engaging me and others in conversation, she managed to wrap herself in a transparent bubble that prevented others from getting close. It took us a long time to get close.

Six and a half years have passed since I signed a document giving her and Gisha power of attorney to represent me in the Israeli court, to allow me to reach my doctoral studies. I remember how she broke the news to me over the phone as she drove back with David from the court hearing.

"The court refused to interfere in the army's refusal to let you reach the campus in Tel Aviv," she said. "I'm sorry. That's just the way it is." Her voice had sounded harsh at the time, but now I realize that she was probably trying to hide her own distress.

"Did they give a reason?"

"It's the same reason they've always given," she said. "That you're active in a terrorist organization, based on secret evidence they showed the justices but not me."

I remember that I laughed. I told her, "Unfortunately, there are only two parties who know that the allegation is false: the Israeli intelligence services and that same terrorist underground to which Israel alleges I belong. But neither of them will come forward to help me."

So many things have changed since then. My life has become intertwined with Sari's, and through her, I can see new worlds. I was actually excited about buying an apartment in Ramallah. But the ground beneath my feet is still not stable. The trip back from Gaza shook me. I'm afraid of what I have gotten myself into, afraid that I won't be able to keep the promises I made to her.

Sari snored lightly. It's amazing how soundly that woman can sleep. Three in the morning: too late for me to fall back asleep. I kissed her gently on the cheek and got up to make coffee.

Sari

A Key Falls in the Forest

It was Saturday, Sukkoth, the seven-day Jewish festival that marks the start of autumn. I was to have four days of vacation, and I agreed to meet a friend for a training run.

I woke at 4:30 a.m.; drank coffee; and drove through the dark streets of Ramallah, Beitunia, and Ein Arik. Men and teenage boys were walking to the mosque for morning prayers. Later, I reached the Ben Shemen Forest and ran with Rotem, a chatty divorced father of two who was training for his first hundred-kilometer race the following month. Bright sunlight, the quiet of the thickets, and conversations about long-distance running techniques.

"You know, while you're running, the adrenaline in your body suppresses the need to urinate, even if your bladder is full. It's OK—your body just suspends nonessential functions in order to pump blood to the muscles," Rotem explained.

After two hours, Rotem went home, and I continued for a longer run, staying on the wide dirt paths to make it easier to find my way back. Occasionally, I came across cyclists, but I ran in a deserted part of the forest, far from the barbeque pits and access roads. I would soon begin training for a new racing season, after a summer rest. I missed the discipline of the training; the readiness in my body; and the cycle of exhaustion, recovery, and anticipation of the next peak. That day, I planned to run thirty kilometers, a taste of the beginning of a new training plan. It was fun running in the forest, without cars and without the pressure of eyes watching me, as they did when I crossed through the villages surrounding Ramallah.

At a corner of the forest close to a military base, on the shaded path that ran along the barbed-wire fence, I checked my GPS watch and saw that I should head back. I had run twenty-two kilometers, and I was eight kilometers from my car. I'd promised Osama that I would be back by ten thirty, but now I would be late. Just to be sure, I used the "Back to Start" function of my watch and ran in the direction of the arrows on the little screen. After three kilometers, I reached into the pocket of my running backpack to eat a date and discovered that the pocket was open. I felt around and found the dates in the left pocket, but the right pocket—where I had put the car key—was empty. I hadn't closed the zipper.

I stopped, breathed, and tried to calm down. *It's not a tragedy. No need to hate yourself.*

Would a towing company break into the car for me? Can you hot-wire a car without a key, as they show in the movies? I traced back my steps, scanning the ground, looking for a spark of shiny metal among the broken tree branches and dust of the path, imagining the joy I would feel at the sight of the tiny word "Ford" printed on the key.

After three kilometers, I turned back in the direction of the parking lot, running slowly, scanning the ground, but without hope.

It was almost noon. The water in my backpack was long gone. In the parking lot, under the glaring sun, I saw the white doors of Bouazizi: quiet, patient, locked. Cars entered and exited. A couple in their forties and their three children sat at a wooden picnic table, feeding a dog the leftovers of their meal. I plastered a smile on my face and approached them.

"I'm sorry to bother you, but could I ask for help? I locked myself out of my car, and I want to call Memsi (the roadside assistance service). Could I maybe use your telephone?"

Memsi told me that they wouldn't come unless I had a key to the car. I ended the conversation and returned the phone to the father of the family.

"You don't have a spare key?" he asked.

"I do, but it's with my boyfriend, and he can't drive here." I imagined them thinking that Osama didn't have a driver's license.

"Where does your boyfriend live?"

"After Maccabim-Reut," I said, the neighborhoods of Modi'in, on the border of the West Bank. I asked to use the borrowed phone again.

"Are you OK?" Osama asked, when I called him from an unfamiliar telephone number. I remembered that he was at his ex-wife's house, that she had asked him to fix a water pipe.

"Yes, but can you go home to find me a few telephone numbers?"

He immediately agreed, but I felt as if I were imposing on him. As if I, too, were a commitment borne out of a love that had since waned, leaving behind just the obligation that he fulfilled faithfully but without enthusiasm. His moodiness had returned in the last few weeks, and also his fears about having children. I wasn't sure of his love anymore. There—in the Ben Shemen Forest, wearing a sweaty, sleeveless running top and shorts, dusty, with nothing but a hat, a fancy watch, and a water bladder that I would need to refill in order not to faint—I felt that worlds separated us.

I would have to meet Osama on Road 443, the road that cuts through the West Bank but is off-limits to Palestinian cars, in order to get the spare key from him and go back to the forest. The family started to pack up their things. I called a taxi company.

"Could you take me from Ben Shemen Forest to Road 443, after Maccabim-Reut?"

"Where exactly do you need?"

The father of the family stood next to me, listening to the conversation, while his wife threw trash bags into the dumpster. I was afraid to displease him, considering that I was using his phone.

"After the checkpoint, in Beit Ur Tahta," I told the taxi dispatcher.

"Where?"

"Do you have any Arab taxi drivers?"

"No, only Israelis."

We agreed that, for a hundred shekels, he would send a driver to meet Osama near the checkpoint and bring me the key. The owner of the phone sat in the driver's seat of his car and looked at me through the open window. Without asking his permission, because I was afraid of the answer, I called Osama.

"Ask where it is once you get to Beit Ur Tahta. It's the place where Palestinian drivers wait to pick up Palestinian workers, after their employers drop them off. You can't get to the main road by car, but the drivers wait near the exit."

I returned the telephone to its owner. "Thank you very much for everything." I didn't meet his eyes, was afraid of what he thought about me and rattled by my dependence on him.

While I waited, I approached another family and asked for permission to give their phone number to the taxi driver so that he would be able to find me in the forest. They were getting ready to start a barbeque, taking plastic containers out of a cooler and fanning the charcoal. I sat near them so they could find me if the phone rang.

Maybe this is punishment for the sin of my excessive ease in transgressing boundaries.

Two hours passed. The family invited me to join them; their daughter insisted that they couldn't eat while I sat alone. I ate two forkfuls of salad, an olive, and a spoon of hummus. I had run thirty-eight kilometers, but I had no appetite.

"His name is Mozart," the mother of the family said, after I complimented her on the little black dog lying under the table. "But he's very old."

"Does someone in the family play music?" I asked.

"And how!" the mother said, the Eastern European accent suddenly obvious in her voice. "Piano. Our daughter—she's amazing!"

"You study piano?" I asked the daughter, a smiling, slim girl with light brown hair.

"Not anymore," she said. "I'm on leave from the army. I have to go back after the holiday." She seemed too young. I had thought she was still in high school.

"Where does your boyfriend live?" the mother asked.

"After Maccabim," I said. They were from Tel Aviv and accepted the answer without interest—they didn't know the area and didn't know that after Maccabim was the West Bank.

"And he can't bring you the key?"

"He can't drive here," I said.

They were kind to and relaxed with each other. They mostly wanted to make sure I ate something and didn't seem to need a lot of details. I felt grateful.

Osama

Access

I dream of an exhibit where I would present all the Israeli permits, Egyptian and Palestinian travel documents, and Jordanian "no objection" letters I have ever received. Maybe I'll also include all the applications for permits I have submitted to Israel.

I'll hold the exhibit in a 67-square-meter gallery. Or maybe 1,967 square meters?

I imagine a space surrounded by three walls. On the upper wall would be famous sayings about travel, crossings, and study. Maybe a picture of Ibn Battuta, the prominent fourteenth-century Muslim scholar and traveler, or pictures of other travelers and scholars of the area. On the lower wall, I would hang quotes from international human rights conventions, with a spotlight on the words: "Every person has the right to freedom of movement and to choose his place of residence."

I don't remember when I first heard the French sayings, "Travel expands the mind," and "The world is a book, and those who don't travel read just one page." Both of them made me laugh. I told myself they mean nothing to Palestinians.

On the first wall, I'd hang the applications for permits and my correspondence with the Israeli authorities. On the middle wall, the longest of the three, the Israeli permits themselves, which would take time to sort. Should I catalog them by color, date, period of validity, or type? Would there be room for all of them on that wall, or would I need to use part of the third wall? Should I hang them next to each other, horizontally, with orderly and uniform spaces between them? Or maybe randomly, to emphasize the arbitrariness of their nature?

I have more than fifty Israeli permits for fifty visits during fifty days of my life.

Maybe I would distribute logic games throughout the gallery to keep the visitors occupied. Would visitors come? I hope so, because I want the exhibit to expose the workings of the occupation to the international community.

Oh yes! If I have room, I'll hang the Israeli Declaration of Independence, which includes a commitment to international conventions regarding freedom of movement and travel.

On the third wall near the gallery exit, a prominent location, I'll arrange the Egyptian documents, in between the sayings about travel above and human rights below. That's the right place for a country of Egypt's status. How can I get visitors to notice that the pages of the passports—where you stamp the visas—are empty? Should I also display the Jordanian applications and visas, to show the many concessions that the Kingdom grants to us Palestinians? Finally, I would display the Palestinian travel document or passport, printed by an authority that doesn't actually control any of the borders I would need to cross to travel or pass. If there's extra room, I would also display the Palestinian Declaration of Independence, even though I'm not sure from whom we've managed to become independent.

What to put in the center of the gallery? Maybe copies of my visas to the United States, the UK, France, Turkey, Cyprus, Malta, and Germany.

I'll show how lucky I am, more than many in the world, especially those in Gaza.

Will visitors come? And what meaning would all that have?

None.

And then what?

I'll turn off all the lights in the gallery, I'll shut the door, and I'll wake up.

Sari

They Are Protecting Me

A Saturday in October, still hot, I decided to run near the house and maybe finish in time to eat hummus with Osama before he leaves for the university. I asked him to try to wait for me.

I left late, and the road from Ramallah to the villages was crowded. Cars sped past me, honking in protest at my attempt to claim space in the shoulder of the narrow, winding road. I reassured myself that after the village of Dir Ibzi', I would loop back up to Ramallah through the settlers' road, a long and steep ascent, deserted on the Sabbath, and then take the quiet road connecting Ein Qinya to Ramallah, surrounded on both sides by olive and fig trees, where herds of grazing goats occasionally crossed.

The conversation yesterday with Osama was difficult. Again. I arrived home from work to our new rental apartment, dropped my backpack, and went to embrace him. He was sitting on the couch, working on his computer, and he barely responded.

"Sweetheart, were you able to get the internet fixed?" I asked. He didn't answer. "Osama?" I tried again.

"I see that we are going to fight," he said. I left the room, went into the bedroom, closed the door, and sat on the bed. After a few minutes, he came into the room and sat next to me.

"I'm sorry," he said. "I'm tired." I didn't answer.

"I'll make dinner," he said and left the room.

How many more conversations like that can we survive?

At 9:15 a.m., my GPS watch recorded twelve kilometers, and I left the village area and ran down to the main road, shared by Palestinians and settlers. I reached the intersection where the signs direct drivers to the settlements, accessible via a wide road with a white line painted in the middle. I turned in the direction of the settlement of Dolev, and amid the quiet and the trees, I passed the entrance to the settlement without looking at it, remembering the time the guard followed me in his car. I'll reach Ein Qinya soon. I'll be home in time to eat breakfast with Osama, if he waits for me.

At the end of the settlement, I turned down the hill, and just before the concrete obstacle that cuts off the village of Ein Qinya from the settlers' road, two soldiers stood. I gave a friendly nod in their direction and kept running, but one of them raised his hand, signaling me to stop.

"Good morning," I said.

"Good morning. Where are you running to?"

"There," I said, pointing to the road behind them, forty meters from the first house in Ein Qinya.

"You don't want to go there," the soldier said with a polite smile. A reservist, maybe twenty-five years old. He had an olive complexion, with black hair and a handsome face.

I returned his smile. "Actually, I do want to go there. I'm on a morning run, so if you'll excuse me . . ."

"You're not allowed to cross there."

"Actually, I am allowed to cross there. It's B," I said.

"What's B?"

"Area B, permitted for Israelis." The Oslo Accords divided the West Bank into Areas A, B, and C, and Israeli military orders determine who may enter which area.

"Over there is a closed military zone," he said.

"May I see the order?"

"It's not written, but look—that's a yellow gate, and you're not allowed to cross it."

"That's not what the rules say."

"Maybe not, but that's how it is. It's for your own good, believe me, so that they don't slaughter you there." He motioned with his hand toward the quiet village, a few dozen meters behind him. I tried to view it through his eyes: the silent houses, the two little kiosks selling snacks and drinks, the concrete school building, the brand-new mosque. There, on the other side of the concrete block. There, underneath the military watchtower. Had he ever been to Ein Qinya? Had he only ever seen it from the window of a military jeep?

"I must say that I run here a lot, and this is the first time I've seen you here," I said.

"Yeah. They called us from the security post at Dolev, told us you were coming."

"So you're here in my honor."

"You could say that."

The other soldier, the younger one, stood behind his partner and did not take his eyes off me. Forty meters to Ein Qinya, and from there, seven kilometers home. Or fifteen kilometers back the way I had come, on a steep road, exposed to the sun, which would be congested with midmorning traffic. I felt a longing for the black dog that guards the entrance to Ein Qinya, the one whose barking and growling symbolize my arrival in a safe place. I couldn't hear him. He only barks after you cross the barrier.

I ran back the way I came, rushing down the hill. My eyes searched for a path on the other side of the wadi that I could use to run home without going down to the main road below. I didn't see one. I accelerated as I passed the entrance to the settlement. Then, on my way down, I called Osama.

"I'll be late. Two soldiers prevented me from going home through Ein Qinya."

"What does that mean? Where are you?" He sounded worried.

"I'll try coming home the way I came, through Dir Ibzi'," I said. "I'll try to get home around eleven, if you'll still be there."

"I'll try," he said.

I wanted us to eat together so that the simple routine of pita and hummus and sliced tomatoes would narrow the abyss that had opened up between us. In Osama's tired smile, an apologetic look, a kiss in the air without touching me, as well as outbursts of irritation, suspicion, and impatience.

I was afraid he would keep retreating further and further away from me, in a silent black storm of anger and anxiety.

I was afraid we would lose each other. I was afraid the settlement's security jeep would come to find me. I was afraid soldiers would wait for me below, at the intersection from which I would try to climb back up to a Palestinian area.

Without a car to hide me, after the conversation with the soldiers who would have radioed their commander, I was exposed. Marked as an Israeli, a lone figure in a white T-shirt and white hat standing out against the black asphalt. What would I do if they also blocked my way to Dir Ibzi'? Maybe I could keep running west, until they lost interest, and then look for a remote village with a public taxi that could hide me until it reached Ramallah?

As I neared the intersection, I saw the settlement's white security jeep, two men standing next to it. One was middle-aged, and the other young, wearing shorts. They had taken off their yarmulkes, there in the intersection from which Palestinians travel from the shared road toward Ramallah.

"Hi, how are you?" the younger one said in Hebrew. I nodded in his direction and drew a wide circle around him with my steps, putting as much distance as possible between us. When I broke into a run, I saw him hold out his hand in a gesture of "stop."

"Where are you from?" he asked hurriedly. "Are you from Dolev?"

He was talking to my back as I continued running up the road. I assumed they wouldn't follow me to the village. Their jurisdiction was limited to the settlers' area. I was afraid they would call the army, the soldiers who don't ordinarily enter Palestinian villages during the day. An image passed through my mind of an army jeep driving up to the village and stopping next to me, and the soldiers speaking to me in Hebrew in front of the incredulous residents. They force me to go back with them, like brothers arriving to bring a rebellious little sister back home.

Osama would be hungry, if he were even waiting for me.

I pondered the possibility that I would be responsible for bringing the army to Dir Ibzi'. The boundaries that I had tried to transgress were closing in on me.

I ran and ran. I no longer knew where to.

Osama

Upside Down

Those who think that people learn from history are stupid, insanely stupid.

We Palestinians contradict ourselves when we chant, "With our soul, with our blood, we will redeem Palestine." We buy Israeli products, throw garbage into the streets of Palestine, allow corrupt officials to govern us, and we don't rebel against them. But at the same time, we're willing to climb onto an Israeli jeep or tank at a demonstration and die in an act of martyrdom.

Israelis are no different. They are willing to die for the sanctity of Israel, but they're not willing to wonder about that gate, on some road close to Modi'in, behind which Arabs live. They're willing to serve in the army and die for it, without challenging what that army does in those cities locked behind the gates.

What are you doing, Osama? When you talk to students about studying the history of science as a social act that can bring about change, what does the history of the development of the computer mean to a young woman living in Beit Ur Tahta, whose father crosses an Israeli checkpoint every day when he returns home from working in a colony, in a nearby Israeli settlement? To the student council member arrested on campus by undercover Israeli soldiers, *mista'arvim*, three days after he wins the elections? To the graduate student whose wife is gunned down on a road outside a settlement, because she lost control of the car, and the security guard said she was a terrorist?

Osama, how do you plan to build a life with this woman when you can't even bring her a spare car key?

Maybe my brother Mohammed was right. I tried to tell him how I felt, to share with him the crippling doubts that had returned. He shook his head over the video call and reminded me of how I'd pleaded with him to plead with Sari on my behalf. "You're upside down, my brother," he said.

Sari

Winds of War

NOVEMBER 14, 2012

"Did you listen to the news?" Osama asked gently.

I answered the phone in the parking lot of the Modi'in train station, on my way to the car at six in the evening, in the November darkness. I had broken my right pinky toe, and the swelling wasn't going to subside unless I stopped walking on it. Not to mention running.

"What, that things have de-escalated?" I said.

"No, sweetheart," he corrected me. "Israel killed a big one, Ja'bari."

"Ja'bari of Hamas?"

"Yes."

"No!" I protested. "The round was over; the fighting de-escalated!"

"No, sweetheart. How were you planning to drive home?"

"Through Beit Ur Tahta."

"OK," Osama approved. "Better not to go near Qalandia."

My thoughts raced back to the last war, in December 2008, when the Israeli army killed hundreds of people on the very first day. So many homes had been rebuilt since then, so many factories and schools. Now everything would be destroyed again. I turned off from Road 443, the Israeli-only road, to a small exit ramp bounded by a yellow metal gate leading to the village of Beit Ur Tahta. I felt relief that the gate was open, and no soldiers were present. Then I felt myself filling with rage. *We were at the end of the escalation*, I shouted silently to the irresponsible politicians running around in my head. *Do your elections justify the destruction that will rain down on both sides?*

I stopped to buy petrol and counted the cash I had, maybe not enough for a full tank. When the elderly attendant saw that I was emptying my wallet, he gave me back the two ten-shekel coins I had scraped out of my pocket.

"Leave yourself with twenty shekels, and we'll fill the tank up to three hundred," he told me. "Come back whenever you want, and we'll add more."

It was quiet in Ramallah too. I turned down the radio. That evening, I didn't want anyone hearing Hebrew through the car's open window.

At home, Osama had prepared spinach and rice, which he served with a plate of lemon and scallions. We entered into the slow pace of a long weekend. The following day was a Muslim holiday, a new year on the Muslim calendar or maybe the declaration of Palestinian independence; I get religion and nationalism mixed up. We ate in front of the television, on the coffee table we'd bought the week before, watching the reports on rockets fired at Rishon LeZion and Be'er Sheva and bombings of Jabalia and Gaza City. The cameras panned over a building turned to rubble and a man kneeling next to what seems to have been the stairwell, cradling in his hands a small body wrapped in a white shroud and rocking back and forth, sobbing. Osama called Mohammed and his sister and spoke to his fearful nieces, laughing loudly to reassure them.

Later, as Osama unpacked books to arrange on the shelves, I saw him pause to read something. I walked over and saw that it was a letter he'd written me but hadn't sent, during a period when he was trying to persuade me to come back to him.

"Can I look?" I asked. He shrugged and handed it to me. I began to read, and he came to stand behind me, to read with me:

I've come a long way since we first started trying. From complete refusal to love, to the most beautiful love of my life. From unwillingness to bring a child into this awful world to readiness to have two beautiful children with you, one who will look like you, with a sharp chin, and who will remind me of other children who have passed through my life. What do you think of Naji as a name?

I folded the letter and returned it to the envelope.

"I'm disappointed," he said.

"Why?"

"Those were beautiful words, pleasant feelings. And it's different now."

I seized the opportunity. Maybe his own words would remind him of what I hadn't managed to get across.

"Do you remember how you felt? Do you understand that that's what I want?" I asked.

"It was a different context," he said.

I felt a flash of anger and despair. The primary thing that had changed was Osama's internal context, that black cloud of moodiness and fear that inflicts pain on him and me. And still, I refused to let him go, because I wanted him so much.

We continued a long weekend of watching the news, calling Osama's family in Gaza, and my outbursts of rage against politicians, generals, and idiocy, idiocy, idiocy, idiocy.

"Sari is confused," Osama said, laughing to his brother Mohammed over the phone. "She's worried about you and is also calling her friends in Tel Aviv, who are fleeing to Jerusalem."

We watched television footage of the demonstration in Ramallah. Hamas flags filled the streets, and the Palestinian Authority permitted it, because you can't challenge Hamas's popularity while Gaza is being bombed. Secular women in T-shirts and tight jeans marched next to bearded men waving green flags and chanting, "God is great!"

I can't join that demonstration, can't chant those slogans. Nor will I join the small demonstration in Tel Aviv on Saturday night, against the war, against the government, against generals taking over the destiny of two peoples. It's too far away, the roads are bad, and I don't know that I still belong to Tel Aviv.

On Friday, I stayed home and propped my foot up on the coffee table, to help the pinky toe heal. I made a new recipe, Vietnamese pho, with chicken instead of pork. I chided Josh over the phone for not taking cover in the stairwell when the sirens sounded in his apartment in Ramat Hasharon. We watched a film on television until Osama started to fall asleep.

On Saturday, I went with Osama to change the tire on my car—one of the potholes on the Ramallah–Beitunia road punctured it. The garage attendant also changed the motor oil, which I hadn't checked until it was almost entirely depleted. Osama continued to the university, and I went home. I called colleagues in Gaza, asked about their families. Hosni's openness surprised me: "I know it's my job to be strong and to reassure the children, but in my heart, I'm also afraid," he said. The day before, an explosion had shattered two windows in his house. But they were OK. The younger son didn't even understand that something was happening, and the grocery store near their house was still open for food supplies.

I cooked spinach with hot peppers, garlic, and chili. For the first time in years, I was worried about gaining weight during these weeks when I wasn't allowed to run. The blind teenager I sometimes see walking around the street knocked on our apartment door to tell me that I had left the car unlocked. I guessed he discovered that while navigating the street by touching the cars. I thanked him and locked it. I checked online for the instructions of the Home Front Command and saw that workplaces in Tel Aviv were to operate after providing guidance about the nearest shelter or stairwell for rocket attacks. I sent text messages to the staff of Gisha—we would go to the office tomorrow as usual.

Osama went to his ex-wife's house again, this time to see her elderly father who arrived for a visit from the Palestinian town of Umm al-Fahm, in Northern Israel. When I called, he told me he had eaten dinner with them. He didn't say when he would come home.

I ate spinach in front of a special edition of Channel 10 news, about the war the Israeli government named Operation Protective Cloud. I wanted to go for a run.

I wondered how long the war would last and how many people would be killed. I wondered where we were headed.

Osama

90 Percent

I came home and found Sari in front of the television, watching the war. With tear-filled eyes, she told me, "Do you remember that woman I told you about, whose son decided to serve in the army, even though neither of them were convinced it was the right thing to do? He was later killed in the West Bank."

"I think so," I said.

"That woman told a journalist that she doesn't want anyone to be killed to avenge her son's death . . ."

I interrupted her impatiently, "I would never forgive someone who hurt my loved ones," but then I remembered the Israeli professor whose daughter was killed by a Palestinian attacker, and the doctor from Gaza whose three daughters were murdered by the Israeli army. They both called for reconciliation. So I calmed down a bit. "I envy people who can forgive their children's murderers," I said.

Then I suggested to Sari that it would be better not to talk about all that right now. This war reminds me of how ugly the people who surround us and surround her are and all the things that would make our life together fail.

But when my brother Mohammed asked about Sari, I felt myself soften. I told him that I felt compassion for her, because she knows people on both sides. Her friend in Tel Aviv decided to take her daughter to Jerusalem to avoid the rockets. And in Gaza, three relatives of her colleague were killed, together with others.

Will things go back to normal after the war this time? I don't think so. Especially after I read an opinion poll in the *Haaretz* newspaper, in which 90 percent of Israeli respondents said they support the continued bombing of Gaza, even after the killing of the ten members of the Al-Dalu family in Sheikh Radwan, not far from the home of my sister Sanaa. The Israeli military dropped a bomb that destroyed the two-story house. Four of those killed were children.

Maybe Dalia, Sari's sister living in the United States, needs to know that children who are the same ages as Menachem, Haim, and Rivka are being killed in Gaza, to make her stop wishing the bombing would continue.

And maybe what Dalia wishes for is the cruelest and most accurate illustration of what is happening here on Palestinian land. People are being killed, and their deaths are funded by others who live thousands of miles from here.

And if only 10 percent fail to support all that, I don't see any hope. I'm sorry.

Sari

A Red Sign

I persuaded Osama to go for a walk with me in Ein Qinya, in preparation for my planned return to running. We parked at the southwestern end of the village, near a lush field of *khubaiza*, common mallow, and walked down the path toward the wadi. Below us were cultivated groves of olive and almond trees interspersed with rows of lettuce, and above us, on the hill, was the road that linked Ein Qinya to the settlement of Dolev. From a distance, I could see the red sign they had installed in my honor, I believed, facing those approaching from the direction of the settlement: "This road leads to a Palestinian village. Entering it endangers your lives!"

The sign had appeared two weeks after I last tried to cross from the settlement to Ein Qinya, a physical instantiation of the verbal warning from the army reservist who blocked my way home, for my own security, he said.

We walked a half kilometer, stopped before the spring, and spread our mat in the center of the abandoned path. We ate pita with hummus and drank tea from the thermos. A young man on a donkey rode by, and we invited him to eat with us. Osama once explained to me the social convention: We have to invite him, and he has to decline. The man smiled, declined, and said that he was going to check on his lands farther down the path.

It was cool, but when the sun peeked out from the clouds, it was hot. On our way back, I removed my sweater. Although he was already late for work, Osama asked a young man walking near our car if it would be OK for us to pick some *khubaiza*, which we both liked sautéing with onions and hot peppers. We brought a plastic bag from the car and quickly drilled a hole in the thick green carpet of leaves.

"It's just seven shekels per kilogram in the store," Osama said, "but it feels good to pick it, no?"

Osama
Mango

"Is that really mango?" I asked my friend Ahmed, who was a year older than me.

The two of us stood across from the home of a wealthy Gazan family, two stories with white pillars near the entrance and a large and neat garden outside.

"Ah yes! It looks like mango," Ahmed answered.

"But it's green. Isn't mango yellow and orange?"

"Maybe it's not yet ripe," Ahmed said.

"Ripe or unripe, I want to taste it," I said.

Ahmed looked at me, wiped sweat from his round, smooth baby face, already streaked with dirt, and said, "The same thing is going to happen to us as happened that day with the oranges."

I laughed. "But you didn't climb the wall fast enough." I didn't want to mention that his weight had slowed him down as we ran from the garden of that neglected house, whose oranges had been abandoned, or so we had thought. We picked a few of them before hearing someone shout, "Hey, what are you doing? Wait!"

I had climbed the wall, jumped down, and ran quickly home, without looking back and without noticing that the owner of the house had caught Ahmed and was slapping him across the face. Ahmed refused to speak to me, and it took me three days to draw him into this mango story.

"But the house with the mangoes is on the main road, and people will see us," Ahmed said.

"But, Ahmed, how often do we get a chance to eat mango? Come on."

"Curse this life," he said. "Two or three slaps across the face won't kill me. I'm fourteen years old now." We laughed, and we were off.

We surveyed the road, climbed the wall, touched the first mango, and I whispered to Ahmed, "It's very tough." Then we heard a shout.

"Hey, what are you doing? Wait!"

I felt an arm grab my shirt, and I tried to break free. I shouted, "Let me go! We've done nothing!"

And then I woke up, startled. Sari slept next to me, snoring peacefully. It was four o'clock in the morning. Thirty years had passed. Time for coffee and work.

Sari

Jewess

"*Yahudia!*" yelled one of the teenagers I passed on the twenty-fourth kilometer of a fifty-kilometer run. In Arabic: "Jewess." There were other words, too, in rapid Arabic, but I only picked out the *Yahudia* clearly. His sentence in Arabic, undoubtedly directed at me, had been preceded by sentences in Hebrew that I understood very well, but I was careful not to turn my head or to display any other sign of comprehension. "What's up?" the shorter boy had asked in Hebrew. He might have been sixteen. And also, "Is everything OK?"

The sign at the entrance informed me that I had reached Beit Ur Tahta, the farthest village I had reached thus far in my trail runs. Soon I would turn back toward Ramallah. I needed to remember to buy ka'ak, a kind of bagel with sesame seeds, at the bakery I had seen at the entrance to the village, because I had already eaten my sandwich of pita filled with sesame paste and dates.

Yahudia? Do they think a settler woman would go for a run in the middle of their village? On the Sabbath? Where did that *Yahudia* come from? I wondered if they would throw a stone. I imagined the stone landing two steps in front of me, because surely they would start with some kind of warning throw. How should I react?

But I had put distance between us, and it was getting harder to hear their footsteps.

This village was different from the others—the main road was wide and well paved, with a white line painted through the middle. On each side, there were sidewalks bound by a safety railing to prevent pedestrians from slipping into the downward-sloping roadside. The houses were large, with front yards fenced in with gates. The best present the village gave me, a relief just before the midpoint of my run, was its flat road, without ascents, something that you never see in this part of the West Bank. On the right was the separation wall, dividing the settlement of Modi'in Illit from the village of Na'alin. On the left, though unrecognizable from a distance, were the familiar trails of the Ben Shemen Forest. They appeared blurry from here, just as the road I was running on in Beit Ur Tahta appeared blurry and unfamiliar when I looked at it from the other side, during my runs in Ben Shemen Forest, me and the other *Yahud* (in Arabic: "Jews"), also known as my running partners.

I didn't have a phone on me. In my running backpack, I had an isotonic drink, an MP3 player, and a note that I had asked Osama to write for me in Arabic: "My name is Sari Bashi, blood type AB+. In case of emergency, call Osama Fahed at . . ."

Like a tag on the collar of a dog, in case it gets lost.

I reached the end of the village, and my GPS watch recorded twenty-five kilometers. Two young women emerged from the thicket, walking toward the village, and paused their conversation to look at me. I ran toward a sign I spotted behind them and saw that I could turn right toward Safa and reach Ramallah that way too. But I had experienced enough new places for one run. I went back to Ramallah the way I had come.

After my shower, my weekly telephone call with my mother, and Osama's class at the university, we sat in the living room, and I told him about my run. His eyes filled with anger when he heard about the *Yahudia*. I found myself defending the teenagers who had mocked me.

"They're right. I am a Jewess."

"Of course. But they don't know the whole story."

"Should we tell them? Could you write me a sign in Arabic that says, 'My name is Sari Bashi, and I'm an Israeli-American Jewish woman in love with a Palestinian man named Osama Fahed. The two of us are just people, and I would be grateful if you could please respect that.'"

"I'll happily write that for you, *habibti*. But do you want the Israeli army to read that sign too?"

A few weeks passed. One morning, I left the house and saw that someone had stolen all of Bouazizi's hubcaps. The tires had been left naked, and I could see the remains of the plastic ties that had been cut. When did this happen? During the night, in front of our apartment? In the parking lot of the Modi'in train station?

I went back inside and called to Osama. As we stood there, assessing the damage, our landlord, Khaled, approached us.

"They only stole from me," I said, looking at the other cars on the street, all of them newer, cleaner, and more expensive than Bouazizi, a Ford Focus born in 2001.

"I don't think it happened here," Khaled said. "There aren't many cars like yours in Ramallah. There's not much use for the hubcaps."

I left for work late, and as I drove down toward Dir Ibzi', before the junction that leads to the road shared by settlers and Palestinians, a car passing in the opposite direction flashed his lights. I thought maybe he was signaling to me to put on my headlights, and I did so. I reached the junction, driving forward a few meters beyond the stop sign to look right toward the settlement, from which the field of vision is limited. The road was clear, and I turned left.

A half kilometer later, on the steep ascent from the intersection, a policeman stood on the side of the road, guarded by a soldier. The police officer motioned for me to stop. He was thin, muscular, with Slavic facial features. He spoke with a faint Russian accent.

"Show me your license and registration."

I showed him.

"Why didn't you make a complete stop at the stop sign below?"

"I did stop."

"You didn't completely stop, with all four wheels."

"Sir, forgive me for correcting you, but I made a complete stop. I stopped a few meters after the stop sign, because until that point, the bushes and the bend in the road block the field of vision. You have to pull forward in order to see if a car is coming."

"It's fine to stop a second time, if the field of vision is encumbered, but you didn't make a complete stop at the sign."

"Sir, I'm sorry, but you're standing a half kilometer from the junction. Maybe you didn't see, but—"

"From here the view is excellent," he said. He had placed his flying checkpoint on the part of the road that looks out over the turnoff from Dir Ibzi'. Only Palestinians emerge from that road, and the safe thing to do is to stop where I did, because from the stop sign you can't see anything.

"Where were you coming from?" he asked.

I saw my chance.

"From there." I pointed to the ascent to Dir Ibzi'.

"Where is there?"

"Dir Ibzi'. I'm a lawyer. I had to meet a client to have him sign a power of attorney. Now I'm driving back to my office in Tel Aviv."

The policeman handed me my license and registration.

"You can drive on," he said. "But don't say you made a complete stop when you didn't make a complete stop."

Osama

Holes

I watched Firas as he tried on clothing, observed that he likes slim-fit jeans that make him seem trim and muscular or sometimes looser, deliberately casual ones with holes sewn into them in a factory in China or Bangladesh. He has grown so much, my son, now a young man. I love him so much. For our upcoming trip to London, he made me buy him a new pair of jeans in Ramallah so that he won't "be ashamed" during the few hours that will pass between landing in Heathrow and his visit to the clothing stores on Oxford Street.

When I expressed a preference for one of the pairs he tried on, he looked at me with a combination of disdain and pity and informed me that I have no sense of fashion. My thoughts raced to London. He was a child, and in the first few weeks, he'd rush home from school to tell me all the new things he'd seen and heard in the city. What would Firas remember from his years there as a child? Where should we go together this time?

Could I become a father again to a new baby? The idea of that suddenly reminded me of an expression I had heard when I was a construction worker in Israel. A woman who lived next to a house we were renovating used to bring us a plate of cookies every morning and ask that we not drill a hole in her head that day.

As they say in Arabic, *Hazaktu rasi.*

No, this is not for me. I'm sorry, Sari. Not now, not in this place, where my son and I can't even fly to London and back from the same airport, because he's an Israeli citizen, via his mother, and I'm a citizen of nowhere, and the airport is off-limits to me.

I paid for the jeans and promised Firas we would buy more in London. He was happy.

Sari

This time, I initiated contact with Chen, the public inquiries officer in the Civil Administration, even before Osama's trip to London, because I wanted a written commitment that Israel would let him return to Ramallah. I was afraid of him leaving, that they wouldn't let him back.

Chen and I exchanged thirteen letters. Chen likes to write letters. Usually, he responds to my requests within three days. He erects an annoying but not insurmountable bureaucratic obstacle, because if I couldn't overcome the obstacle, the game would end prematurely.

"You didn't attach a power of attorney form."

"Our records indicate that the request has not been submitted."

"He should apply at the liaison office near his place of residence."

"He should submit an application for a staying permit."

Six days after Osama left for London, I got a letter from Chen, announcing that Osama's passage to the West Bank via Allenby Bridge had been "coordinated as per his request."

I filed the response in the huge binder with Osama's name and the case number of the petition I had filed in the Supreme Court seven years earlier. I thanked David for the representation—he still signs the letters.

On the day of Osama's intended return, at 3:00 p.m., I got a text message from Osama that he had crossed the Jordanian side of Allenby Bridge. By the time I spoke to him again, he had already reached the Israeli side and was informed that "there's no coordination." They told him to go back to Jordan.

I called David and asked him to speak with Chen. Chen likes order, so if he knew there was a contradiction between his written commitment and the conduct of the soldiers at the crossing, he might intervene on our behalf. I think Chen enjoys tasks like these, intervening in mishaps that take place without his approval to show that the military bureaucracy is usually good; however, in every well-run system, mistakes happen occasionally.

By the time David got in touch with Chen, the soldiers had already started sending Osama back to the Jordanian side, almost by force. Osama called me as they were trying to get him to board the bus back to Jordan. I heard him pleading with them, in English and in Arabic: "Please, just wait one moment. There's a mistake. It will just take half an hour . . . Will you please speak to my lawyer in Hebrew?"

He persuaded a soldier to take the phone from him, and I explained to her that we had a written commitment from the Civil Administration to let him reenter the West Bank. She told me she would check with her commanding officer. But the phone rang again a minute later, and I heard Osama's pleas: "Will you talk to me? Can I say something?"

I realized the soldiers weren't willing to wait. Osama's voice sounded more and more desperate. I wanted to tell him not to resist, not to give them an excuse to use violence against him. I heard him say, "You don't need to force me; you know that I will go with you."

Finally, he addressed me, in despair: "They say I have to get on the bus to Jordan."

"If they say that, then you have to go, sweetheart."

"You don't understand. It will take hours to get back from Jordan, and the intelligence officers there will make my life hell."

"It's OK, sweetheart. We're working on it. It will just take time."

I imagined him returning to Amman, a city he hates, to wait for permission to return home. I thought of getting on a bus to the Jordanian border so I could travel to Amman and join him. I could take a vacation; we could turn the exile into a holiday at the Dead Sea or in Aqaba.

I hate Jordan.

As soon as Chen entered the picture, things moved quickly. The officer who yelled at David, the female soldier who hung up on me, the male soldier who had returned Osama to Jordan—all got an order from Chen. The crossing had been coordinated.

"What happened was wrong," he told David over the phone.

I updated Osama, who was on the bus back to Jordan. I told him that the officer on the Israeli side was supposed to explain to the Jordanians that they could return him to the Israeli-controlled side of the border. I promised him he would be allowed to enter Ramallah that same night. I offered to drive to the border crossing, to wait for him in Jericho so that we could drive home together.

"Don't bother, sweetheart," he said, and his voice was distant and exhausted. "I'll be very late."

I'm trying to persuade Osama that he can trust the world, that the ground on which we are building a life together is stable enough to support the tiny feet of the children I want to have together. Chen had to choose now to amuse himself with mishaps in his usually efficient military bureaucracy?

Osama

The Fault of Someone There . . .

A security official wearing a black shirt and black pants escorted me outside the building. He was a native Arabic speaker, probably Druze. "Look at me," I said to him. "Talk to me." He ignored me and called for a soldier to come over. "This guy needs to get on the bus," he said in Hebrew. The soldier was Black, maybe Ethiopian, and he raised his gun in my direction. I boarded the bus from Jordan to the Israeli side for a second time. I was the only one on the bus. The Jordanian bus driver had taken me for the trip there and knew very well what I had been through, but he still made me pay for the ride again, and he didn't even give me a ticket, presumably so that he could pocket the money. I didn't expect anything, but it felt so ugly, that none of these three men, who had also experienced oppression, and with whose plight I empathize, displayed any sense of solidarity. I felt how even the small amount of peripheral power they wielded erased any sense of humanity. They were doing their jobs.

When I got off the bus, they brought me to a group of Jordanian security officials within the border office. "He was rejected," the bus driver told the officials. One of them was praying on a rug. When he finished, he telephoned what he called the "other side," spoke for a few minutes, and then told me I could get back on the bus.

On the Israeli side, an officer wearing a yarmulke, who introduced himself as Ron, was waiting for me as I got in line for the metal detector. He apologized in English and ordered my suitcase brought to me, then accompanied me through the security stations so that I would get through quickly. Ron spoke in Hebrew to the clerk responsible for registering my name and details: "This man was here today, and they didn't let him enter. Now it's OK." The clerk asked why they didn't let me in, and Ron whispered in Hebrew something I couldn't hear.

He apologized again and wished me luck. When he shook my hand, he said in English, "The thing is that there were two other Gazans here today who didn't have coordination, and they waited for hours before we sent them back to Jordan. It's not your fault, and it's not my fault either. It's the fault of someone there." He waved his hand in the air in no particular direction.

One of the "accomplishments" of the Palestinian Authority was their "coordination" at border crossings. To return to the West Bank from London, I had to fly into Jordan (because the Israelis don't let us open an airport or use theirs), cross through Israeli security, and then through the rubber stamp of PA security officials. Israel insists that requests for coordination be submitted through the Palestinian Authority, even though it has no power to actually let Palestinians in or out of the West Bank.

Thank you, Abu Mazen.

Sari

Diving

At the tree-lined bourgeois swimming pool in Ramallah, women and men removed their clothing, grilled meat on the barbeque, drank beer, jumped into the water, and played ball. It was thirty degrees Celsius. Ramadan again. The world was on edge from hunger, thirst, and nicotine cravings. The sound of the muezzin calling afternoon prayers rang out as I pointed out to Osama the skimpy bikini of a blond woman, foreign, who sat on the edge of the pool, sipping beer and dangling her legs in the water. Osama dove into the deep end, and I stretched out on a lounge chair. We searched for each other from time to time with looks and with caresses that we allowed ourselves in that bubble of forbidden deeds, surrounded by an unforgiving city.

Our lives are intertwined. Our love is deepening. Our domestic routine is pleasant. We laugh, talk, share our lives.

We managed to make a life together inside the pressure cooker that is our maqluba world. But none of this can overcome Osama's refusal to have a child with me.

Our story will end with us switching places. Osama will take off for some distant land across the sea, and I'll stay here, go back to living in Tel Aviv. Maybe I'll have a child with a nice man I met recently, an Arab Jew, as Osama would call him, who also wants to separate parenthood from couplehood. He loves men and can't have a child with another man, and I also love a man with whom I can't have a child.

My eyes burned from the bright sun reflecting off the pool. I covered them with an eye cover I had saved from the last flight I took. As I lay there drowsily, a cacophony of children's shouts and their parents' replies in Arabic filled my ears.

Osama applied for a job abroad, and I am interviewing candidates to be the father of a child we'll raise together in Tel Aviv.

Will the child be Zionist?

Osama's refusal insults me. How can he give up on us? He refuses to stray beyond his comfort zone, a zone in which there are no children, and soon there also won't be me.

Osama

Yes . . . No

We used to pluck the leaves of a tree whose name I forgot, or the petals of a rose, playing "she loves me . . . she loves me not."

I decided to look deeply within myself. Anything not to leave things as they are now. At forty-five years old, I'm supposed to know how to make a decision.

I thought about traveling, starting a new life in another country with Sari, walking along the beach without a permit from Israel, maybe life in the United States, maybe even becoming a citizen, maybe and maybe . . .

I'm afraid to be tied down to a child.

When I did the exercise Sari suggested and imagined what would happen ten years from now if I agreed to have a child, the first thing that came to mind was "divorce." I know myself. I can't have another child whom I won't be able to protect. I can't give my children a father who could be taken away from them at any moment.

But I love her so much.

I'm lost.

Sari

Al-Afiyeh

At the peak of exertion, when I'm panting and struggling, I don't like to feel the curious eyes of onlookers, so I chose a deserted place for speed training for a hundred-kilometer race. I drove to the Israeli city of Modi'in, to a deserted area next to a construction site, with a quiet path, good for running intervals. I had set aside sixty-five minutes in total for a warm-up, six intervals, and a cooldown, to finish in time for the 7:40 a.m. train.

After the first interval, I felt tired. During the second interval, I pushed with all my strength, and my running watch showed a heart rate of 180 beats per minute, but my pace was slow compared with the previous week. I finished the interval and felt a wave of nausea. During the subsequent intervals, too, I got my heart rate up to the maximum, but my pace was slower than four minutes per kilometer.

OK, I thought, *maybe I'm coming down with a cold, or maybe it's because my period is approaching.* A few days later, I went for another interval training session in Modi'in before getting on the train to work. Again, maximum heart rate but a slow pace.

My period didn't yet arrive, but that Friday I ran forty kilometers in Ramallah—looping in and out of different neighborhoods, running past closed shops in the downtown and the lively restaurant area of the Old City, viewing people's weekend lives at different stages of the morning—and I felt good, light and swift. Later that day, I had a work meeting in Tel Aviv, which I cut short in order to get home more quickly.

I understood that I was in trouble when I saw the soldier laughing as he spoke to a driver ahead of me in the line for the flying checkpoint, the surprise mobile checkpoint, in Beit Ur al-Fauqa. This must mean the soldier was Druze, part of an Arab religious minority in Israel whose men serve in the Israeli military. Jewish soldiers don't joke with Palestinians. So he would speak to me in Arabic, discover that I'm Jewish, and refuse to let me drive home, because the road he is blocking leads directly to Area A, forbidden to Israeli citizens. I'll tell him that I'm driving to a meeting with a client, and maybe he'll let me through.

"*Al-afiyeh*," he greeted me in Arabic, when I opened the car window.

"*Shalom*," I answered in Hebrew. There was no point trying to fool him.

"I said to you, '*Al-afiyeh*,'" he rebuked me in Arabic.

I hesitated. "*Al-afiyeh*," I answered.

He continued to speak Arabic. "Give me your ID card."

I gave it to him.

"Where are you going?"

"Ein Arik," I said, choosing a village that Israeli citizens are permitted to enter. My accent in Arabic is atrocious, especially when I pronounce the guttural letter *ein*.

"Have a good trip."

"Thank you," I said in Arabic, and continued driving home, marveling at how people cling to their preconceptions, even when faced with strong rebutting evidence. He didn't expect to see a Jewish woman in this part of the West Bank, so he didn't see her.

Osama

Hot Summer

"Can we talk a little?" Sari asked just after we finished dinner.

I don't remember who cooked, but I think we ate fish.

I do remember that it was August, the summer of 2013, because that day I had finished preparing my classes for the new semester and was ready for a break. Sari and I had been living together for fifteen months, and the last few months had been tense.

"Of course," I said, worried, as I usually am when Sari wants to talk.

"I know that the topic of children is hard for you," she said as we sat on the couch. "And you know that we won't stay together if we don't have children."

My heart beat faster. I said to myself, *What's new here? What does she want this time?*

Then Sari threw the grenade. "I think I'm pregnant."

Silence. Maybe she said something more, but I didn't hear.

No, it's impossible . . . it must be a mistake. How will I explain this to Firas? How can I go through this again? To repeat the mistakes of the past, to try to provide stability and security to a child, when the ground beneath my feet is shifting? And here, in this place that floods you with anxieties, that trains you to obey the dictates of fear? Will I carry the new child in my arms, terrified, moving him from room to room, waiting for the next bombing?

Sari kept talking, but I didn't hear anything. I remembered the look of confusion and fear on Firas's face when Nisreen and I told him we were separating. And now my daily attempts to get him on the phone, to let me pick him up from his friend's house, to talk to him.

And then, like a pleasant flame suddenly igniting, out of nowhere, another thought crossed my mind: *Why not?* Maybe it's an opportunity to make up for past mistakes. And then another thought engulfed the previous one like a warm blanket: *What if it's a girl?* Wow. That would be sweet news.

No. I can't do this. No. I have to tell Sari: This is not what we agreed to.

PART FOUR

New Country

Sari

Lisbon

In the little hotel on the southern coast of Portugal, I complained to Laura, my old friend, about a member of Gisha's board who was raising objections to the plan I had proposed to hire a new executive director who would take over when I took my maternity leave. I was on vacation, the last trip before giving birth and maybe also before moving to the United States, Europe, or any other place that isn't Israel or Palestine.

"Why are you angry at him?" Laura asked, and I gave her a list of the reasons my anger was justified.

Nine years earlier, on a different trip with Laura, to Vietnam, I was gestating Gisha, my first baby. Each time we reached a city large enough to have an internet café, I would send emails to David about the project we had started to develop. I remembered the dinner I had hosted in my mother's apartment in New York, in which I passed around a draft of the logo that David's son had designed to get feedback from the guests. I remembered the founders' meeting, in which

I was appointed executive director, a title that amused me at the time, because there was nothing and no one to direct. All I had was a desk in David's office and our nascent attempts to offer legal representation to Gaza residents. A few months later, my small database of clients included a doctoral student, Osama Fahed, who was trapped in Ramallah.

In the first year of founding the organization, I did a lot of things for the first time: First court petition, first marathon, first grant I raised, first employee I hired, first news release, first court hearing. And first victory—for a medical student, originally from Gaza, who got permission to reach his clinical studies at the Muqased Hospital in East Jerusalem, after the court petition I filed led to the army relenting. I introduced the organization in the first-person plural, hoping that no one would notice that "we" was actually just me.

"You work for Gisha?" people sometimes ask me, and I say yes, proudly, still surprised that people who don't know me know the organization. My greatest success is that it has an independent existence, which, I hope, will continue without me.

Years ago, I sought the guidance of a management consultant, expressing impatience with staff members I didn't know how to manage. She gave me an assignment: Fall in love with your staff, focus on the good things they do, and empower them.

I followed her instructions. I love them. I admire them. I learned to listen to them, to support them and to be a leader among them. And in a week, I will call a special staff meeting and announce that I'm leaving.

I touched my expanding stomach, still too small for maternity clothing but stretching the waistline of my regular pants. I caressed it, the daughter whom I prayed would be born. I love her. I love her father. I was on the verge of achieving a dream—a good life with Osama, and a daughter.

I'll find a new job, even abroad. I've built a network of connections and also a good reputation.

"Do you remember what you told me?" I asked Laura. "That in

addition to the positive messages I should communicate to the staff, I should also give them room to grieve?"

She nodded, and I added, "You're reminding me that I should also give myself room to grieve."

Osama

Norwegian Sun

A classmate from my doctoral program wrote me that the University of Trondheim in Norway was looking for a lecturer in its interdisciplinary faculty. At night, I searched online for information about the university. The students there would laugh if I were to teach a class in English. Or—am I supposed to learn Norwegian?

Sari wrinkled her nose when I told her.

"Do you know that the sun doesn't even rise there in winter?"

Yes, Sari, I thought to myself. *I know that I will stay here, but maybe I haven't told you often enough that it's not because of the sun . . .*

A few days after Sari returned to Ramallah from a trip abroad, she called me in the middle of the day, worried about some doctor's comment on her twenty-six-week ultrasound scan. It was one of the endless prenatal tests she was undergoing in Tel Aviv. All of them without me.

"Don't worry, sweetheart," I found myself saying as I took out another cigarette. "If it doesn't work this time, we'll try again."

The day before yesterday, I took Firas out for the evening. When we returned home, on the floor near the front door, I found huge plastic bags, some bearing the names of Israeli companies that sell children's clothing. In a thick black marker, someone had written "3 months" and "6 months" in Hebrew. I realized that Sari had come back from visiting Yael, her friend from Tel Aviv who has a three-year-old daughter. I peeked inside the bags and saw a sea of pink. A wave of exhaustion washed over me.

I went outside to smoke a cigarette. The floor beneath our apartment was rented by a day-care center, and I made sure the ash didn't blow into the courtyard, near the slide and colorful climbing blocks. The quiet felt good. At least at this time of night, the cries of children underneath our window had fallen silent.

I emptied the ashtray.

How will our daughter move between the two worlds we are trying to connect?

Sari

High Value

MARCH 2014

On a stormy winter Tel Aviv evening, I fought the wind and rain as I walked to the hotel where I was supposed to meet Laura, my friend visiting from abroad. We were to have dinner together, and I was going over in my head which restaurant to pick that would serve something that would stay in my system. Since the end of my second trimester, it had become nearly impossible to keep food down, and I'd been transferred to a high-risk obstetrician for follow-up.

As I waited for her, I checked my phone for the results of my last blood test. An indicator called ALT, which reflects liver function, was at 787, while the normal value ranges between 5 and 40. The lab report included a note shaded in red: *The test was conducted twice.*

"I noticed a very high value on the blood test," I told the receptionist at the clinic. "Can it wait until tomorrow, for my appointment with the high-risk obstetrician?"

She asked me for my ID number and said she would check with

the on-call doctor. A few minutes later, I heard her voice again. "Stay on the line. Don't hang up."

Laura arrived in the lobby and approached me. "I think I have to go to the emergency room again," I told her.

"Are you afraid?"

"I'm tired."

At the hospital, they checked my blood pressure and connected me to a monitor to check fetal heart rate. I was soon joined by Eyal, the medical resident I knew from previous referrals to the obstetric emergency room.

"You're here again?" he asked with a smile.

"You're the ones who keep bringing me back here all the time."

"Actually, I'm the one who keeps releasing you all the time," he corrected me and looked at the printed clinic referral, the fetal monitor, and the blood pressure monitor. He smiled again.

"It must be a mistake," he said. "We'll run the blood test again, and I'll try to get you home soon."

I sent a text message to Osama: "I'll probably be released soon, and I'll sleep at Yael's."

But when the blood test result came back, there was no mistake. They found the condition they had been searching for during a month of vomiting, weight loss, and the fetus's too-slow growth. I stared in disbelief when Eyal told me they would schedule a cesarean section for the following day.

"But she's too small. I'm only in week thirty-three!"

"She'll be fine. She'll stay here, in the NICU."

Osama was sleepy when I called him. "Tomorrow? Are you sure?" I felt guilty for having the baby without him, as if I had proved him right, that he wouldn't be able to protect his child.

That night again I vomited the entire contents of my stomach. In the morning, Josh and Yael arrived and stayed with me while they did additional tests and gave me a shot of steroids to strengthen the fetus's lungs. During the afternoon fetal monitor, the nurse stared at the printout and then called for the resident to come.

I managed to call Osama on the way to the operating room.

"Her heart rate went down," I told him. "They're doing the operation now, urgently. I'll leave my phone with Josh."

Yael hugged me before they rolled me into the hallway of the operating rooms.

"You're going to be a mother!" she said and kissed me on the cheek.

Osama

My Daughter Will Be Born Today

I drove to the university, choosing back roads to avoid traffic and noise. I wanted to be alone. Near the wadi, at the edge of Ramallah, I stopped on the side of the road for a cigarette. The road was empty of traffic, and I heard the buzz of insects. An orange-and-black butterfly flitted above me and then disappeared.

When Sari called to say the doctors had decided to take the baby out, she said, "Her life is in danger, and so is mine."

Could that really be true?

Her life is in danger, and I can't be with my child. I'd missed Firas's birth, too, until I couldn't stand it and sneaked into Israel to see him three days later. That was before they built the separation wall.

What have I done to myself? What will my life look like? What will I say at my lecture today? Then I stopped myself, told myself sternly, *You are accustomed to living in different worlds. Today is no exception.*

When I reached the campus, I didn't tell anyone what was going on. I was in my office, but I wasn't at the university at all. Why and how I managed to teach that day, I have no idea. I tried to put myself together for the 2:00 p.m. lecture on how science was taught in refugee camps in the West Bank and Gaza Strip of the 1950s. I told the students at the start of the lecture that I was waiting for an important phone call, and that if it came, I would have to answer it. Then Josh's name appeared on the screen of my phone. I asked the students to review the article we were discussing and stepped outside the lecture hall.

My child will be born today.

Sari

Waking Up

I awoke feeling dazed. Yael and Josh explained that the baby was OK; she was in the neonatal intensive care unit, the NICU. Josh had seen her.

I realized I wasn't pregnant anymore. I was afraid to look at my stomach, the stomach that hadn't had time to grow round during my abbreviated pregnancy, rife with vomiting. I touched it and felt surgical staples above my pelvis.

A nurse transferred me to the maternity ward and began infusing magnesium into my veins. I fell asleep. The next day, the nurse showed me how to squeeze colostrum from my breasts into a tiny syringe. "Like squeezing an orange," she said. Her name was Anna, and she was plump, with a big heart.

In the afternoon, they let me get out of bed, and Josh pushed me in a wheelchair to the NICU. The incubator looked like an aquarium, but instead of a fish swimming inside, it held a baby. Her eyes were closed, and she was naked except for a diaper, with electrodes and tubes connected to her thin, almost translucent skin. There was a huge monitor above her with numbers running constantly, making endless, monotonous beeping. The room was white and sterile, with harsh fluorescent overhead lights. She was very skinny, with chicken legs. Every once in a while, she scrunched up her face.

I asked Josh to wheel me back to bed.

Osama

Josh

"*Mabruk!*" Josh said. "Adase arrived." I held myself, so as not to cry, and because it was cold in the hallway. Adase was the nickname we had given her as a fetus, meaning "lentil" in Arabic. Two students walked by, their voices echoing in the empty space.

"How is Sari?"

"She's OK. But she hasn't come out of the anesthesia yet."

"And the baby?"

"In an incubator. But she's breathing on her own, without support."

After the lecture, I looked at the text messages and pictures that Sari's friends had continued to send me. Liquids from the womb and blood clots were spread on the baby's reddish skin and mixed into her thick black hair. Why did the nurse's hand look so big in the picture?

The campus emptied out, and I walked to the car. I felt sad. Bitter. Angry. My child was born, and I can't protect her. I can't even meet her.

Sari

The Father's Name

The next day, I discovered I couldn't raise my head without searing pain. They told me it was a side effect of a failed attempt at a local anesthetic. The resident had injected the needle into the wrong place. Days passed. Josh updated me on the baby's condition. He had registered as her father so that they would let him enter the NICU. Yael had registered as my sister, or maybe as Josh's sister? It was hard for me to keep track. They tried to get Laura in—she had delayed her return to the United States to stay with me—but I got confused and contradicted the version they told the head nurse, and Laura was stripped of her NICU visiting privileges.

Osama

Your Name

I want to tell you a little about your name. First, your mother loves giving names to all the things and subjects in her life. When we were sure she was pregnant, that you had been created, you were the size of a lentil. That's the source of your nickname.

Second, we tried to find a name that would link Arabic with Hebrew and with Iraq, and we wanted it to be an old name. *Forat* ("Euphrates" in English) is a river in Iraq (why make Iraq part of your name? Ask *Sido* ["grandfather" in Arabic]), on whose banks sprung the first civilization that knew how to write. We got a book on Forat, the Euphrates River, from an Iraqi friend of your mother, who was happy about your name. I hope you will like books and museums and music.

Third, Firas, the sweetest sixteen-year-old in the world, said yesterday that Forat has a nice meaning, but he prefers Reem (a very common Arabic name for girls). Who is Firas? He is your brother, and your mother and I think you will fall in love with him because he's wise and handsome. Firas suggested names like Mira, Miss, Reem, and Reema, and he's still working on it.

By the way, Mahmoud Darwish helped me arrive at the name Forat. Who is Mahmoud Darwish? You will get to know him as you get older. The nicest surprise is that you and he share a birthday.

I can't reach you, and reaching you is the only thing I want to do. To see you, to embrace you and your mother, to touch you, to look at you, to feel you, to feel myself.

I hope to breathe you in.

Sari

Football

"From the very beginning, she was breathing on her own," Josh told me. "I sent photos to Osama and your parents."

Yael brought me to the breastfeeding room, to the pump that I used to try to make my breasts produce milk. I wanted to vomit from the pain that exploded every time I lifted my head.

I started to get phone calls and text messages: "Congratulations, Sari!"

"I don't feel happy," I told Josh and Yael. "I don't feel anything."

They brought me a huge bouquet of flowers. "From Osama," Josh said. I guessed that Josh had bought it for him—how exactly was Osama going to send me flowers? They photographed me with the flowers, lying down.

"I'm OK," I told Osama over the phone. "The headache will pass."

"What do the doctors say?"

"To drink a lot of water and take paracetamol."

Osama laughed bitterly. "That's what they told me in prison."

"You don't want to request a permit for Osama?" Yael asked. "Or there's no chance?"

"Actually, now there are grounds—a first-degree relative hospitalized long term." They told Josh that the baby would stay in the hospital until her weight reached two kilograms. She was born 1,491 grams and had lost weight since then. It would take a long time. "But I'm afraid that if they know Osama has an Israeli wife, it will lower the chances of them ever agreeing to change his registered address to Ramallah."

The days passed, but the headache persisted. I lay in bed. Every three hours, I forced myself to get up, go to the breast-pumping room, and connect myself to the pump. Each pumping session yielded just a few drops, which I put into a bottle and, ashamed of myself, placed it on top of her incubator so that the nurses could add it to her feeding tube. She was a fetus prematurely plucked from the womb, now lying in an incubator. Every once in a while, she would move a hand or foot, each the width of a twig.

Josh told me the meaning of the numbers on her monitor: pulse, body heat, oxygen saturation, and number of breaths per minute. My head weighed a thousand tons.

"Sweetheart, can we talk again about the possibility of requesting a permit?" I asked Osama by telephone.

"What do I have to do?"

I asked Hadas to call him to explain the process. The chances of success were low. He'd have to first submit the request to the Palestinian Authority. The Israeli authorities would likely refuse to recognize our marriage or his paternity. It could negatively impact his request to change his address. Osama had different fears.

"I don't want to expose myself to them. I don't trust them."

"Who?"

"The Israeli authorities and the Palestinian authorities."

"But what are you afraid of?"

"Sweetheart, please. Let it go."

There was silence. I looked at the clock on the telephone. I would have to get up in twenty minutes to pump milk. Anna, the nurse, had told me that if I ate more and got stronger, I would produce more milk.

Outside the door—the squeaking of visitors' chairs and the sound of a girl running in the hallway. My world had contracted to my room in maternity ward A and the pumping room attached to the NICU. It was quiet after eight and noisy until then, during visiting hours for women who had given birth to healthy babies.

"Will you play football today?" I asked Osama.

"Yes, after I tutor Firas for his chemistry exam."

Ramallah and Osama were a thousand kilometers away from me. I felt like I would never make it home.

"Osama," I said, staring at the white tiles on the ceiling. "I'm sorry."

"Let it go, sweetheart," he said. "I'll call you later. I need to leave now, to go to Firas."

Osama

My Daughter's Eyes

In the video that Sari filmed, ten days after her arrival, the baby opened her eyes to reveal long eyelashes. I heard Sari in the background, encouraging her to stay awake for Baba. The color of her eyes was deep black, with a touch of blue, but maybe that was a distortion of the camera.

Welcome to the world, my love, Forat.

Adase.

Sari

Passover Discount

The day before Passover eve, I bathed Forat in the sink of the NICU and weighed her: 1,934 grams. Her release was conditioned on her weight reaching two kilograms, but the Ichilov Hospital NICU was known to give a 50-gram discount. I figured the staff would want to whittle down the NICU population in advance of the holiday, when most of the doctors and nurses would be on vacation, so maybe they would be willing to knock a few more grams off the price of release.

"Good morning to the wonderful doctors and nurses of the NICU," I wrote in Forat's name, in a note intended for the doctors who would do the following morning's rounds. "Tonight the Festival of Liberty begins. Can you weigh me again this morning to see if I can also go free?" I stuck the note behind the feeding chart on Forat's heated bassinet.

The next morning, as I was dressing to leave Yael's apartment, where I'd been staying since my own release weeks ago, I got a call from the NICU. They approved Forat's release.

I packed my belongings, thanked Yael for hosting me, and grabbed the infant car seat I had borrowed from a friend of a friend. I listened to the nurse's briefing and received instruction sheets for feeding, sleeping, hygiene, and immunizations. I expressed breast milk in the pumping room. I said goodbye to Nirit and Avner, the parents of a baby girl born the same day as Forat, but at an earlier stage of pregnancy. They were the only ones who knew that Josh was not Forat's father, and that her father was waiting for her in Ramallah.

"Give her an early lunch," Avner told me. "So you don't get caught in Passover seder traffic."

At the age of one month, Forat went outside for the first time. Despite the cloth I had hung over the infant seat for shade, she squinted her eyelashes at the sight of the bright natural light. On our way from the hospital plaza to the underground parking garage, she fell asleep. I attached the infant seat to the car, and we drove to Ramallah.

Sixty-five kilometers and seventy-five minutes later, I stopped at the entrance to the apartment. Forat woke up, hungry and screaming. Osama opened the door of the house to see the tiny, red, furious baby. I held her out to him. He hesitated, afraid—and then took her from me. "She's so small!" He brought her closer to his face. I hurried to heat the bottle of breast milk I had brought from the car.

"Do you want to feed her?" I asked him.

Osama smiled and said something that I couldn't hear over the screams of our hungry daughter.

Sari

In Motion

AUTUMN 2020

Three and a half years after Forat came into the world, her brother Adam was born. The children speak Arabic, Hebrew, and English, sometimes in the same sentence. Six-year-old Forat, curious and smart, asks a lot of questions. We don't always know how to answer them. Few people have the benefit of moving, as she does, throughout the space between the Jordan River and the Mediterranean Sea, and she has a lot of observations about it: who can drive which car, who can pass through which checkpoint, who speaks which language. The first time I heard Forat refer to herself as Jewish was when soldiers stopped us from crossing a checkpoint. "But, *Ima*," Forat said, "we're Jews."

Osama continues teaching at the university. I transferred the management of Gisha to a new director, who is doing wonderful work. I feel pride and satisfaction in watching my "baby" excelling without me. Not long after Forat's birth, the Israeli authorities agreed to change Osama's address from Gaza to the West Bank. Since then, we have traveled the world a lot, living in South Africa and the United States for periods of a year or two. Each time we return to the Ramallah area, and I think we are still searching for our place in the world.

I still work in the human rights field—engaging in writing, advocacy, research, and legal projects—and as the years pass, I am increasingly drawn to communications and public-oriented work, using lectures, op-eds, and news coverage to pick apart the fears and assumptions that lead people to believe that others are less deserving of dignity, rights, and resources.

When I first moved to the West Bank, I kept my identity mostly hidden. But my way of being here has evolved with time, and with the growth of the children. I speak to them in Hebrew, and when Forat began to answer me in Hebrew, at the top of her lungs in the supermarket, it became harder to maintain a low profile. I want her to know that she need not be ashamed of who I am and of who she is. I also want the people around me to know who I am so that they won't think I'm a settler. Palestinians are afraid of settlers, and their fears can endanger me. In the street, in the Ramallah area, I pass for a Palestinian woman, and when people hear my accent in Arabic, they assume I'm a foreigner. In the villages, the situation is more complicated, because villagers expect that the "foreigners" coming to visit are settlers who don't mean well. In familiar settings—among neighbors, the children's schools, neighborhood shops—I try to find a way to let people know who I am so that we can get past the awkwardness and move on.

"Where are you from?" people sometimes ask.

"From among your cousins," I sometimes answer, a nod to Ishmael (Ismail) and Yitzhak (Isaac), the sons of Abraham (Ibrahim), from whom Jews and Muslims are believed to descend. Sometimes I say I'm from Tel Aviv.

I borrow salt from the neighbor upstairs, a religious woman who is different from me in many ways but tolerant and generous to me. We are both raising small children, both dealing with the pressures of work, the challenges of motherhood, and dilemmas about the future.

I still miss Tel Aviv. The hills here are charming, but I miss the expanse of the sea, and Yarkon Park, and the citrus groves that surround Tel Aviv to the east, where I used to run.

Osama and I haven't changed the world with our choices. The occupation and regime of discrimination have not ended. They are becoming more sophisticated in their ugliness. But we managed to build a good life together, amid the oppression and attempts to instill fear. Our love is an ordinary, flawed love—and at the same time, like every love, unique and perfect too. For that we are grateful. And we are grateful to you for reading our story.

Epilogue

JULY 2025

This English edition comes to light at a time of unspeakable violence, destruction, and loss in Israel-Palestine, particularly in Gaza. The childhood home that Osama describes in the book, the richness of his family's social life in their home by the sea, the market where his mother shopped—all have been ravaged by war. Since October 2023, Osama's family has been on the move, sheltering in relatives' homes, in a wedding hall, in a language training center, in a greenhouse, and in other makeshift structures. Israeli air strikes have destroyed the universities where his nieces and nephews were studying, and like many young people in Gaza, they're struggling to see what their futures hold. His strong and resilient mother, who left Gaza five months into the war, misses her family and neighbors, and she is trying to return home.

In Israel, society is becoming even more deeply militarized, politicians are undermining public structures that previously held a modicum of integrity, and many Israelis who can leave . . . are leaving. A number of my Israeli friends mentioned in this book have upended their lives and moved abroad, out of fear for what the future in Israel holds for them and especially their children.

In the West Bank, where we live, settlers, backed by the Israeli government, are taking over more and more land, using violence to displace Palestinians from their homes and prevent them from farming their land. Travel has become even more restricted, and the Israeli military has closed roads leading from Palestinian cities, towns, and villages to main roads. The roadblocks deter people, including us, from attempting to travel between cities, because we don't know if we'll be able to access intercity roads or how long it will take to pass checkpoints.

Gisha is still doing important work, now helping medical patients and their companions in Gaza overcome the Israeli government's refusal to allow evacuation for treatment abroad. Osama continues teaching at his university, including remotely teaching Palestinian students from Gaza who logged into his class on their phones, from shelters and relatives' homes to which they fled. Despite the escalating violence in the West Bank, our children's school has remained open, giving them much-needed routine and stability. Forat, now eleven, and her brother, Adam, aged seven, are painfully aware of the war and its dangers, mostly for their relatives in Gaza but also for themselves. We try to give them information that will help them digest the nightly Israeli military incursions in the West Bank, the Iranian missile strikes that have sent us sheltering in our walk-in closet, and my somewhat anxious shushing in the frequent moments when we drive toward Israeli military checkpoints.

So many things are collapsing in Israel-Palestine right now. Hatred, fear, trauma, and pain dominate its social, political, and emotional landscape. Whether or not the future will be better or worse depends on us. We have a lot of work to do to build up the power we'll need to replace the current regime with one that provides justice and accountability and allows all people in Israel-Palestine to live in peace, dignity, and security. As horrible as the current circumstances are, when things collapse, there are opportunities to fill the vacuum with something better. We who believe in justice have both the opportunity and the responsibility to work as hard and as smartly as we can to create a just future and prevent something worse from filling the void.

Despite how difficult these many months have been—and maybe because of how difficult they have been—I experience a deep and daily sense of gratitude. I look at the peaceful faces of my children, sleeping warmly and safely in their beds, and think of the many parents in Gaza, including my in-laws, experiencing the pain of not being able to protect their children. My gratitude for the relative safety of our family is genuine, deep, and maybe sometimes a little desperate. I'm grateful for the love that infuses our messy home; for the strength and beauty of my children, who are forging their path through this upside-down world; and for Osama, who continues to delight me with his resilience, his easy laughter, and his curious, frank way of exploring life.

And I am deeply grateful to you, my English-language readers, for taking the time to read our story. Please know that despite the terrible violence engulfing Israel-Palestine, there are good, loving people here who are working for a better future.

Acknowledgments

And more thank-yous from each of us:

From Osama:

Thank you to *Maqluba*—the book that saved us every time I made a mistake or caused harm.

And thank you to Gaza, which perhaps is the main reason I met Sari.

From Sari:

My life was turned upside down.
Should I say thank you for that?
To Gisha, which introduced me to Osama.
To running, which led me back to him.
To Osama, who gives me a life of maqluba.

Upside-Down Chicken, Rice + Vegetables (Maqluba)

Ingredients:

1.5 kg/3.3 pounds chicken parts, rinsed that's all?! ☹
1.5 cups long brown rice (Basmati is especially good)
1 large onion, diced
1 small cauliflower, broken into florets
1 medium eggplant, sliced
2 medium potatoes, peeled and sliced
2-3 tomatoes, sliced
1 3/4 tsp salt plus more for salting the vegetables,
1/2 tsp ground black pepper
1 Tbsp maqluba spice blend*
Oil for frying (canola oil is good)

Preparation:

1. Fry the cauliflower, eggplant and potatoes in oil until they soften slightly. Alternatively, you can roast them in the oven. Sprinkle with salt.
2. In a separate, large and wide-bottomed pot, fry the onion. Add the chicken parts, 3/4 tsp salt and the black pepper. Add water just until it covers the chicken. Bring to a boil and simmer for ten minutes.
3. Rinse the rice well. Mix in the maqluba spice mixture and a teaspoon salt.
4. Remove the chicken and liquid (soup)

from the large pot. Line the bottom of the pot with the tomato slices. Arrange the chicken parts, <u>without</u> the liquid, in a layer on the bottom of the pot. Sprinkle them with half the rice mixture. Arrange the vegetables in a layer above the rice and sprinkle the rest of the rice mixture in a layer on top. Add 2.5 cups of the chicken cooking liquid to the pot and save the rest as soup stock for another day. The liquid need not cover the top layer of rice - the steam will cook it, so long as the pot is tightly covered.

5. Cover securely, bring to a boil, lower the heat and cook for at least an hour. If using white rice, you can reduce the cooking time to at least a half hour.
6. Remove the pot lid and cover the pot with an upside-down large, wide plate or tray whose diameter is larger than the diameter of the pot. Carefully turn the pot over onto the platter. You can "drum" on the pot with spoons before you lift it to coax the contents to fall onto the platter. Remove the pot from the platter.
7. You can garnish with toasted pine nuts, parsley, almond slivers or raisins if you like.

* Maqluba spice mixture may be available at Middle Eastern spice stores, or you can make it on your own using this version:

1 tsp. cardamom
1.5 tsp cinnamon
Pinch of ground cloves
3/4 tsp allspice — just put a pinch!
½ tsp ground black pepper
1 tsp nutmeg
1 tsp sweet paprika
1 tsp hot paprika